DISCOVERING
THE LAST GOD

DISCOVERING THE LAST GOD

Prabhuji

DISCOVERING THE LAST GOD
by Prabhuji

Copyright © 2025
First edition

Printed in Round Top, New York, United States

All rights reserved. None of the information contained in this book may be reproduced, republished, or re-disseminated in any manner or form without the prior written consent of the publisher.

Published by Prabhuji Mission
Website: prabhuji.net

Avadhutashram
PO Box 900
Cairo, NY, 12413
USA

Painting on the cover by Prabhuji:
"Discovering the Last God"
Acrylic on canvas, New York
Canvas Size: 24"x24"

Library of Congress Control Number: 2025903816
ISBN-13: 978-1-945894-71-8

Contents

Preface 1
Introduction 5

Section I: The ontotheological conception of God

Chapter 1: The problem of nihilism 23
Chapter 2: The history of the concept 27
Chapter 3: The distance from the Divine 43
Chapter 4: The birth of ontotheology 59
Bibliography Section I 65

Section II: Transcending the personal God

Chapter 5: Christian excavations 71
Chapter 6: Christophany: the intimate relationship with the Divine . 93
Chapter 7: The death of Christ 101
Bibliography Section II 123

Section III: From participation to emanation

Chapter 8: The path of participation: the Thomist dualism 127
Chapter 9: Emanation and the return to the One in Plotinus .. 135
Chapter 10: The three fundamental hypostases of Plotinus 141
Bibliography Section III 155

Section IV: The forgetting and becoming of Being

Chapter 11: The divorce between being and thinking 159

Chapter 12: Truth as correction (*orthótes*) in Plato 171

Chapter 13: The opening to Being: a new beginning............... 183

Chapter 14: Existential analytics, poetry, and manifestation of Being 191

Chapter 15: A first approach to God 199

Chapter 16: The unity of humanity in Being............................. 211

Bibliography Section IV.. 219

Section V: From ontotheology to the unknown God

Chapter 17: The unknown God 225

Chapter 18: The ontological death of *Dasein*............................. 237

Chapter 19: Heidegger's Ontological-Hermeneutic Turn............ 243

Bibliography Section V... 263

Section VI: The journey toward the Last God

Chapter 20: The six assemblies toward the last God................. 267

Chapter 21: A new philosophical framework 285

Chapter 22: Language as the house of being 301

Chapter 23: Being and God in the quadrature.......................... 315

Chapter 24: The dawn of the last God...................................... 331

Chapter 25: The opening to the "Retroprogressive Path" 341

Bibliography Section VI.. 349

Appendixes

About Prabhuji.. 353
The term *prabhuji* by H.G. Swami Ramananda 371
The term *avadhūta* 375
About the Prabhuji Mission.. 389
About the Avadhutashram 393
The Path of Retroprogressive Alignment 395
Prabhuji today... 397
Titles by Prabhuji.. 402

ॐ अज्ञानतिमिरान्धस्य ज्ञानाञ्जनशलाकया ।
चक्षुरुन्मीलितं येन तस्मै श्रीगुरवे नमः ॥

> *oṁ ajñāna-timirāndhasya*
> *jñānāñjana-śalākayā*
> *cakṣur unmīlitaṁ yena*
> *tasmai śrī-gurave namaḥ*

Salutations unto that holy Guru who, applying the ointment [medicine] of [spiritual] knowledge, removes the darkness of ignorance of the blinded [unenlightened] and opens their eyes.

This book is dedicated, with deep gratitude and eternal respect, to the holy lotus feet of my beloved masters His Divine Grace Bhakti-kavi Atulānanda Ācārya Mahārāja (Gurudeva) and His Divine Grace Avadhūta Śrī Brahmānanda Bābājī Mahārāja (Guru Mahārāja).

Preface

The story of my life is an odyssey from what I believed myself to be to what I truly am... an inner and outer pilgrimage. A journey from the personal to the universal, from the partial to the whole, from the illusory to the real, from the apparent to the true. A wandering flight from the human to the divine.

Everything that awakens at dawn rests at dusk; every lit flame eventually extinguishes. Only what begins, ends; only what starts, finishes. But what dwells in the present is neither born nor dies, for that which lacks a beginning never perishes.

As a simple autobiographer and narrator of significant experiences, I share my intimate story with others. My story is not public but profoundly private and intimate. It does not belong to the turmoil of social life, but is a sigh kept in the most hidden depths of the soul.

I am a disciple of seers, enlightened beings, shadows of the universe who are nobody and walk in death. I am just a whim or perhaps a joke from the heavens and the only mistake of my beloved spiritual masters. I was initiated in my spiritual childhood by the moonlight, which showed me its light and shared its being with me. My muse was a seagull that loved to fly more than anything else in life.

In love with the impossible, I traversed the universe, obsessed with the brilliance of a star. I traveled countless paths, following the traces and vestiges of those with the vision to decipher the hidden. Like the ocean that longs for water, I sought my home within my own house.

I do not claim to be a guide, coach, teacher, instructor, educator, psychologist, enlightener, pedagogue, evangelist, rabbi, *posek halacha*, healer, therapist, satsangist, psychic, leader, medium, savior, guru, or authority of any kind, whether spiritual or material. I allow myself the audacity and daring to represent nothing and no one but myself. I am only a traveler whom you can ask for directions. With pleasure, I point you to a place where everything calms upon arrival... beyond the sun and the stars, your desires and longings, time and space, concepts and conclusions, and beyond all that you believe you are or imagine you will be.

I paint sighs, hopes, silences, aspirations, and melancholies, inner landscapes, and sunsets of the soul. I am a painter of the indescribable, inexpressible, and indefinable, and unconfessable of our depths... or maybe I just write colors and paint words. Aware of the abyss that separates revelation and works, I live in a frustrated attempt to faithfully express the mystery of the spirit.

Since childhood, little windows of paper captivated my attention; through them, I visited places, met people, and made friends. Those tiny mandalas were my true elementary school, high school, and college. Like skilled teachers, these *yantras* have guided me through contemplation, attention, concentration, observation, and meditation.

Like a physician studies the human body, or a lawyer studies laws, I have dedicated my entire life to the study of myself. I can say with certainty that I know what resides and lives in this heart.

My purpose is not to persuade others. It is not my intention to convince anyone of anything. I do not offer theology or philosophy, nor do I preach or teach, I simply think out loud. The echo of these words may lead you to the infinite space of peace, silence, love, existence, consciousness, and absolute bliss.

Do not search for me. Search for yourself. You do not need me or anyone else, because the only thing that really matters is you. What you yearn for lies within you, as what you are, here and now.

I am not a merchant of rehashed information, nor do I intend to do business with my spirituality. I do not teach beliefs or philosophies. I only speak about what I see and just share what I know.

Avoid fame, for true glory is not based on public opinion but on what you really are. What matters is not what others think of you, but your own appreciation of who you are.

Choose bliss over success, life over reputation, and wisdom over information. If you succeed, you will know not only admiration but also true envy. Jealousy is mediocrity's tribute to talent and an open acceptance of one's own inferiority.

I advise you to fly freely and never be afraid of making mistakes. Learn the art of transforming your mistakes into lessons. Never blame others for your faults: remember that taking complete responsibility for your life is a sign of maturity. Flying teaches you that what matters is not touching the sky but having the courage to spread your wings. The higher you rise, the more graciously small and insignificant the world will seem. As you walk, sooner or later you will understand that every search begins and ends in you.

Your unconditional well-wisher,

Introduction

Since the dawn of civilization, an intimate and enduring relationship between humanity and the sacred has been evident. Humans' inquiry into their own existence and place within the whole is reflected in the expression of art, philosophy, and religion. The earliest artistic manifestations, such as cave paintings, display figures with extraordinary characteristics that have revealed that the notion of the divine is not a recent invention for social and political control. Both in Eastern traditions and Western thought, divinity has often been interpreted as a myth or a literary construct serving hegemony. While these explanations provide valuable perspectives, the concept of the sacred is not fully exhausted by mere sociohistorical interpretations.

From the earliest cultural evidence, the figure of a deity is inseparably linked to human consciousness and identity. This fusion between the idea of the divine and the human reflects a dimension that transcends the material. It points to human being's deepest concerns and their tireless search for meaning in a cosmos they perceive as vast and enigmatic.

The presence of the sacred in the development of human thought highlights the need to recognize its central role in the evolution of systems of reflection and understanding. From the earliest organized communities to the elaborate philosophical and theological doctrines, the perception of the Divine has constituted a core around which the interpretation of the world has been articulated. This integration emphasizes that the Divine is not merely a cultural phenomenon. It expresses the profound human quest to understand its essence and purpose in a universe whose vastness and mystery have continued to fascinate and challenge us.

However, God has been conceived and represented differently throughout history. The conception of God has followed a long and complex path, from the religions of the Paleolithic, with their hypothesized religious beliefs and behaviors for that era, to the more refined philosophical and theological conceptions. It transitioned from the anthropomorphic figures of primitive religions to metaphysical abstractions. This extensive journey can be described as an evolution from a personal God to an abstract divinity, reflecting the development of theological perspectives and changes in understanding reality, nature, and existence.

In the early stages of prehistory or history, the perception of the Divine emerged as a reflection of human interaction with forces considered essential for survival, such as the sun, fertility, and hunting. This conception, rooted in observing natural phenomena, was translated into rituals of sacrifice and offerings, practices that can be identified in the complex traditions of pre-Hispanic civilizations in the Americas. The rituals expressed their beliefs and connected them to the Divine, that is, to a superior entity with the power to influence the fundamental aspects of existence.

As societies experienced significant changes, the representations of divinity also transformed. The evolution from a relationship with impersonal forces to an anthropomorphic representation marked a crucial point in cultural development. Divine figures began to acquire specific human characteristics, reflecting an abstraction process that allowed for a more understandable interaction with the sacred. This process restructured the organization of societies and contributed to a more cohesive perception of collective identity. At the same time, it gave divinity a character that facilitated its integration into common consciousness and redefined its meaning in the human experience.

The development of anthropomorphic divine representations involved a reorganization of how groups of humans understood their environment and their own position in the universe. This was not simply a change in the form of religious symbols but a shift in the way humanity articulated its relationship with the transcendent. Adopting deities with human attributes allowed societies to establish a closer connection and channel for symbolic interaction that reflected the complexities of human existence, including desires, fears, and aspirations.

The transition from the veneration of natural forces to a more personalized conception of divinity highlights a seminal change in collective consciousness and how cultures interpreted the sacred. This plurality of expressions and their development show how humans, over the centuries, sought to make sense of a world they often perceived as unpredictable. The emergence of divine figures with human qualities transformed religious imagination and, in addition, laid the foundations for subsequent philosophical and religious reflections. These representations impacted human thought, influencing how various traditions reflected on the relationship between the finite and the infinite, the contingent and the Absolute.

The gods of ancient polytheistic religions, such as those in Greek, Roman, Egyptian, and Mesopotamian mythologies, possessed human characteristics, both in appearance and behavior. These deities interacted directly with humans, actively influencing their lives, society, and world affairs. The Greek Olympic pantheon is a notable example of this conception, where gods like Zeus, Hera, Apollo, and Athena were seen as beings with personalities and human attributes, though endowed with supernatural powers. They ruled over various aspects of nature and human life but also displayed emotions, rivalries, and relationships similar to those of humans.[1] The humanity of the gods allowed

---

1. Burkert, Walter. *Greek Religion* (Cambridge, Massachusetts: Harvard University Press, 1985), 129, 182–183.

people to relate to them intimately and personally, offering sacrifices and prayers in hopes of gaining their favor or avoiding their wrath.

The move toward a personal and unique God is evidence of the emergence of Judaism, Christianity, and Islam. In the monotheistic Abrahamic religions, God remains a personal entity, though not anthropomorphic in the strict sense. God is conceived as a supreme being, omnipotent, omniscient, and omnipresent, who cares for humanity and establishes a moral code for its followers. This personal God has a direct and meaningful relationship with each individual, offering comfort, guidance, and salvation.

With the progress of societies and the intensification of philosophical reflection, the tendency to conceptualize God in a less personal and more abstract manner emerged. This transition was not immediate but rather gradual and incremental, developing through a series of philosophical and theological advancements. A transcendental innovation can be found in classical Greek philosophy, especially in Platonic and Aristotelian thought. Plato introduced the idea of a "Supreme Good" or "Form of the Good," which transcends the sensible world and is the source of all reality and knowledge.[2] Although not a god in the personal sense, this Supreme Good possesses a divine character fundamental to the structure of reality.

---

2. Plato. *The Republic*. Translated by G. M. A. Grube, revised by C. D. C. Reeve (Indianapolis and Cambridge: Hackett Publishing Company, 1992), Book VII.

In addition, Aristotle developed the idea of the "Unmoved Mover" or "First Mover."[3] This concept describes a first cause not caused by anything else, a Being that is pure actuality and perfection. The Unmoved Mover is eternal, unchanging, and necessarily existent. Although it does not relate to the world personally, it is the ultimate cause of every movement and change in the universe. This idea profoundly influenced medieval scholasticism, especially through Thomas Aquinas, who identified Aristotle's Unmoved Mover with the Christian God.[4]

To analyze the relationship between the Christian God and humanity, St. Thomas Aquinas introduced the concept of "participation," a principle that will be addressed in detail in later chapters. This theoretical framework holds that beings, that is, all creatures, participate in the supreme Being, while maintaining their ontological individuality. God creates humans as beings distinct from Him, endowed with autonomy and freedom. This ontological distinction has shaped the theological and philosophical understanding of the relationship between God and humanity in the West, particularly in Catholic doctrine.

---

3. See Aristotle, *Physics*, Book VIII, in The Complete Works of Aristotle, vol. 1, ed. Jonathan Barnes, trans. R. P. Hardie and R. K. Gaye (Princeton, NJ: Princeton University Press, 1984), 250b15–259a13, 128–44.

4. Wippel, John F. *The Metaphysical Thought of Thomas Aquinas: From Finite Being to Uncreated Being* (Washington, D.C.: Catholic University of America Press, 2000), 440.

Introduction

The notion of "participation" in the thought of St. Thomas is rooted in Aristotelian and Platonic metaphysics. From the Aristotelian tradition, Aquinas inherits a view of reality where contingent beings derive their existence from a first cause, the "Pure Act," which is God. However, the Thomistic innovation lies in how it reconfigures this inheritance by integrating the Platonic concept of participation, in which beings receive their existence from a supreme principle without diluting their own existence. In this framework, participation does not suggest mere causal dependence but rather a profound ontological link that allows the human being to exist while at the same time being oriented toward its ultimate end, which is God Himself.

The doctrine of participation implies that although human beings and all creatures come from God and depend on Him for their existence, they are not identified with divinity. The creature maintains its condition of "other," reflecting the idea of a multiplicity of beings participating in the one Being without merging with Him. This separation allows St. Thomas to argue that the creature can know and love God, but always in a limited way and by analogy since human knowledge cannot fully grasp the divine essence. This point is fundamental to understanding the relationship between the finite and the infinite. While the human being participates in the divine being, it does so partially and imperfectly, which ensures its autonomy while always keeping it in a state of ontological dependence.

Contrary to this notion of participation in Thomas Aquinas, Plotinus' vision offers a radically different view through his doctrine of emanation, a central concept in his Neoplatonic system. For Plotinus, the One, or the Absolute, is the source of all being, from which all things emanate in a necessary and eternal process. This emanation does not imply creation *ex nihilo* but a natural irradiation, similar to the light produced by the sun without being exhausted. In this schema, the cosmos and, therefore, the human being are not independently created entities; rather, they are extensions of the One. Therefore, the relationship between the Divine and creation is one of continuity rather than separation. The multiple unfolds from the unity and, at the same time, aspires to return to it through a process of spiritual and mystical reabsorption.

The main difference between Plotinus' perspective and that of Thomas Aquinas lies in the conception of the ontological independence of the human being. In the Thomistic framework, while dependent on God, humans retain an identity that allows them to be autonomous moral and spiritual agents. This autonomous space is essential to Christian theology, as it justifies the notion of free will and the possibility of merit and guilt. However, in the Plotinian view, individuation is illusory to some extent; the true and essential reality is unity with the One, and any form of distinction is considered a lower degree of reality. Multiplicity is not an end in itself, but a means for the soul to experience and transcend toward its divine source.

The doctrine of emanation in Plotinus carries significant metaphysical and epistemological implications. Since creation is an extension of the One, all knowledge is, ultimately, a process of reminiscence and return to the source. In its journey toward understanding, the human soul must purify itself and rid itself of the shadows of multiplicity to achieve a mystical union with the Divine. This process transcends discursive knowledge and presents itself as a direct intuition of the ultimate reality. For its part, Thomistic thought maintains a clear distinction between creator and creature, allowing knowledge to develop through human natural faculties, illuminated by divine grace, but without losing its rational character.

The comparison between these approaches reveals certain conceptual differences that have important practical implications for humans' spiritual and moral lives. Aquinas' approach favors a life of virtue and rationality, in which grace perfects nature. On the other hand, Plotinus' vision orients or directs the soul toward a more introspective asceticism, seeking a mystical union that transcends language and thought.[5] Participation in Thomas Aquinas and emanation in Plotinus, rather than mere metaphysical theories, represent different paths toward understanding transcendence and the human being's place in the cosmos.

---

5. Plotinus, *The Enneads*, vol. 5, Enneads V.1–9, trans. Arthur Hilary Armstrong, Loeb Classical Library no. 444 (Cambridge, MA: Harvard University Press, 1984), 29 (V.1.6).

While this theophilosophical debate shaped the Western vision of God and human beings, Eastern traditions conceived of the Divine in an abstract and impersonal way. For example, in Hinduism, we find the idea of Brahman, the ultimate reality, pure consciousness, the absolute and impersonal principle underlying all that exists. More than a deity in the anthropomorphic sense, Brahman is the essence of all beings and the source of everything that is. Vedantic wisdom refers to Brahman as *neti-neti* (not this, not that), emphasizing its indefinable, imperceptible, unqualified, and inconceivable nature. Brahman transcends all description, conceptualization, and human understanding, a reality surpassing all relative dualities and particularities. Similarly, in Buddhism, God is not discussed in traditional terms. The dharma (the cosmic law and natural order) and the Buddha nature (the awakened and enlightened pure consciousness) represent abstract principles that transcend personal conceptions of divinity. According to Buddhism, the ultimate essence of reality is emptiness (*śūnyatā*), a state of non-duality that challenges all categories and concepts.

In modern and contemporary Western philosophy, the idea of an abstract God has taken various forms. One of the most significant developments has been the conception of God as consciousness or Being. The German philosopher Georg Wilhelm Friedrich Hegel was a key proponent of this idea. In his philosophical system, Hegel describes God as the Absolute Spirit, a reality that manifests itself through the dialectical process of history and human culture. The Absolute Spirit is not a personal being separate from the world but the totality of reality that develops and understands itself through history.[6] For Hegel, God is consciousness unfolding through time, reaching self-awareness in human self-consciousness.

Hegel's identification of God with the Absolute Spirit facilitated the integration of the personal and abstract conceptions of God throughout this philosophical journey. This integration, which has impacted current philosophy and theology, has sought to preserve the intimate and meaningful relationship that people can have with the Divine while equally recognizing the transcendent and indefinable nature of ultimate reality. Notable examples of this include Karl Rahner and Paul Tillich. Karl Rahner, a 20th-century Catholic theologian, developed the idea of the "Absolute Mystery" or "Absolute Horizon." He identified God as the ultimate and incomprehensible reality and argued that this Absolute Mystery is revealed and made accessible to humans through experience and history. According to him, God is both the transcendent horizon of our existence and the intimate presence in our personal lives and the world.

The theology of Paul Tillich presents, for its part, another type of integrative perspective that describes

---

6. Hegel, Georg Wilhelm Friedrich. *Encyclopedia of Philosophy* (New York: Philosophical Library, 1959), 196.

God as the "Ground of Being" or "Being Itself." Tillich argues that God is not a being among other beings but is the foundation of all existence and the power of being that sustains everything that is. At the same time, he emphasizes that this fundamental reality manifests in our experiences of ultimacy when we face questions and situations that touch on the ultimate meaning and purpose of our lives.

Finally, transitioning to an abstract conception of God has ethical and social implications. If we understand God as the fundamental reality underlying all things, then every human being and, in fact, every entity in the universe participates in this same divine reality. This idea of inclusivity leads to an ethic of respect, compassion, and justice based on recognizing the unity and interconnectedness of all existence.

In this context, the present study will address the philosophy of Martin Heidegger, whose thought unfolds a singular analysis of the idea of God, closely linked to the problem of Being (*Sein*) and human existence (*Dasein*). Heidegger sees Being as the fundamental reality underlying everything that exists.[7] Therefore, instead of conceiving it as a being, he invites us to consider it the original condition enabling beings' existence. This ontological distinction allows the traditional question about God to be displaced toward a more radical reflection that questions the very foundations of classical metaphysics.

---

7. Heidegger, Martin. *Being and Time*, ed. by John Macquarrie and Edward Robinson (Oxford: Basil Blackwell, 1962), 27.

Introduction

Heidegger's exploration of the human being understood as *Dasein*, that is, as being-there-in-the-world, introduces a dimension in which the experience of Being constitutes the starting point for any inquiry into the Divine. Instead of addressing the idea of God as if it were an external object or as a being with defined attributes, Heidegger seeks to understand it from the existential openness of the human—to Being. In this sense, the search for the meaning of Being, as it is lived in *Dasein*, serves as the pathway to think what he calls "the Last God."

As we will see in detail, the "Last God" idea embodies a possibility that exceeds conventional theistic representation. It points to a horizon where divinity, rather than adopting anthropomorphic or personal forms, emerges as a presence that questions and transforms the human being in its totality. This revelation is not a direct presence nor characterized by the tangible closeness of a divine being, but it is understood as an event that reconfigures the very understanding of Being and its relationship with *Dasein*. In this way, the Divine is presented as an immanent transcendence that provokes human beings to reconsider their existence and relationship with the sacred. This approach encourages a critical revision of the categories and assumptions of traditional theology and philosophy, inviting a path of reflection that transcends the boundaries of established metaphysical thought.

The search for the sacred in Heideggerian thought is a challenge and not mere intellectual speculation. As such, it urges us to embark on a journey toward the essence of the Divine, that is, toward what Heidegger understands as an experience of the limit of understanding. As we will see, this journey will allow us to redefine our relationship with the Divine and discover a new connection with the totality of Being. In a state of openness, *Dasein* discovers the sacred as a dimension that transcends and grounds human existence. The "Last God" represents or stands as an invitation to go beyond the limits imposed by traditional representations of divinity. It is not a Being to which one has access through dogmas or formulas. On the contrary, it is a mysterious presence that transforms the understanding and meaning of the sacred.

This journey will take us from the concept of a personal God to the abstract God and, finally, to the Last God. Recognizing that the Divine transcends our human categories and concepts returns us to humility and openness to the mystery of existence. In this context, we will present a new approach characterized by contemplation, meditation, and other forms of spirituality that will open us to the presence of the Divine. Guided by Heidegger's ideas, the search for the Last God leads us into the unknown and, likewise more importantly, into the unknowable, into the depths or essence of Being and our consciousness.

रुद्रारगौतस्
... रुपी
... येतु
... स्वको
... ।।ष

SECTION I
THE ONTOTHEOLOGICAL CONCEPTION OF GOD

Chapter 1

The problem of nihilism

This study begins with what is commonly referred to as "the problem of nihilism." This doctrine asserts that reality and existence lack inherent meaning, as nature has no ultimate purpose or grand plan concerning humanity. The approach in question, which Martin Heidegger mentions in several of his works, entails denying God and any other figure or supreme value that could be conceived as transcendent to humanity. Heidegger identifies that this disorientation is a byproduct of a more serious issue. Humanity has fallen into an ontological crisis as a result, paradoxically, of its effort to understand itself as a being.

The first problem Heidegger highlights is "the forgetting of Being." In its quest to explain everything through thought, Western philosophy has excluded the essence of existence from its frameworks and conceptual categories: Being. Philosophy has constructed a cognitive structure capable of classifying and systematizing reality in many ways, but it has failed to consider the ontological dimension that sustains everything. It has designed an

Section I: The ontotheological conception of God

explanatory map but has ignored that which underlies all things: the Being that grants beings their condition of being, whether they are living or inert. Heidegger attributes this emptiness to "conceptualization," that is, the tendency of the philosophical tradition, beginning from Plato to equate thinking with the activity of conceptualizing. Under this paradigm, the act of thinking is reduced to assigning concepts to objects of knowledge, a practice that, as he emphasizes, confines understanding to the domain of the ontic to the detriment of the ontological. Rather than allowing the mind to open to Being itself, concepts put reality into the schemes of prefabrication, thereby preventing its true nature from revealing itself.

Furthermore, this problem means that, under the epistemological structure developed to understand the world and humanity's position, philosophy has reduced the possibility of thinking to merely categorizing objects and beings. Thus, even when the object of study was not a tangible being, this approach has treated it as if it were, leading to an ontological confusion that equates Being with a being. Being, which is not a being but the source of all beings, has been confined and conceptualized, denying its true nature and relegating it to oblivion for not fitting into the preconceived categories of philosophical epistemology.

Philosophy has, consequently, prioritized its own conceptual structure over the reality it seeks to understand rather than approaching it in a way that respects its inherent nature. This act of conceptualization has led to a distortion where Being has been ontified and, in doing so, has hidden itself from philosophical vision. Every attempt to think about Being within the limits of the conceptual apparatus constructed by philosophy has resulted in its continuous disappearance. Therefore, the very effort to conceptualize Being has led to its concealment.

Heidegger emphasizes that this problem has implications that go beyond mere epistemological discussions. The confusion that has reduced Being to a being has impacted how humans think about themselves, preventing them from accessing their own Being, and their most authentic essence. This has led to reducing humans to merely conceptualized beings, framed in philosophical categories and, later, also in scientific ones. The dimensions of humans that do not fit into such ontic structures have been systematically removed from the field of knowledge, thereby limiting "understanding" to what is empirically demonstrable.

Modern philosophy, and science as its extension, has limited human self-understanding by eliminating what cannot be subjected to its own empirical and conceptual categories. This ontological limitation has resulted in a constant reification of reality and the human being as well as in a reductive conceptualization of the figure of God. Institutionalized religion has adapted the notion of God to this framework, presenting Him as an accessible figure who fits into a conceptual scheme as a personal deity. This has prevented us from perceiving

Section I: The ontotheological conception of God

God in His own essence, beyond a reflection created in the image of the human being.

The problem is relevant because, before the rise of the Platonic Academy and the establishment of philosophy as a discipline, humans had tried to understand themselves by turning to art and religious meditation. These efforts sought to capture the relationship with Being or the Divine, that is, with what is inconceptualizable. The inability to approach our own essence and meaning has led to what Heidegger, and Nietzsche who came before him, described as nihilism, a position often translated into skepticism or relativism.[8] In its various forms, this nihilism suggests that nothing transcends our conceptualization of reality and ourselves; and that everything is ephemeral or temporary and devoid of their own or inherent meaning. This work aims to address this problem. To do so, we accept Heidegger's invitation to explore and overcome conceptualization to get closer or return to Being and God, specifically to "the Last God," but this time perceiving Him in His own terms and immanent nature.

---

8. Nietzsche, Friedrich. *The Will to Power*. Edited by Walter Kaufmann. Translated by Walter Kaufmann and R. J. Hollingdale. New York: Vintage Books, 1968.

Chapter 2

The history of the concept

In light of the general context described, we will begin by offering a brief history of the concept and the problem of conceptualization in the Western philosophical tradition. This will help us position ourselves and define the scope of the issues presented in the introduction and in the previous chapter. Since its origins, concepts have been interpreted according to each era's philosophical and epistemological problems, allowing for their constant redefinition over time. In Greek philosophy, the systematic study of the concept has a crucial starting point in the reflections of Plato and Aristotle. For Plato, as we mentioned before, concepts are not simple mental representations derived from experience; instead, they refer to the eternal Ideas or Forms. These Ideas exist in a transcendent and unchanging realm, and the sensible objects in the physical world are mere imperfect reflections of these metaphysical realities. For example, the concept of "justice," for Plato, points to an ideal Idea that transcends any particular manifestation of justice in the empirical world. In other words, the concept of "justice" as such does not derive from or arise out of any manifestations of justice that may occur in the sensible world of experience.

In contrast, Aristotle offers a more empirical and concrete conception of concepts. For him, concepts are formed through a process of abstraction based on sensory experience. That is, instead of situating them in a transcendent world, Aristotle holds that concepts arise from analyzing the common properties among objects, being universals that can be applied to multiple individuals. His work *Organon* lays the foundations for logic and defines concepts as categorical predicates, an approach that will shape the development of logic and the philosophy of science moving forward.

During the Middle Ages, Christian philosophy incorporated Aristotle's notion of the concept into its theological framework. Thomas Aquinas adapts Aristotle's theory of concepts to explain how the human mind can know both material and divine realities. In his view, concepts are formed through abstracting from sensible data, but this process is illuminated by divine reason. In scholasticism, concepts play a fundamental role as intermediaries between human reason and knowledge of the Absolute. This view positions the concept as a bridge between the finite and the infinite, uniting logical categories with theological realities.

For his part, John Duns Scotus examined the concept from a perspective that integrates knowledge, metaphysics, and language, offering an approach of great precision within the medieval scholastic framework. His vision significantly influenced the theory of knowledge and logic, addressing the concept as a universal mental representation that allows the human mind to grasp the essence of objects.[9] Concepts are abstractions that mediate between concrete individuals and intellectual understanding. Through them, the intellect can know universal realities starting from the sensory experience of the particular. Scotus argues that concepts have formal universality; although they derive from the experience of individual objects, they acquire a universal character in the mental realm. For example, the concept of "humanity," instead of referring to a particular human being, refers to the essence shared by all human beings. This universality does not imply, as in Platonism, that concepts exist outside the mind but rather that they are constructions of the intellect that abstract the essential characteristics of multiple individuals.

One of Scotus's most relevant contributions to the issue of concepts is his position on universals, which is framed within moderate realism. For him, universal concepts have their foundation in reality, as they reflect the true essences of particular objects, but their universality only exists in the intellect. That is, essences (such as humanity or animality) are real in individuals, but their universal character only manifests in the mental

---

9. Duns Scotus, John. *Duns Scotus: Philosophical Writings.* Translated by Allan B. Wolter, OFM. (London: Thomas Nelson and Sons, Ltd., 1962).

Section I: The ontotheological conception of God

process of abstraction. This approach balances the reality of individual essences with the universalization that occurs in understanding.

Scotus also introduces a fundamental distinction between univocal and analogous concepts, especially in his treatment of Being. A univocal term is applied uniformly to everything. In contrast, analogous terms vary in meaning depending on the context in which they are used, such as the attribute "good." For Scotus, the concept of being is univocal, so it is applied uniformly to both God and creatures, even though their modes of existence are radically different. Scotus differs from the dominant scholastic view represented by Thomas Aquinas, who argued that Being cannot be applied analogously to God and creatures since their existence is essentially distinct. On the other hand, Scotus maintains that although God and creatures differ radically in their modes of existence, the concept of being must be applied in the same way to both to avoid conceptual ambiguities. Scotus's position on the concept reflects an integration between his moderate realism regarding universals and a theory of knowledge based on the univocity of essential concepts. This synthesis allows him to preserve both the formal universality of knowledge and the ontological uniqueness of individuals, overcoming the limitations of his predecessors and providing a coherent framework for understanding how the human mind apprehends reality.

In this context, Scotus introduces the notion of haecceity (in the Latin *haecceitas*, meaning "this-ness" or

Chapter 2: The history of the concept

"this-hood") as one of the crucial themes of his work. This term refers to the metaphysical principle that grants each entity its irreducible individuality. Unlike notions such as essence or nature, which describe the shared properties of individuals of the same species, haecceity addresses what makes each individual unique and irreplaceable. In order to understand this concept, it is necessary to place it within the context of the theory of individuation, which seeks to determine what makes an individual unique, even when it shares the same essence with others. Traditionally, philosophy held that essences or natures explain the common characteristics among individuals; for example, all human beings share the essence of "humanity." However, this explanation does not clarify what makes an individual particular, that is, what makes it this individual and not another. Scotus proposes the concept of "haecceity" to resolve this problem. According to him, haecceity constitutes the principle that makes a being this particular being, but without adding an additional quality to its essence. While nature or essence defines what a being is (such as "human"), haecceity determines who that particular being is (for example, "John"). In this way, haecceity grants the individual a singularity that cannot be shared by any other.

In Scotus's metaphysics, this principle of individuation is presented as a solution to earlier theories. For example, Thomas Aquinas argued that the individuation of material beings is explained through matter. According to Aquinas, individuals are distinguished from one

SECTION I: THE ONTOTHEOLOGICAL CONCEPTION OF GOD

another by the particular matter they possess. However, Scotus considered this explanation insufficient, arguing that matter, on its own, cannot fully explain the uniqueness of each being. For Scotus, haecceity is a formal principle that, in combination with matter, explains what makes a being unique and irreplaceable. The importance of haecceity is not limited to human beings, extending to all entities. Scotus uses this concept to explain the individuality of both material and immaterial beings. Even angels, who lack matter and share the same essence, differ from one; thanks to their haecceity. This principle allows Scotus to preserve the notion of individuality in any being, highlighting the ability of haecceity to explain uniqueness within his metaphysical framework.

Furthermore, the ideas of univocity and haecceity allow Duns Scotus to propose a new metaphysical map concerning Being, God, and humanity, from which he addresses other fundamental issues such as creation. To do this, the Scottish philosopher introduces two new fundamental terms, "facticity" and "contingency," which are linked to divine freedom. The term "facticity" takes on special importance in the relationship between God, creation, and the world's facts, within which Scotus explains the distinction between what is necessary and what is contingent. At the heart of Scotus's thought is his assertion of the radical contingency of the created world. From this perspective, it is possible to identify two types of realities: necessary and contingent. The former are those that, by their nature, cannot be otherwise, such

Chapter 2: The history of the concept

as logical or mathematical truths, for example "2 + 2 = 4." These truths are immutable and do not depend on divine will.

On the other hand, contingent truths, which include the facts of the world, could have been different. The world we inhabit is not the only possible one; God, in His absolute freedom, could have created a different world or even created nothing at all. This sovereign choice of God reveals the world's factual nature. The term "factual" refers, in this context, to the facts that shape reality: contingencies that are not necessary in themselves and, therefore, depend entirely on divine free will. The factual is that which exists due to a contingent will of God, but which could not have existed or been different. In this way, the distinction between the necessary and the factual that Scotus introduces highlights the absolute dependence of creation on divine will. The existence of the world does not obey an intrinsic necessity but is the product of God's free choice. Therefore, what makes creation contingent, and thus factual, is precisely the lack of a logical or natural necessity that determines its existence; what exists is the result of a free decision.

This distinction is quite different from the approach of earlier thinkers like Thomas Aquinas, who emphasizes the relationship between God's necessary being and the contingent being of creation while stressing the intrinsic rationality of the world. On the other hand, Scotus maintains that divine freedom implies the absence of

SECTION I: THE ONTOTHEOLOGICAL CONCEPTION OF GOD

a necessary reason to explain each fact. As mentioned earlier, God, in His freedom, could have arranged a different reality, highlighting and explaining the factual and non-necessary nature of the events we observe. The Scotist concept of facticity also has an ontological dimension. The factual refers to what could have been different while also depending on an external foundation for its existence. In this case, that ultimate foundation is God, whose being is necessary and does not depend on anything else. Therefore, the factual refers to that which, although present in the world, that is, although real, does not exist necessarily and could not have existed. This contingent nature is explained by divine freedom, whose decision grants being to everything that exists.

Scotus's analysis of facticity has important philosophical implications, especially in ethics and theological fields. In the field of moral theology, the contingency and facticity of the world offer a particular perspective on divine commandments. According to Scotus, not all moral precepts are equally necessary. While some precepts are absolute, such as "thou shalt not kill," which he considers an immutable natural law, others, such as the command to observe the Sabbath, could have been different or might not have existed. This distinction between universal and contingent precepts reflects the flexibility of moral norms based on divine freedom and historical circumstances.

With the arrival of modernity, the debate about the nature of concepts intensifies, especially with the rise of rationalism and empiricism. René Descartes places concepts in the realm of innatism, arguing that certain concepts, such as "God" or "the self," are innate in the human mind and do not come from experience. For Descartes, clear and distinct concepts are essential for true knowledge, and human reason can access the Truth through these innate concepts. In contrast, British empiricism, represented by John Locke, rejects the idea of innate concepts and asserts that all concepts come from experience. In *An essay concerning human understanding* (1690), Locke argues that at birth, the mind is a *tabula rasa*[10] (Latin for "blank slate") and that concepts are constructed by combining simple ideas obtained through the senses. According to this view, the concept of "cat," for example, is formed by observing several particular cats, which allows one to abstract their common characteristics. For his part, Gottfried Leibniz attempts to reconcile Cartesian rationalism with Locke's empiricism. In his view, concepts are innate predispositions in the soul, though their development requires interaction with the world. It is through experience that these potentialities are actualized and perfected, making a synthesis between innate reason and sensory data possible.

German idealism introduces a true revolution in the understanding of concepts, especially with the

---

10. John Locke, *An Essay Concerning Humane Understanding: In Four Books*, 4th ed. (London: Printed for Awnsham and John Churchill, and Samuel Manship, 1700), Book II, chap. I, sec. 2, 41.

Section I: The ontotheological conception of God

thought of Immanuel Kant and G.W.F. Hegel. Kant, in his *Critique of Pure Reason* (1781), argues that concepts are not merely derived from experience nor innate in an empirical sense; rather, they are *a priori* forms that the understanding uses to structure experience. The categories of the understanding, such as causality, substance, or unity, are necessary for any experience to be possible. Concepts, therefore, do not merely describe reality but constitute it. Without them, we would not be able to perceive the world coherently. Hegel takes this conception further by viewing concepts as dynamic entities that evolve through a dialectical process. For Hegel, concepts are not fixed or timeless. They unfold historically, reflecting the development of reality itself. The concept of "being," for example, can only be understood in its relation to "non-being" and "becoming," not as a static entity. In this sense, and similarly to Kant, for Hegel, concepts actively participate in the constitution and historical transformation of reality rather than simply being tools we use to describe it. In other words, in the eyes of German idealism, reality constitutes itself as such by being thought and understood.

The 20th century witnesses the development of two key philosophical approaches regarding concepts: analytic philosophy and phenomenology. In the analytic tradition, figures like Gottlob Frege and Bertrand Russell focus on the logical analysis of concepts. For Frege, concepts are functions that assign truth values to the objects they apply.[11] Conceptual analysis, therefore, consists of clarifying the conditions under which a concept can be applied to a particular object, allowing for a more rigorous understanding of language and its structure. Later, Ludwig Wittgenstein introduced a different approach, arguing that concepts are not static and their meaning depends on their use in language or, more specifically, on language games. That is, the social context determines the meaning of terms and, thus, the nature of concepts.

On the other hand, Edmund Husserl's phenomenology offers a different perspective. For Husserl, concepts are fundamental for intentional consciousness, implying how the mind directs itself toward objects. Through his phenomenological reduction, he seeks to unravel how concepts emerge from experience and structure our relationship with the world. His approach focuses on subjectivity and how concepts condition the way we perceive.

In contemporary philosophy, the study of concepts has been radically transformed by thinkers like Michel Foucault, Gilles Deleuze, and Jacques Derrida. In the development of his philosophical work, Foucault explores the linguistic construction of reality through an approach focused on analyzing discourse and the relationships between power and knowledge. Unlike traditional philosophical approaches, Foucault does

---

11. Frege, Gottlob, *The Thought: A Logical Inquiry*. Mind, Vol. LXV, No. 259 (July, 1956), 292.

Section I: The ontotheological conception of God

not understand language as a passive medium for describing an objective and independent reality. Discourse is more than a set of words that refer to objects or facts. Every society defines rules that determine what is accepted as "truth." For him, language is an active force that participates in creating and structuring reality. It reflects the power structures determining what can be said, thought, and known in a given time and society.[12] Thus, instead of simply communicating information, language also imposes limits on what constitutes reality.

These categories through which we understand the world are not universal or permanent but historical and contingent, shaped by the power relations of each historical period. An emblematic example of this dynamic is the transformation of the concept of "madness." Before the Modern Age, madness was not considered a mental illness that required diagnosis and treatment by experts. However, with the rise of the human and medical sciences, madness was "constructed" discursively as a pathology. This discursive shift transformed the notion of madness. By defining it as a condition that must be treated, it hence directly contributed to the establishment of psychiatric hospitals. As we see, discourse is not neutral; on the contrary, it is rather a mechanism for regulation and social control.

---

12. Foucault, Michel. *History of Madness*, edited by Jean Khalfa and translated by Jonathan Murphy and Jean Khalfa (London: Routledge, 2006), xx–xxi.

Chapter 2: The history of the concept

The relationship between power and knowledge is fundamental in Foucault's work. According to his analysis, power and knowledge are not separate entities; where there is knowledge production, there is simultaneously a form of power that structures it. Therefore, knowledge creation is conditioned by power configurations that classify what is true or false. Scientific, medical, or legal discourses determine what is true and thus create norms that shape social life and human relationships. In this way, power-knowledge constructs the epistemological reality through which it designs social and political reality. Moreover, Foucault introduces the "order of discourse," which refers to the rules and restrictions that determine what can be said in a given context. This order encompasses mechanisms of exclusion, such as censorship, the prohibition of certain topics, and classification practices that determine what is meaningful and what must be ignored. Thus, discourse produces subjects and objects of knowledge with which it establishes the legitimate ways of understanding the world. For example, medical discourses define what a healthy body is and thereby construct concepts like health and illness.

Foucault employs archaeology and genealogy of knowledge to understand how discourses have shaped reality over time. Archaeology analyzes the discursive structures that have defined what is considered

Section I: The ontotheological conception of God

"knowledge" at different historical moments.[13] This approach does not seek to trace a linear evolution of knowledge, but rather to identify the discontinuities that have transformed our way of thinking. For its part, Genealogy investigates the power mechanisms that sustain and reproduce those discourses. It aims to demonstrate how power-dominance relations have shaped discursive practices and how "truth" is always mediated by struggles for power. Foucault's theory of the linguistic construction of reality has important philosophical implications. First, it questions the idea of an objective and independent reality that can be discovered through reason or science. In line with Foucault, what we call "reality" is always conditioned by power struggles. This leads to a relational and contingent conception of knowledge: there is no single truth, but multiple truths that emerge in specific historical and social contexts. Thus, reality is presented as that which has been constituted and conditioned by discourse and the power relations that prevail at a given moment.

This approach also implies a reconsideration of the traditional notion of the subject. Foucault rejects the conception of an autonomous and rational subject controlling language and knowledge. On the contrary, he argues that the subject itself is a product of discourse. That is, the categories through which

---

13. Foucault, Michel. *The Order of Things: An Archaeology of Human Sciences* (New York: Vintage, 1994), xxi–xxii.

Chapter 2: The history of the concept

we define our identity, such as gender, race, class, or health, are not innate but are discursive constructions that vary with time and place. In this way, subjects are not stable beings but the result of discursive practices that constitute and delimit them.

Foucault's approach is reinforced in the works of subsequent authors, such as Deleuze and Derrida, among others. In his work with Félix Guattari, Deleuze maintains that concepts are not mere representations of what exists; they are philosophical creations that produce new realities. Concepts, therefore, are in constant transformation and creation, serving as tools for new forms of thought. Derrida, for his part, from the perspective of deconstruction, investigates how concepts are structured by binary oppositions and how these oppositions are inherently unstable. Derrida maintains that no concept has a fixed essence and that its meaning always depends on its relationship to what it excludes, to its otherness. This view reveals, confirming the stance of both Foucault and Deleuze, the indeterminacy and impossibility of definitively fixing the meaning of concepts. The importance of this line of thought in contemporary philosophy is that it questions the foundations of the history of philosophy itself. That is, even philosophical theories and proposals are power discourses that, through language, have designed and delimited ontological and metaphysical, and ultimately also ethical, parameters through which we understand the world. Foucault, Deleuze, and other authors follow the "philosophy of suspicion," viewing philosophy as a powerful tool humans use to understand the world based on each historical moment.

The "philosophy of suspicion" should not be understood as a mere attempt to discredit and corner or challenge philosophy or theology. On the contrary, Foucault's philosophy, especially that of Nietzsche, who came before him, allows us to exercise a critical attitude that encourages us to return to earlier philosophers. In the context of this book, rereading and analyzing these lines of thought will help us unravel discursive and turns of thinking whose consequences have been important, and in many cases negative, for the subject of Being and God.

Chapter 3

The distance from the Divine

The medieval period witnessed a close and complex relationship between scholastic philosophy and theology, creating a robust intellectual structure that fostered a solid analysis of God and the connection between divinity and humanity.[14] The rediscovery of Aristotle, driven by Latin translations made by scholars such as William of Moerbeke, significantly impacted scholasticism. Aristotelian principles were integrated into scholastic discourse, such as the distinction between substance and accident, act and potency, and the theory of the four causes. These provided tools for a more detailed examination of the structure of Being and its dependence on a pure act identified with God, without composition or potentiality.

In this era, rooted in the contributions of Plato and Aristotle, essential questions were addressed, which spurred a renewal of philosophical concepts and

---

14. Klima, Gyula, Fritz Allhoff, and Anand Jayprakash Vaidya, eds. *Medieval Philosophy: Essential Readings with Commentary*. (Oxford: Wiley-Blackwell, 2007), 3.

Section I: The ontotheological conception of God

redefined abstract thought processes. The goal was to achieve a more detailed and accurate conception of Being and, at the same time, to chart a renewed path toward understanding the essence and existence of God. Scholasticism employed a method that unified the rigor of logic with theological reflection, allowing for a meticulous and orderly analysis of metaphysics. Aristotelian contributions enriched new theories of divine transcendence and its relationship with the cosmos. They focused on causality and formal logic alongside Platonic ideas of dualism between the world of Ideas and concrete reality. This rational framework transcended simple faith and integrated reason and theology into a coherent discourse. The new conceptual constructions went beyond defining God as the absolute principle and explored the interaction between human finitude and the infinite, between the soul and the totality of Being.

Among the most prominent thinkers of this time was Thomas Aquinas. He combined Aristotle's logic with Christian doctrine to develop arguments that demonstrated the existence of God and could be understood both by reason and by faith. The five ways of Thomism represent a key example of how rational reflection and theological knowledge could converge to forge a bridge between the observable and the transcendental.[15] This method solidified medieval

---

15. Aquinas, Thomas. *Summa Theologica*. Translated by the Fathers of the English Dominican Province (New York: Benziger Bros., 1947).

philosophy as a space where rational investigation and revelation shared a common purpose: offering a deeper and more cohesive understanding of Being and the relationship between humanity and the Divine.

This period focused its attention on the existence of God and His attributes, such as omniscience, omnipotence, and absolute goodness. Debates concerning God's essence required analogical language to refer to the Divine but avoid a literal interpretation that would confuse the created with the creator. Aquinas' theory of the analogy of Being became a fundamental tool. It emphasized the ontological difference between absolute Being and finite beings without falling into contradictions.

The influence of Aristotelian metaphysics manifested clearly in the work of the Italian theologian, especially in his concept of *actus essendi*, or the "act of being," as the principle that grounds the existence of everything that is. This concept transformed the perception of reality by asserting that, in God, being and essence are identical, while in creatures, these elements are distinct. This highlighted the ontological dependence of the contingent on the necessary, offering an explanatory framework for the participation of the finite in the absolute. The approach revitalized the view of the universe as a hierarchical order in which each being occupied a place oriented toward the Supreme Being.

Anselm of Canterbury, with his famous ontological argument, also exemplified the use of reason to address the existence of God. According to Anselm, the notion of a being "than which nothing greater can be conceived"[16] implied its existence as a being that exists in the mind and in reality, is greater than one that exists only in the mind. This reasoning sparked extensive debates and was criticized by Gaunilo of Moutiers and, later, by Thomas Aquinas, who preferred an approach based on experience and the observation of the sensible world, meaning, an *a posteriori* analysis.

Another central aspect of scholastic development was the attempt to harmonize human freedom with divine omniscience. Medieval philosophers faced the challenge of reconciling God's absolute knowledge with free will. The dilemma was whether God's prescience influenced human decisions or if it could coexist with freedom. Thomas Aquinas proposed that God, being timeless, sees all events in an eternal present, which preserves human autonomy without sacrificing divine omniscience.

Plato's theory of Ideas also notably influenced reflections about universals, a topic of great relevance in scholastic thought. As a proponent of moderate realism, Thomas Aquinas argued that universals existed in the mind of God as eternal archetypes. At the same time, nominalists, in contrast, saw them as mere linguistic constructs without independent existence. This debate was crucial in defining the foundations of ontology

---

16. Oppy, Graham; Rasmussen, Josh; Schmid, Joseph (2023), "*Ontological Arguments*," in Zalta, Edward N.; Nodelman, Uri (eds.), *The Stanford Encyclopedia of Philosophy* (Fall 2023 ed.).

Chapter 3: The distance from the Divine

and epistemology at the time, and it affected how the relationship between human knowledge and ultimate reality was conceived.

The contribution of medieval philosophy to the development of thought that integrated faith and reason was fundamental. This approach ensured that theology was not reduced to irrational belief. Instead, it acquired the status of a systematic discipline in which the existence and attributes of God could be deduced from logical and rational foundations.

One of these debates is the "problem of universals." Philosophy has explored the relationship between individual objects and the general qualities that these objects share. This metaphysical problem addresses the difficulty of explaining how different objects can share the same property or class. Specifically, it seeks to determine whether universal properties, such as "red," "roundness," or "justice," are real entities of objects independent of the mind or whether they are merely mental constructs. This dilemma arises when we observe that particular objects share similar qualities. Take, for example, a red rose. Although each red rose is a unique individual, all red roses share the common quality of being roses and being red or belonging to the categories "rose" and "red." What does it mean to say something is "red" or "just"? Do "redness" or "justice" exist as real, independent entities, or are they merely projections that the mind creates from observing empirical objects presented to us through the senses?

SECTION I: THE ONTOTHEOLOGICAL CONCEPTION OF GOD

This discussion distinguishes three key philosophical positions: realism, nominalism, and conceptualism. Realism holds that universals exist independently of the particular objects that manifest them. Two approaches stand out within this position: Platonic realism and Aristotelian realism. The former, as presented by Plato, argues that universals exist in a transcendent realm separate from the material world. According to this view, the sensible objects of the world participate in the eternal Forms or Ideas.[17] For instance, all red things participate in the "Idea of redness," which exists in an abstract plane beyond space and time and whose existence is not relative to the red things that participate in it as an Idea. For his part, although a disciple of Plato, Aristotle modified this perspective by asserting that universals exist as present in the particular objects themselves rather than in a separate realm. In this sense, universals do not exist outside individuals but rather reside in them. For example, the Idea of humanity is present in each human being but not as a separate and independent entity apart from the human beings in which it manifests. Despite this important difference, both conceive universals as ontological realities, whether in a transcendent (Plato) or immanent (Aristotle) way.

Nominalism, in contrast to realism, denies the real existence of universals. For nominalists, universals are not entities in themselves, neither dependent nor

---

17. George, Grote. *Plato, and the Other Companions of Sokrates*, vol. 2, 2nd ed. (London: John Murray, 1867), 266, chap. XXV.

Chapter 3: The distance from the Divine

independent, and only concrete individuals have real existence. Universals are merely names or labels we use to group objects that exhibit similarities. For example, calling several objects "red" does not imply the existence of an independent "redness" outside of them, nor does it mean that "redness" is inherent in them. Redness, in contrast, would be a linguistic convention derived from observation. One of the most influential proponents of this perspective was William of Ockham, who argued that it is unnecessary to postulate the existence of additional entities like universals. According to him, only concrete individuals exist, while universals are general terms the mind uses to describe and classify these individuals and their similarities.

Conceptualism, for its part, occupies a position between realism and nominalism. According to this view, universals are not autonomous entities existing outside the physical world; neither are they mere words. Universals exist as abstract concepts in the human mind. In other words, when we observe various objects that share a common property, such as "redness," we form the concept of "redness" in our minds even though that concept has no existence outside of the mind. This position was defended by philosophers such as Peter Abelard, who argued that although universals do not exist in extra-mental reality, they cannot be reduced to mere names and thus do not simply arise from language. For Abelard, universals are mental concepts that allow us to group, classify, and understand particular objects based on the properties they share.

Section I: The ontotheological conception of God

The debate surrounding universals has significant implications in various branches of philosophy, from ontology and epistemology to logic and language. In the ontological realm, which is the study of Being in general, the position one adopts regarding universals directly affects the conception of reality. In its various versions, realism posits the existence of abstract or general entities that transcend the physical world, while nominalism reduces all existence to particular individuals. In the epistemological realm, the theory of universals influences our understanding of knowledge. If universals exist as autonomous realities, then by knowing properties like "justice" or "redness," we are accessing objective aspects of the world. However, if universals are merely mental constructions, as suggested by nominalism or conceptualism, knowing these universals would be more of an intellectual operation without an extra-mental correlate rather than a discovery of independent realities.

Similarly, how language refers to classes of objects or properties is also directly tied to the conception of universals. If universals are merely names, as nominalism maintains, then language has a purely conventional character. If, on the other hand, universals are real entities, then language reflects essential and structural aspects of the world. The theory of universals, therefore, opens a debate between realism, nominalism, and conceptualism regarding the properties shared by particular objects and their place within the metaphysical order.

CHAPTER 3: THE DISTANCE FROM THE DIVINE

In this context, we will now focus on the third of these positions, which synthesizes the previous two and begins to lay an epistemological foundation within modern philosophy. As we have seen, conceptualism defends the idea that universals are mental concepts that allow us to group, classify, and thus understand particular objects according to their properties. This position is articulated around two fundamental properties: extension and comprehension. These properties establish both the scope and the degree of precision with which a concept can include multiple elements while simultaneously specifying the essential characteristics that define it. In a rigorous philosophical framework, these notions are essential for delimiting a concept's degree of inclusivity and intelligibility since their inversely proportional relationship conditions how conceptual thought is organized. The extension of a concept refers to the set of individuals or entities it encompasses. A relevant example of this is the concept of "animal," whose extension is considerably vast as it includes a variety of living beings, from insects to mammals. This property allows the concept to encompass many entities, though with a more general level of detail.

In contrast, comprehension or intension refers to the defining notes that constitute the essence of the concept. The greater the comprehension of a concept, the more precise and detailed the characteristics that define it will be. However, its extension will decrease, applying to a more limited number of entities. For example, the

Section I: The ontotheological conception of God

"Siamese cat" concept has a greater comprehension than "animal," as it specifies unique characteristics of a particular species, even though its extension is smaller, referring only to cats. The interaction between extension and comprehension is inversely proportional. This means that as the extension of a concept increases, comprehension becomes vaguer, as it becomes necessary to include fewer specific properties. A concept with great extension tends to be more general, sacrificing precision.

This phenomenon is especially evident when attempting to encompass totalities, like Being, which is one of the broadest concepts in the history of philosophical thought. The concept of Being is the most extensive one that can be conceived, as its field covers the totality of what exists, what is, and what there is, from physical entities to abstract and immaterial ones. Due to this extreme breadth, the understanding of Being becomes blurred, making its conceptual apprehension difficult. When attempting to encompass all that exists, the concept of Being loses specific content, significantly reducing its intelligibility. This immediately reveals the limitations of conceptual thought itself when dealing with notions that exceed its ability to delineate clearly.

Since ancient times, the concept of "universality" in the philosophical tradition has generated a reflection that extends beyond epistemology, delving into ontological and metaphysical terrain. The discussion of universals is not limited to understanding their function as instruments of knowledge; rather, it expands toward questions concerning Being in its utmost expression. This ontological dimension introduces a degree of complexity that conceptualism struggles to encompass despite its valuable contributions to epistemology. The human cognitive capacity to organize, categorize, and distinguish the particular within sensory experience allows for a form of knowledge useful for ordering the multiplicity of the perceptible world. However, this conceptual structure reaches an impassable threshold when addressing the totality of Being.

Moreover, within the purely epistemological realm, conceptualism, which postulates the non-independence of universals outside the human intellect, provides an effective explanatory model for understanding how individuals can identify and relate singular entities in a shared environment. This approach is essential for understanding the formation of mental categories that enable our comprehension of the phenomenal world and interaction with it. However, its applicability is restricted when facing transcendental universals, such as Being itself or the notion of the Divine. Attempting to apply the categorical structure of conceptualism to the understanding of Being entails a reduction that overlooks its ontological depth.

In examining Being as a universal, the categories produced by conceptual thought prove insufficient because they cannot capture its true essence. Integrating Being into a categorical system involves reducing it to just another object among others, stripping it of its

SECTION I: THE ONTOTHEOLOGICAL CONCEPTION OF GOD

fundamental role as the basis of being and knowledge. This reveals to us that, by its very nature, Being, as a universal, transcends any attempt at conceptualization that seeks to fit it within human categories, thus challenging the capacity of reason to comprehend it in its entirety. This limitation also reveals the inherent boundaries of a mode of thought that attempts to classify reality without grasping its ultimate foundation.

The incapacity of conceptualism to address the universality of Being leads us to explore other philosophical perspectives that can achieve a more integral understanding of reality. The knowledge that transcends mere categorization and approaches the essence of existence must surpass the strictly epistemological framework of conceptualism. The limitations of conceptualism become more apparent or clearer when the universal in question is God, whose essence defies any attempt at rational conceptualization. In this context, ontological reflection and metaphysical thought open up a space to investigate the nature of Being more profoundly, free from empirical or logical analysis. Attempting to confine the notion of the divine within cognitive categories constitutes a reduction of an idea that, by its very nature, escapes the parameters of reason. Thus, the classical metaphysical tradition has maintained that God requires a different approach that transcends traditional analytical tools. Otherwise, defining God within categorical frameworks will only obscure its true nature.

Chapter 3: The distance from the Divine

The philosophical challenge of addressing these concepts cannot be ignored. Both Being and the Divine represent frontiers that question the sufficiency of the categories and concepts useful for understanding the multiple and the finite but incapable of encompassing the Absolute. This limit, however, does not imply the abdication of the effort to know. On the contrary, it is an explicit recognition that there are dimensions of reality whose understanding demands an approach that transcends the thinking structures that try to reduce the incomprehensible (Being) to the familiar (being). Only in this way can we continue the search for a truth that, though unattainable in its entirety, remains the driving force behind the highest philosophical thought.

Martin Heidegger's hermeneutic philosophy focuses on the rigorous exploration of the tension between conceptual clarity and the complexity of existence, which the author traces back to the roots of Plato's thought. As we will see in detail later, for Heidegger, the point at which Plato redefines Being as an abstract entity marks a decisive turning point in the trajectory of Western philosophy. This Platonic reinterpretation is key because it marks a deviation from the pre-Socratic philosophers like Heraclitus and Parmenides, who understood Being as a fundamental reality that escapes the restrictions of abstract conceptualization. This Platonic transformation of Being into an abstract idea has significant implications. First, it weakens the intuitive connection with the Divine and, as a result, strips the

Section I: The ontotheological conception of God

understanding of divinity of its vital and immanent character. Thus, the Divine is reduced to a purely intellectual construct, lacking existential resonance. Heidegger sees in this turn a prelude to the systematic approach that characterizes much of later philosophy, especially analytic philosophy, where conceptual precision and eliminating ambiguities become the primary goals. This same desire to structure knowledge within universal categories leads to the "forgetting of Being."

The first consequence of this forgetting is the imposition of a categorical system that seeks to encompass the totality of reality but paradoxically excludes Being itself, which withdraws and evades. This withdrawal of Being implies an irresolvable conflict: universal and abstract concepts aim to encompass a necessary essence, but concrete human existence, with all its singularity and contingency, cannot be captured by such structures. Being resisting encapsulation in an eidetic framework carries with it human existence, which also cannot be fully defined by universal categories. As a result, concrete existence is ultimately addressed through general notions on the one hand and as empirical, quantifiable data on the other. This conceptual dilemma, born of the transformation imposed by Plato, culminates in the difficulty of conceiving the relationship between humanity and the Divine outside purely intellectual schemas.

Therefore, Heidegger argues that reflection on God and the essential relationship between the human

Chapter 3: The distance from the Divine

being and the sacred requires a form of thinking that escapes the limitations of traditional conceptual systems. This reflection transcends philosophy, understood as a mere analysis of concepts. It opens a path toward more integral thought that can encompass the totality of existence without reducing it to abstract formulas. In his proposal, Heidegger calls for a break with philosophy understood as simple categorization, inviting a form of thought that recognizes the insufficiency of conceptual tools to capture the essence of Being. This intellectual renewal points toward an approach to reviving human experience in all its singularity. It also suggests that philosophy must transform into a dialogue that surpasses the limits of abstraction and acknowledges the complexity of Being and existence in its totality.

Chapter 4

The birth of ontotheology

In the early stages of this study, we can say that ontotheology, as a philosophical category, tries to capture God within the conceptual parameters of ontology. This implies that God is preconceived as a being that can be assigned a place within the order of existence. Ontotheology approach arises or starts from the intersection of two fields: First, ontology, understood as the study of Being as such, and second, theology, which is the discipline addressing issues related to the Divine. By integrating the Divine into the ontological domain, ontotheology brings God into the realm of rational thought, subjecting Him to the analytical tools historically used to study reality in its various forms. In this sense, ontotheology attempts to make God an object of study comparable to other objects in reality, approaching Him with the categories of being.

The term itself implies a transition of the Divine into the realm of what can be thought and classified within the system of Being. aiming for an understanding from the perspective of reason. This means that, in

SECTION I: THE ONTOTHEOLOGICAL CONCEPTION OF GOD

ontotheology, God is no longer seen as purely transcendent and unreachable but as an entity to which existence and essence can be attributed in a way similar to any other ontological object. This attempt to bring God into the realm of the intelligible is seen in major philosophical traditions from Aristotle to Kant, shaping a process by which metaphysics also becomes rational theology.[18]

As we explored in the previous chapter, this ontotheological tendency originates in the medieval synthesis carried out by Thomas Aquinas, who proposed unifying Aristotelian principles with Christian doctrine. In this context, God is conceived as the pure act of being, an *actus essendi* that constitutes the foundation of all reality without losing its transcendental nature. When God is seen as the first mover, the ontotheological structure arises, which tends to think of the Divine in terms of being and existence. The integration of God into metaphysical thought thus involves a dual articulation. On one hand, God is the principle that gives coherence to the totality of Being; on the other hand, His transcendence is projected in intelligible and structured terms that allow for His approach within philosophical rationality.

The impact of scholasticism extended beyond the Middle Ages, laying the foundation for advances in philosophy and theology in subsequent centuries.

---

18. Kant, Immanuel. *Critique of Pure Reason*, translated by Paul Guyer and Allen W. Wood (Cambridge University Press, 1998), A629/B657.

Chapter 4: The birth of ontotheology

Discussions about the divine nature, creation, and contingency paved the way for philosophers such as Descartes and Leibniz, who explored new ways to integrate philosophical reflection with metaphysics and emerging sciences. In Descartes, for example, the existence of God is the principle that guarantees the certainty of all knowledge, while in Leibniz, God is conceived as the necessary being that ensures the pre-established harmony of a rational universe. In these systems, the Divine is considered a being that guarantees the world's order, a foundation that, while absolute, becomes the object of rational demonstration. This rationalizing approach to God as an intelligible principle is also evident in Kant, who, while recognizing that God is inaccessible as theoretical knowledge, considers Him a necessity of practical reason. Here, the concept of "God" becomes a regulative idea. This postulate serves as a horizon for reason but is still formulated in terms of Being within the structure of human thought.

As we will see in more detail later, Heidegger's thought challenges this structure and its framed tradition. His philosophy suggests that conceiving God as a being instrumentalizes the Divine, as it reduces His transcendence to fit within the limits of human reason. According to Heidegger, ontotheology is the culmination of the metaphysical will that seeks to frame and delimit the Absolute within the parameters of the rational. The direct result of this "de-absolutization" of the Absolute is the transformation of the Divine into

Section I: The ontotheological conception of God

a mere element of the ontological system, stripping it of its character as the "totally other" or of "radical otherness." As we will elaborate later in this study, ontotheological thought, instead of questioning Being, focuses on its representations. Placing in the foundation a conceptualized God ends up concealing Being. Thus, Being is eclipsed by the attempt to find a final principle that gives coherence to the whole within a framework limited by human understanding.

The ontotheological notion of God implies an intrinsic tension between His character as a foundation and His transcendence. God is approached as the Supreme being—the being that gives meaning to all others. This foundational character, which presents Him as the Being that guarantees the totality of existence, is problematic from Heidegger's perspective, as it implies an instrumental view of the Divine, subordinating it to the structure of Being as a whole. This critique also resonates in some developments of contemporary philosophy, where it is argued that ontotheology represents a kind of "reduction" of the Divine by including it within the realm of the sayable and conceptual. For example, in the thought of Emmanuel Levinas, there is an objection to ontotheology because reducing the Divine to a being loses God's radical otherness. For Levinas, God must be "understood" in His infinity and not as an object of knowledge. Similarly, Jean-Luc Marion opposes the ontotheological tradition by proposing a conception of

God that transcends the categories of being. In Marion's view, God is equivalent to what cannot be reduced to the object of human understanding nor become the object of rational appropriation.

We see that ontotheology's attitude has deeply influenced Western thought. It has reduced the transcendence of Being to an ordered and coherent representation within the limits of rationality. The subordination of the mystery and transcendence of the Divine to ontological categories constitutes a double problem. It exhibits a form of "conceptual violence" as it seeks to subject the Absolute to the parameters of the intelligible. On the other hand, it prevents any genuine approach to the Divine that is not mediated by the conceptual and logical apparatus that defines the metaphysical tradition.

Since ancient Greece, philosophical exploration has tried to enclose the Absolute in definable categories. In trying to achieve greater understanding, the infinite was reduced by it to the finite. This approach has been fundamental in philosophy's history and later Christian theology, influencing how the nature of the Divine has been understood and discussed. The theology of medieval Christianity made the fundamental error of interpreting the kerygma, the message of Jesus, with an ontotheological attitude that incorporated a visual conception of divinity. God acquires ontic characteristics through which Christianity tries to explain and know Him. The personification of God

Section I: The ontotheological conception of God

reflected, using Foucault's terminology, a desire to control and experience the Divine in human and understandable terms, revealing the intimate connection between religion and metaphysical philosophy in their effort to explain and grasp the Absolute.

This anthropomorphization caused "the forgetting of Being." Heidegger argues that this forgetfulness is due to "ontological confusion," that is, to confusing Being with a being. This confusion is typical of an eminently epistemological philosophy. Moreover, it also permeates metaphysics and, ultimately, the Western religious conception of God. According to Heidegger's argument in *Identity and Difference* (1957), traditional philosophy has been based, since Aristotle, on the notion of being.

As a result, traditional metaphysics, anchored in Platonic-Aristotelian philosophy, unfolds by opening a dual field of study. On the one hand, it deals with the subject of beings in general, while on the other, it appropriates God, who is perceived as the supreme being. This dual unfolding means that, for Heidegger, medieval philosophy and metaphysics, which had such influence on Christianity, are already determined by an ontotheologizing attitude toward God. As a result, rather than bringing us closer to God, they adapt God to their conceptual parameters. That is, this conception cannot address the subject of God as a transcendence beyond a being. This has led to the forgetting of Being and, more dramatically, the forgetting of the ontological difference between Being and the beings.

Bibliography Section I

- Burkert, Walter. *Greek Religion*. Cambridge, MA: Harvard University Press, 1985.
- Duns Scotus, John. *Philosophical Writings.* Translated by Allan B. Wolter, O.F.M. London: Thomas Nelson and Sons, 1962.
- Foucault, Michel. *History of Madness*. Translated by Jonathan Murphy and Jean Khalfa. London: Routledge, 2006.
- Foucault, Michel. *The Order of Things: An Archaeology of the Human Sciences*. New York: Vintage, 1994.
- Frege, Gottlob. "*The Thought: A Logical Inquiry.*" Translated by A. M. and Marcelle Quinton. Mind 65, no. 259 (July 1956).
- Grote, George. *Plato, and the Other Companions of Sokrates*. Vol. 2. 2nd ed. London: John Murray, 1867.
- Hegel, Georg Wilhelm Friedrich. *Encyclopedia of Philosophy.* New York: Philosophical Library, 1959.
- Heidegger, Martin. *Being and Time*. Translated by John Macquarrie and Edward Robinson. Oxford: Basil Blackwell, 1962.
- Kant, Immanuel. *Critique of Pure Reason*. Translated by Paul Guyer and Allen W. Wood. Cambridge: Cambridge University Press, 1998.
- Klima, Gyula, Fritz Allhoff, and Anand Jayprakash Vaidya, eds. *Medieval Philosophy: Essential Readings with Commentary*. Oxford: Wiley-Blackwell, 2007.

SECTION I: THE ONTOTHEOLOGICAL CONCEPTION OF GOD

- Locke, John. *An Essay Concerning Humane Understanding: In Four Books*. 4th ed. London: Printed for Awnsham and John Churchill, and Samuel Manship, 1700.
- Nietzsche, Friedrich. *The Will to Power*. Edited by Walter Kaufmann. Translated by Walter Kaufmann and R. J. Hollingdale. New York: Vintage Books, 1968.
- Nielsen, Kai. *Reason and Practice: A Modern Introduction to Philosophy*. New York: Harper & Row, 1971.
- Oppy, Graham, Josh Rasmussen, and Joseph Schmid. "*Ontological Arguments*." In *The Stanford Encyclopedia of Philosophy*, edited by Edward N. Zalta and Uri Nodelman. Fall 2023 edition. Accessed January 9, 2025.
- Plotinus. *The Enneads*. Translated by A. H. Armstrong. Vol. 5, Enneads V.1–9. Loeb Classical Library 444. Cambridge, MA: Harvard University Press, 1984.
- Siecienski, Anthony Edward. *The Filioque: History of a Doctrinal Controversy*. Oxford: Oxford University Press, 2010.
- Watt, Stephen. "*Introduction: The Theory of Forms* (Books 5–7)." In Plato: Republic, translated by Desmond Lee, vii–xxv. London: Wordsworth Editions, 1997.
- Wippel, John F. *The Metaphysical Thought of Thomas Aquinas: From Finite Being to Uncreated Being*. Washington, D.C.: Catholic University of America Press, 2000.

SECTION II
TRANSCENDING THE PERSONAL GOD

Chapter 5

Christian excavations

Being, nothingness, and creation from a philosophical perspective

Understanding the notion of creation from a philosophical perspective is essential. In Genesis, creation is associated with goodness, as God, after creating, says:

וַיַּרְא אֱלֹהִים אֶת־כָּל־אֲשֶׁר עָשָׂה וְהִנֵּה־טוֹב מְאֹד [...]
(בראשית א', ל"א)

And God saw all that He had made, and behold, it was very good [...]

(Genesis, 1:31)

First, it is important to highlight the close connection that Genesis points out between creation and goodness. However, this connection must be understood starting from Being, which relates both realms. In other words, everything that God has created is an entity that has existence, and by having existence, by being, it is inherently good. This relationship indicates that goodness is a fundamental quality of everything that exists, as its mere existence is a manifestation of the divine creative act. It follows that creation and Being are sources of goodness, as both are attributes derived from God. However, this does not mean that everything that exists, everything that is, is good by default. For, although God created everything with goodness, human beings, by exercising their freedom, have chosen non-being over Being, thus perverting good and turning it into evil. Being is linked to divine goodness and non-being to humans. This dilemma is also presented in Genesis, from which the humans emptied Being of its fullness, or *pleroma*. This is conveyed in the following verse, where we read:

וַתֵּרֶא הָאִשָּׁה כִּי טוֹב הָעֵץ לְמַאֲכָל וְכִי תַאֲוָה־הוּא לָעֵינַיִם וְנֶחְמָד הָעֵץ לְהַשְׂכִּיל וַתִּקַּח מִפִּרְיוֹ וַתֹּאכַל וַתִּתֵּן גַּם־לְאִישָׁהּ עִמָּהּ וַיֹּאכַל:
(בראשית ג', ו')

And the woman saw that the tree was good for food and that it was a delight to the eyes, and the tree was desirable to make one wise; so she took of its fruit, and she ate, and she gave also to her husband with her, and he ate.

(Genesis, 3:6)

Creation can be defined as "giving being," while sin, in contrast, can be interpreted as "removing being."

Chapter 5: Christian excavations

Sin, in essence, represents a direct denial of creation, opposing participation in Being. When we speak of creation, we refer to an act that involves harmony with Being. Thus, while creating establishes an integration into Being, sin deprives that integration, as sin strips Being of its essence, aligning itself with nothingness, that is, with negating all Being.

As we have called it here, this dilemma fits perfectly with how the ancient Greeks referred to Being and nothingness. Specifically, for the ancient Greeks, the idea of nothingness did not have an autonomous existence; only Being existed. The Greek language did not have a specific word for "nothing." Instead, to negate Being, they used the expression *me on*, composed of the terms *me* and *on*, which mean "no" and "being," respectively. Therefore, the expression they used to refer to "nothing" was "not-being." In this sense, since nothingness is understood as a negation of Being, we cannot conceptualize it without first postulating the existence of Being. This means that the relationship between Being and nothingness is configured in terms of participation and deprivation. If creation involves a process of affirmation and construction, sin acts as a force of negation and destruction. Creation and sin, therefore, position themselves as opposing forces in the unfolding of Being.

From a philosophical analysis, we can emphasize the importance of Being as the primary ontological foundation, while nothingness is understood exclusively as the negation of this foundation. Similarly, since Being is linked to good and non-being to evil, we can also affirm that if we do not presuppose the existence of good, it would be impossible to conceive of evil. In this context, evil is interpreted as an accident of Being, requiring the existence of a substance to empty it of Being. Therefore, evil cannot exist by itself and is not an independent entity; its existence depends on Being, which, as such, is foreign to it or, we could also say, is other to it. Essentially, evil is to good as non-being (nothingness) is to Being, ultimately leading us to affirm that evil corresponds to nothingness.

The assertion that nothingness does not have its own ontological existence leads Heidegger to formulate his famous expression: "the nothing noths." This implies that nothingness, when manifesting in Being, progressively empties it, stripping it of its essence. Nothingness, when actualized in the realm of Being, gradually deprives us of the fullness of our Being, leaving us increasingly empty. Thus, the expression "the nothing noths" means that nothingness dissolves Being until it becomes nothing, that is, "gradually noths it." In other words, if nothingness had its own ontological existence, Being could not be, for nothingness, which is precisely the negation of Being, would not allow its generation and existence. That is why the ontological debate about Being and nothingness, linked with the question of good and evil within the creation framework, is not a trivial debate, but a fundamental philosophical issue.

CHAPTER 5: CHRISTIAN EXCAVATIONS

Individual and universal consciousness

The issue we have just addressed, which has allowed us to connect Being and non-being with good and evil, has other important ramifications. Specifically, in this section, we will refer to the subject of the "I," the thinking subject, or individual consciousness. Based on what has been stated in the previous paragraphs, we can affirm that Being refers to itself intrinsically, insofar as Being simply expresses existence and being in a de-individualized manner.

In this sense, Being, as existence, entails a denial of individual consciousness. This is because personal consciousness places a "separate I" at the center of perceptions of good and evil. The "I," or personal consciousness, decides between one or the other, defining good according to what the "I" itself determines. This is shown in the biblical narration of the tree of the knowledge of good and evil. In this process, the "I" appropriates the criterion of Being, which implies that Being ceases to be the central axis of existence and is replaced by a "historical I" or "separate I."

Furthermore, individual consciousness is strengthened by decentering the fact of existence itself, of Being. In turn, by affirming individual consciousness and appropriating the criterion of morality, the "I" implicitly denies universal Being. In a sense, both deny each other. Affirming universal Being involves rejecting the prerogative of individual consciousness to define good and evil autonomously. This means that individual consciousness can deny universal Being by "eating from the tree," appropriating a criterion that belongs to Being as if this rule were intrinsic to consciousness itself. Alternatively, consciousness can choose not to appropriate this criterion, resolving itself in Being. This resolution takes place in Being, as it is Being that establishes the criterion for consciousness, not the other way around. From a philosophical perspective, sin equates to denying the universal Being to appropriate and corrupt its goodness. Individual consciousness imposes a new criterion of morality, of good and evil, disconnected from universal consciousness, where Being itself beats. This is why Latin borrowed the Greek term *diábolos* (in Latin *diábolus*) to signify that the devil is that which divides or separates.

Evil, in its essence, is considered a deprivation of Being. This deprivation, rooted in separation or disunion, amounts to a self-alienation that denies Being and generates individual consciousness with an identity that seeks to negate us as beings of Being. The existence of beings is primary, while nothingness is characterized by its capacity for active negation, stripping us of our essence. It is crucial to distinguish between the destruction of our conceptions of Being and the gradual process by which nothingness strips us of our Being. When emptied of Being, we lose the essential aspect of our authenticity; that is what we are. For this reason, it is essential to free ourselves from our false beliefs about our identity to rediscover who we are.

Chapter 5: Christian Excavations

The generation of individual consciousness is known as the egoic phenomenon. This term refers to the absence of our true essence in the present rather than to a specific person or concrete entity. This stripping, caused by nothingness, deprives us of our essence, leading us to an existence devoid of the fullness of Being that should define us. Evil, ultimately, manifests as a lack and involves the deprivation of what is essential for Being to achieve its full realization. Understanding this process leads us to recognize the interaction between nothingness and existence and to understand how the absence of authentic presence shapes the egoic phenomenon. The nature of evil is self-separation or disunion (*diábolos*) from Being, which strips beings of their Being, resulting in an incomplete existence lacking essence. The existence of evil is fundamentally an accident of Being, as it depends on the existence of Being to manifest. This diminishes its fullness and obstructs its completeness. In this sense, evil acts as a parasite of Being, depriving it of its complete and perfect essence. For this reason, we can say that, in essence, sin, original sin, is a force that subtracts Being and prevents its full realization.

Being and the Good

Even with what has been stated previously regarding Being and the Good, transcendental philosophy shows us that one cannot affirm that they are identical in an absolute sense. This intimate relationship between Being

Section II: Transcending the personal God

and Good, however, does demonstrate a significant co-belonging that philosophy has referred to as "the problem of the transcendentals."

From an essential perspective, beings, insofar as they exist, are defined by being good, beautiful, true, one, and by being itself. The existence of any entity is inextricably linked to its goodness; to be good is to fully realize its own nature. In classical philosophy, a good person is synonymous with a true person. Similarly, we consider a chair to be good when it authentically fulfills its essence; that is, it possesses all the essential qualities that define it as a chair. This intrinsic goodness manifests in its functionality and the complete realization of its purpose. The interrelationship between "Being" and "good" implies that the mere existence of anything includes its inherent goodness, and this goodness is measured in terms of authenticity and fullness as it reflects being what one truly is. However, the complexity of this interrelationship requires an analytical approach and a nuanced understanding. Recognizing this distinction is essential to avoid oversimplifying philosophical concepts that, while related, maintain their own specificities and meanings within the framework of transcendental thought.

As we have said, the goodness of beings is measured by their conformity with their own nature and essence. In this way, beings are considered good when they reach their full potential and fulfill their true identity. This intrinsic relationship between "Being" and "good" highlights the interdependence of these concepts in the metaphysical understanding of reality. People are beautiful and good when they fully realize their essence; in this context, the terms "beautiful" and "good" become almost interchangeable. The concepts of being, beauty, truth, and goodness are intimately connected and, to some extent, interchangeable.

In contrast to good, and as we have argued above, evil is a form of negation of Being; in other words, the absence of a good that should exist. For example, a chair with two legs will not have all the qualities necessary to fulfill its purpose and nature, and therefore, it lacks an essential characteristic. This situation shows that evil consists in depriving beings of their essential qualities rather than adding them. Therefore, the exact definition of evil is not an ontological presence but the lack of a necessary good.

According to Thomas Aquinas, evil, strictly speaking, cannot be considered a creature, as it was not created and therefore lacks ontological essence.[19] In other words, there are no beings whose essence is evil. Rather than being a creation with an independent essence, evil is conceived as the absence of good, a defect in the existing Being. This is why we previously stated that evil equates to non-being. This perspective emphasizes that evil must be defined by the lack of perfection or fullness

---

19. Thomas Aquinas, *Of God and His Creatures*, trans. Joseph Rickaby (London: Burns and Oates, 1905), Book III, Chapter VII, "That Evil is not a Nature or Essence."

instead of having a positive reality. Without this lack, without evil, any existence or creation would be good or complete by definition. This means that the essence of evil is not ontological but manifests historically. Evil enters human life through the human being itself, yet it is not a creation of humanity.

Good and evil: Being and non-being

We have affirmed that evil gradually empties the human being of Being. With this emptiness of Being, the human being introduces non-being into history. Thus, evil can be understood here as the Being stripping itself of itself, alienating itself, and allowing the prevalence of non-being in human existence. Human beings, through their sinful nature, make way for non-being, and this phenomenon is integrated into the historical experience of humanity.

If we consider that evil is the negation of Being, then good will represent the affirmation of Being. The norm that governs good is Being, while the norm that governs evil is non-being. Being evil would, as such, imply not being what one truly is and living misaligned from one's own essence. We have previously linked this self-alienation or disunion from universal Being to the emergence of individual consciousness. By separating from universal consciousness, individual consciousness gives rise to the ego within itself, that is, an "I-other" in relation to the "I-Universal Being," which, by separating, becomes

Chapter 5: Christian excavations

deficient and incomplete. The egoic phenomenon is, precisely, a lack or deficiency. Goodness manifests in being authentically what one is; consequently, being good means being truly what one is in essence.

St. Augustine asserts that humans are born with the inherent condition of being, but they are immersed in a deep solidarity when entering the human species. This solidarity suggests that we are all one, so any action an individual performs involves everyone else. This is known as the transcendental unity of the human species. In other words, any act committed by a person is an act in which all humanity participates. St. Augustine refers to this absolute participation as the "federal being of humanity," alluding to the union of all humanity in a pact represented by Adam. This means that Adam's actions have repercussions on all his descendants. This view emphasizes the solidarity and essential unity of the human species in terms of moral and spiritual responsibility and consequences.

From this perspective, humanity shares a common destiny where the actions of one affect all, thus reinforcing the idea of an indivisible human community in which our individual decisions have collective implications. From the Christian perspective, Adam did not act alone. On the contrary, we were all in Adam, participating in his action. For this reason, we cannot say with certainty that we would have acted differently in his place. This Augustinian view implies that all human beings are intrinsically connected. We belong to a single unity, like the branches or roots of the same tree. Anything that affects the roots inevitably affects the stems, fruits, and leaves. St. Augustine presents humanity as a single body, where any good or bad action performed by one person is effectively performed by all.

Just as Adam's actions have universal repercussions, the glory of Christ, who is the second Adam, resides in all of humanity. All human beings participated in Adam's original sin; analogously, all humanity is represented in Christ, thus receiving life. From this perspective, both natures coexist in every human being: that of Adam, which represents non-being, or individual consciousness, and that of Christ, which symbolizes Being, or universal consciousness. What is important is to transcend the nature of the former, the separation and egoic individuation, to access the latter's universal nature. In this context, the words of John the Baptist become clear when he says:

> He must increase, but I must decrease.
> (John 3:30)

Individual consciousness must be relegated, as every human being is born with this fallen condition, manifested in a consciousness centered around the "I." We can only repair this fracture or existential disunion by transcending this condition and reaching or integrating into a universal consciousness. This fall or fracture refers to the fact that, upon birth, each person carries the individual consciousness that characterizes the first Adam. However, every human being is simultaneously called to reduce the dominance of their individual consciousness in order to (re)integrate into pure, universal consciousness.

It should be noted, however, that it is impossible to attain this universal consciousness without first negating the individual one. In clearer terms, without first renouncing the state of the first Adam, born of the flesh, it is impossible to enter into the state of the second Adam, who is born of the spirit. This is why the Bible says in the *Epistle to the Romans*:

> We know that our old self was crucified with him so that the body ruled by sin might be done away with, that we should no longer be slaves to sin—because anyone who has died has been set free from sin.
>
> (Romans 6:6–7)

The main point of this idea is the urgent need to let the first Adam die to be reborn as the second Adam. In individual consciousness, also known as the flesh, all human beings are destined for death, while in universal consciousness, or the spirit, all human beings can attain eternal life. Therefore, the transcendence of the spirit is emphasized in contrast to the flesh, stressing the need to overcome our individual limitations to reach a full and universal existence. "Dying to the self" is a

SECTION II: TRANSCENDING THE PERSONAL GOD

key concept of the New Testament that symbolizes the essence of Christian life. It highlights the importance of abandoning individual consciousness, or evil, to access a higher, fuller, and more benevolent existence.

This transition means that the New Testament calls for taking up the cross and following Christ, taking a crucial step toward spiritual rebirth. The old self dies in this process, and the new self, rises as mentioned in John (3:3–7). Christians experience a new birth at the moment of salvation and continue dying to themselves during the process of sanctification. Thus, dying to oneself, or the "separated self," is a singular event but one that also extends throughout the life of true Christians.

Jesus repeatedly emphasized to his disciples the need to take up their cross, an instrument of death, and follow him. Anyone who desires to follow him must deny themselves, meaning they must renounce their own egoic life and individuation. This was an indispensable requirement for being considered a true disciple of Christ. This is why Jesus himself warned that attempting to save our egoic life, or "independent self," would inevitably result in losing our life to the kingdom of God. This context helps us understand Jesus when, through Luke, he clearly stated that those who are not willing to sacrifice their personal lives for him cannot be his disciples (Luke, 14:27). On the other hand, those who give up their lives, or individual consciousness, for his sake will find eternal life (Matthew, 16:24–25; Mark, 8:34–35).

Chapter 5: Christian excavations

Christian ethics

In this chapter, we have linked Being with divine goodness, opposing it to non-being, that is, to nothingness and evil. We have also defined nothingness and evil as the absence of goodness and good, associating them with the creation of an individual "I," which, by asserting itself, empties Being of its essence. In this sense, Christianity preaches that embracing Christ means renouncing our particular "I" to reunify with Being and merge with absolute goodness.

This small map now opens the door to Christian ethics. In the first letter of Paul to the Corinthians, we read the following:

> Everything is permissible, but not everything is beneficial. Everything is permissible, but not everything is constructive.
>
> (1 Corinthians, 10:23)

This verse expresses the essence of authentic Christian ethics. By saying that everything is permissible, it is revealed that ethics does not reside in the dichotomy between what is forbidden and what is allowed, but in the freedom to discern what is beneficial to the community and what is not. There are thoughts, feelings, attitudes, and actions that contribute to our growth, development, and elevation as human beings.

Similarly, there are others that do not contribute to this because they merely favor the agent or a community at the expense of others. As a manifestation of Christian ethics, Kantian ethics is not defined by an extensive list of prohibitions. On the contrary, everything is permissible, but humans must always discern and choose what elevates them spiritually; that is, what they aspire to make a universal law. Therefore, instead of simply avoiding what is forbidden, it is about adopting a perspective that actively promotes goodness and prosperity in all aspects of life.

> "What then? Shall we sin because we are not under the law, but under grace? By no means!"
> (Romans, 6:15)

In this verse from the Epistle to the Romans, Saint Paul addresses Christians, explaining that we are no longer under the law, as the law is now subordinate to us. This is because, under the reign of grace, Christ has perfectly fulfilled the law in our place, and we participate in that fulfillment through faith. Therefore, Christians are not called to fulfill or obey the law, but to enjoy it, renewing it with every moral decision. The Christian is devoted to the absolute and universal, not to the particular and individuated. Through free will, the Christian is responsible for cultivating an intimate relationship with the Divine. In this relationship, the personal God transcends and sublimates, giving way to the impersonal

God, the absolute and universal consciousness where the human being reintegrates fully. The ethical issue is inseparable from ontological and theological issues to the point where neither can be understood on its own, as expressed clearly in the Epistle to the Philippians, where it is stated:

> Finally, brothers and sisters, whatever is true, whatever is noble, whatever is right, whatever is pure, whatever is lovely, whatever is admirable—if anything is excellent or praiseworthy—think about such things.
>
> (Philippians, 4:8)

Christ: the universal archetype

Beyond being a historical figure, Jesus embodies a level of pure consciousness, known as Christ consciousness, which Carl Jung refers to as "the archetype of consciousness" or the "Self." Archetypes are innate patterns in the human psyche that profoundly influence our perceptions and behaviors. The fundamental patterns outlined by Carl Jung, known as archetypes, are essential parts of his psychological theory. According to Jung, archetypes reside in the collective unconscious and act as universal frameworks that shape our experiences and reactions to various situations. These structures inherent in the human mind manifest in all societies' myths, dreams, and cultural expressions, reflecting common aspects of the human condition. Moreover, they guide our understanding of the world, facilitating the connection between individuals of different cultures and eras who share similar symbols and narratives.

The truth of Christ does not lie in the mere factual existence of Jesus but in the archetype, he represents, which constitutes a universal model of the human being shaped by universal consciousness. This archetype's validity is independent of Jesus's historical existence, as it does not depend on him. Although the historical Jesus represents a complete manifestation of this archetype, what is essential is the archetype itself, not the specific individual. This archetype of universal consciousness surpasses the limitations of individual existence and presents itself as a model of perfection accessible to all. Unfortunately, most Christians focus only on the historical figure and center their devotion on the individual named Jesus.

Christ's consciousness represents a spiritual ideal that all of us can aspire to. This ideal transcends belief in miracles and leads to a profound understanding of an essential archetype; it focuses on an archetypal connection and trust beyond historical facts and personalities. To have faith in Christ means trusting that we can give our spirit with complete confidence.

In biology, there is a clear distinction between genotype and phenotype. The genotype refers to the complete set of genes and genetic information constituting an individual of any species. This genetic composition is passed from generation to generation, ensuring the continuity of hereditary traits. On the contrary, the phenotype is an individual's physical and observable expression of these characteristics. While the genotype remains constant, the phenotype may vary due to the interaction between genes and the environment. Therefore, the phenotype is the external and tangible manifestation of the genetic information contained in the genotype. The gene is the genotype, while the individual would be the model carrying that type.

Following this analogy, the historical Jesus can be considered the phenotype and Christ as the archetype. The phenotype, as a "phenomenon," is the visible manifestation, while the archetype is the underlying foundation of what is shown. Jesus would be the manifestation of Christ, that is, the archetype that is the basis of that manifestation. The relevance of Jesus lies in his ability to embody this archetype, showing how it is possible to live in harmony with universal consciousness. While his historical existence provides valuable context, the essence is the universal principle he embodies. This archetype guides humanity, indicating a path to spiritual elevation and overcoming the "separated self." Thus, it promotes integration and connection with the totality of Being. In this sense, we can affirm that Christic consciousness transcends the barriers of time and space, inviting all human beings to recognize and live according to this universal truth.

Section II: Transcending the personal God

Christic consciousness

Pure consciousness, or *logos endiatikos*, can only be attained through *logos prosforikos*, or "the proclaimed word or language." This language is not static; in the process, it is enriched by the various consciousnesses and masks it assumes. The notion of *logos endiatikos* refers to an internal understanding that is fundamental and abstract. However, this state of consciousness cannot be attained or communicated without *logos prosforikos*, that is, through articulated language. In this context, language becomes indispensable for expressing and transmitting this internal consciousness.

It is important to note that language is not a fixed or immutable entity. On the contrary, it is continually enriched through the various individual consciousnesses and the multiple "masks" it adopts in its use. These "masks" represent the different forms and contexts in which language can be applied and understood. In communication, language adapts and expands, integrating individuals' various perspectives and experiences. Pure consciousness depends on language to manifest, while this language is enriched and evolves thanks to the various forms of consciousness and contexts in which it is employed.

Properly understood, Christianity centers on an encounter with Christ that is experienced at the innermost core of the human being. It encompasses both the individual and collective spheres and resides at the heart of reality. This experience manifests through a personal Christic faith that emulates Christ's perspective and attitude and adopts what is known as the "Christic principle." This approach goes beyond mere belief and points to a comprehensive transformation that fundamentally alters the understanding and experience of existence as a whole. It is a faith that promotes inner metamorphosis, reconfiguring both perceptions of the world and interactions with the surrounding reality.

One can transcend their egoic nature by embracing, accepting, surrendering to, and trusting in Christic consciousness through faith. This trust enables overcoming the sinful inclinations inherent to the human condition and leads toward fully integrating individual consciousness into universal consciousness. In turn, this transition allows the individual's life to be elevated above sinful tendencies, achieving an authentic and meaningful transformation.

Chapter 6

Christophany: The Intimate Relationship with the Divine

Following everything discussed in the previous chapter, we can understand Christianity as an "ecclesial mutation" in Christian self-understanding that surpasses both medieval Christendom and modern Christianity. Viewed from this perspective, Christ, as the mystical core of faith, assumes greater relevance than the Church in its sacramental dimension and social aspect. This is not an entirely new idea. In fact, many prominent Christians throughout history have, for this reason, often been uncomfortable with the ecclesiastical institution. Meister Eckhart, a 13th-century German theologian and mystic, stands out among the eminent Christians who transcended Christendom and institutional Christianity, which can be called even corporate Christianity. Eckhart was accused of heresy for his teachings on a direct relationship with God and his rejection of ecclesiastical mediation. Although he died before a final decision was rendered, the Church condemned several of his doctrines. Eckhart

Section II: Transcending the personal God

was not the only one to be condemned. Below are several examples:

- Marguerite Porete, a 14th-century French mystic, wrote *The Mirror of Simple Souls*. She was executed by burning because of her teachings, considered heretical by the Inquisition, as she rejected the hierarchical structure of the Church and emphasized direct union with God.
- Girolamo Savonarola, a 15th-century Dominican monk who preached against ecclesiastical corruption. Excommunicated and executed, his criticisms of papal authority and his call for a radical moral and spiritual reform cost him his life.
- Jeanne Guyon, a 17th-century French writer and mystic, was imprisoned for her teachings on inner prayer and the passivity of the soul, which were seen as dangerously quietist.
- St. John of the Cross, now venerated as a saint and doctor of the Church, was imprisoned in his lifetime by his fellow Carmelites due to his mystical experiences and his efforts to reform the order.
- Tertullian, an influential 2nd-century theologian who separated from the official Church to join the Montanist movement, which was considered heretical due to its rigorist and prophetic beliefs.
- Origen of Alexandria, a prominent 3rd-century theologian and scholar whose teachings on the pre-existence of the soul and the eventual salvation of

all beings, were condemned by the Church after his death.
- Joaquín de Fiore, a 12th-century monk known for his apocalyptic vision of history and the arrival of a new age of the Holy Spirit. His ideas were condemned at the Fourth Lateran Council in 1215.
- Dante Alighieri, the famous author of *The Divine Comedy*, was excommunicated for political reasons, though his work had a decisive influence on Christian theology and thought.
- Nicholas of Cusa, a 15th-century philosopher and cardinal whose ideas on the infinitude of God and His relationship with the universe were viewed with suspicion.
- St. Teresa of Ávila, though later canonized, faced resistance and suspicion because of her mystical experiences and her reforms within the Carmelite Order.
- St. Augustine, recognized as one of the greatest doctors of the Church, whose ideas, particularly about predestination, caused controversy.
- St. Thomas Aquinas, whose teachings on Aristotelian philosophy were initially received with suspicion and only fully accepted after his death.
- Teilhard de Chardin, a 20th-century Jesuit and paleontologist whose ideas on evolution and the Omega Point were censored by the Church.
- Thomas Merton, a 20th-century Trappist monk whose writings on mysticism and his interest in

interreligious dialogue created controversy in some ecclesiastical circles.
- Henri Le Saux (Abhishiktananda), a 20th-century Benedictine priest and mystic whose efforts to integrate Hindu and Christian spirituality were viewed with deep suspicion.
- John Wycliffe, considered a precursor of the Reformation, whose teachings were condemned posthumously. In a symbolic act of rejection, his remains were exhumed and burned.
- Jan Hus, whose reformist ideas led to his excommunication and, ultimately, execution by burning.
- Giordano Bruno, a 16th-century philosopher and priest who was burned at the stake for his revolutionary cosmological and theological ideas.

These cases show that those who have sought a more direct and intimate relationship with the Divine have often come into conflict with the ecclesiastical authorities of their time due to their innovative and sometimes controversial teachings. This way of understanding Christianity, based on the Christic existence, is simultaneously ancient and contemporary, and it promotes a double liberation. On the one hand, it emancipates from the fixed and determined political order that characterized Christendom; on the other, it frees from identifying the Christian Being with the mere acceptance of a specific set of rules, laws, and

Chapter 6: Christophany: the intimate relationship with the Divine

regulations. This vision generally fosters a more intimate and mystical relationship with Christ, in which personal transformation and direct connection with the Divine are essential.

For many years, I have divided religion into three categories: religionism, religiosity, and religion. Religionism encompasses the dogmas and beliefs that form the theological structure of a faith. On the other hand, religiosity includes the culture and art that develop around temples, reflecting the influence of religion on daily life and cultural expressions. Finally, religion refers to an intimate approach to God, where spiritual experience and direct connection with the Divine are fundamental. We could also call religion "religiophany," a term that emphasizes the personal and mystical experience of faith, highlighting the intimate connection with the Divine and transcendental manifestations. This term thus refers to the internal and profound experience of religion.

This division allows us to understand how faith manifests in beliefs and practices, cultural expressions, and the personal search for a relationship with the Divine. Moreover, it clearly distinguishes between Christianity, Christendom, and Christophany. Christianity includes the dogmas, doctrines, and fundamental beliefs that form the theological foundation of this faith. On the other hand, Christendom encompasses the cultural, historical, and sociopolitical influence of Christianity, manifested in its architectural, artistic, and traditional legacy. Finally, Christophany focuses on the mystical experience of faith, highlighting the intimate connection with the Divine and the individual's spiritual transformation. Those who reduce Christianity to the only path to salvation do not understand any religion, for they confuse the relative with the Absolute. To think that Christ is the only way to God closes the mind to other forms of divine understanding and even prevents full access to the essence of Christ.

The etymology of the term "Christophany" comes from the combination of two Greek roots: *Christós* (Χριστός) and *phanía* (φανία). The word *Christós* (Χριστός) is translated into English as "Christ," and it originates from the Hebrew *mashíaj* (משיח) meaning "anointed." In Christianity, Christ refers to Jesus of Nazareth, considered the Messiah and Savior. On the other hand, *phanía* (φανία) derives from the verb *phaínō* (φαίνω), which means "to appear or manifest." This root is also present in terms like "theophany" (manifestation of God) and "epiphany" (divine appearance or manifestation). Combining these two roots, we obtain "Christophany," which literally means "the manifestation of Christ." Thus, "Christophany" refers to the appearance of Christ, whether in visions, mystical experiences, or any form of direct divine revelation.

In light of what has been explained, we consider that the Church and the Christian religion must evolve from collective and rigid structures to a more intimate conception. This new way of living Christianity in the

Chapter 6: Christophany: the intimate relationship with the Divine

third millennium seeks to surpass the Christendom of the second millennium. The Middle Ages represented the era of Christianism or Christian religionism. Then came Protestantism or Christendom, meaning Christian religiosity. We suggest advancing toward a retroprogressive religious Christophany that alludes to a transcendent experience that reveals Christ to us. Therefore, the fall of religionism and religiosity of any belief is highly positive because it allows us to live religion more intimately and authentically. As individualized subjects, or as "Adams," we have hidden ourselves with the fig leaves of the egoic phenomenon. This step will bring us closer to Being, that is, to the absolute goodness of creation.

It is necessary to emphasize the experiential dimension of Christianity and underline that Christ is not solely the heritage of Christians. Speaking of Christophany implies adopting a Christian identity beyond legal, social, or institutional belonging and doctrinal consensus. Based on a direct experience of the Divine, this identity seeks to reflect the same trust in the Spirit that Christ Jesus had. In its essence, Christophany promotes a personal and intimate connection with divinity, fostering an essential and meaningful transformation in the way we understand and practice the Christian faith in the contemporary era. We aspire to an integral and retroprogressive transformation of Christianity, transcending doctrinal acceptance toward a spiritual experience that integrates all human existence.

Section II: Transcending the personal God

This seeks to renew and revitalize the practice of the Christian faith in the third millennium. Moreover, only Christophany will allow authentic religious experience to open the necessary pathways to transcend all egoic phenomena. Then, individuated, separated, and fragmented consciousness will reintegrate into universal consciousness.

Chapter 7

The death of Christ

וַיֹּאמֶר אֱלֹהִים נַעֲשֶׂה אָדָם בְּצַלְמֵנוּ כִּדְמוּתֵנוּ וְיִרְדּוּ בִדְגַת הַיָּם וּבְעוֹף הַשָּׁמַיִם וּבַבְּהֵמָה וּבְכָל־הָאָרֶץ וּבְכָל־הָרֶמֶשׂ הָרֹמֵשׂ עַל־הָאָרֶץ:

(בראשית א', כ"ו)

And God said: "Let us make man in our image, after our likeness; and let them have dominion over the fish of the sea, and over the fowl of the air, and over the cattle, and over all the earth, and over every creeping thing that creeps upon the earth."

(Genesis, 1:26)

According to this quote from the book of Genesis, God created humankind in His image and likeness. If we analyze this from the perspective of St. Thomas Aquinas and St. Augustine, we will understand that the "image" refers to a metaphysical aspect, while the "likeness" encompasses a moral dimension. Being created in the image of God implies that we reflect

Section II: Transcending the Personal God

His essence. Like Him, we are rational, free, volitional, spiritual, unique, and personal beings. Being a person entails being a rational substance. For example, although a dog, a cat, or a donkey are substances, they lack rationality and, therefore, an animal cannot be considered a person. In contrast, like a human being, an angel is a rational substance and, therefore, can be considered a person. The essential difference between angels and humans lies in the fact that angels are pure spirits, while humans are spirits tied to matter. Despite this difference, both are recognized as persons. Hence, the three substances that qualify as persons are God, angels, and humans. Each possesses the rational capacity that defines a person, although at different levels of existence and with different essential attributes.

Although God is a divine person and we are human persons, we share fundamental characteristics. This concept is expressed as *ad imaginem Dei*, or "in the image of God." In Christianity, Jesus Christ is seen as the perfect and faithful representation of God the Father. This distinction is crucial. To be *imago Dei* means "to be the image of God," while to be *ad imaginem Dei* means "to be in the image of God." Human beings are not "the" image of God, but we exist "in" His image, reflecting certain aspects of His divine nature.

This reflection helps us understand the special relationship between divinity and humanity according to Christianity. First, the existence of the Father is

CHAPTER 7: THE DEATH OF CHRIST

acknowledged, whom we understand as God. Second, Jesus Christ is considered the perfect model or the image of God. Finally, human beings are recognized as beings created according to, or in the image of, this model. This tripartition implies, however, that although we have been created according to this divine model, we are not the model itself; that is, we are made in the image of the model without being the model as such. This difference rests on an important aspect that should also be carefully considered: the image of God in human beings is considered metaphysical, while the likeness is understood in moral terms.

According to Christian theology, God possesses two types of attributes: communicable and incommunicable. Communicable attributes are those that God can share with created beings. For example, God can communicate His holiness, intelligence, love, justice, and mercy to us. In contrast, God's incommunicable attributes, such as omnipotence, omniscience, and omnipresence, cannot be shared with humans. When we assert that we have been created in the image of God, we are indicating that human beings possess God's communicable attributes. This means that in our human nature, we can reflect, albeit in a limited way, aspects of divine holiness, intelligence, love, justice, and mercy.

This understanding underscores the dignity and purpose of human beings in creation, highlighting our ability to reflect God's qualities in our lives and actions. While we do not reach the absolute perfection of His incommunicable attributes, our existence is marked by the possibility of manifesting the communicable ones in our interaction with the world and others. The likeness, on the other hand, is of a moral nature because the more we partake in God's holiness, the more we resemble Him. For example, the fallen angel and the archangel Gabriel share the same metaphysical image but not the same moral likeness. Similarly, a saint and a villain are ontologically identical but differ in morality. As human beings, we cannot be more or less "persons" in an ontological sense, but we can morally elevate or degrade ourselves. This implies that we can strive to improve in virtues and morality without altering our ontological essence. While the essence of our humanity remains unchanged, our actions and choices determine our moral excellence. Religious life does not make us more persons; instead, it optimizes and elevates each individual, fostering a gradual process of likeness to the Divine, divinizing our existence.

When referring to God as a person from a Christian perspective, we intend to indicate that in Him reside both will and intelligence, that is, rationality. According to Christian doctrine, the interaction with God is precisely based on relating to Him as a personal being. However, this viewpoint was not fully endorsed by St. Thomas Aquinas or all of Christianity, and certainly not from the perspective of the religious Christophany we have just presented. God is invariably conceived as a being in the realms of religionism and religiosity, although this

CHAPTER 7: THE DEATH OF CHRIST

conception does not strictly apply in the formal religious sphere. St. Thomas Aquinas argues that describing God as a person is an imprecise use of language because, in a strict and proper sense, we do not possess complete knowledge of the true nature of God. Therefore, St. Thomas adopts negative theology, emphasizing that we know more about what God is not than what God is. This negative approach highlights the transcendence and mystery of the Divine, underscoring that human understanding is limited in the face of the immensity of the Divine.

This debate leads us directly to one of the central issues of Christianity: the doctrine of the Holy Trinity. This expression and concept is used to denote that in the unity of the Most High, three distinct Persons exist: the Father, the Son, and the Holy Spirit. Although substantially equal, they differ from each other. The interrelationship between these three entities is known as procession, while the union between them is called *perichoresis*. This word comes from the Greek terms *peri* (around) and *choro* (to yield or make space), which express a unity that manifests itself in its diversity. Therefore, we will talk about three distinct persons because the Son is not the Father, and the Holy Spirit is neither the Father nor the Son. For example, consider Julius, Daniel, and Peter: while they are distinct, they share the same humanity. There are not three different humanities, but only one. Their personalities may differ, but their nature is identical. The Father is the Creator, the Son is the Redeemer, and the Holy Spirit is the Sanctifier. The Holy Spirit represents the mutual love between the Father and the Son and provides humans with the strength necessary to fulfil the commands of the Father. For His part, the Son redeems humanity, allowing it to be justified before God.

Although the Holy Trinity has been aimed at explaining the nature of God from Christian theology, we consider that this explanation has ultimately reduced God to a mathematical nature. Essentially, God is neither strictly three nor one, as the concept of number is inadequate to refer to divinity. He is not only one because the Father, Christ, and the Holy Spirit are three, but He is also not reducible to three because as Jesus Himself says:

> Jesus said to him, "Have I been with you so long, and yet you do not know me, Philip? Whoever has seen me has seen the Father. How can you say, 'Show us the Father'?"
>
> (John, 14:9)

In this quote, Jesus does not say, "Whoever has seen me has seen the Son," but rather, "Whoever has seen me has seen the Father." This indicates a co-belonging between them that transcends any mathematical relationship. This apparent nuance caused a significant theological conflict in the year 1000, known as the *Filioque* controversy or

CHAPTER 7: THE DEATH OF CHRIST

dilemma.[20] Eastern Christians held that the Holy Spirit proceeds only from the Father, while Western Christians claimed it proceeds from both the Father and the Son. The controversy lies in that if the Holy Spirit is the Spirit of the Father, it could not be the Spirit of the Son, according to the Eastern perspective.

In contrast, Western Christians argued that the Holy Spirit is the Spirit of the Father and the Son. In this mystery of co-belonging, the Holy Spirit is the same as the Father and the same as the Son. Thus, whoever receives the Holy Spirit receives both the Father and the Son. Whoever loves the Father also loves the Son and vice versa. Accordingly, they are neither fully three nor fully one. This mutual relationship of love suggests a complex unity that transcends traditional numerical categories, reflecting an intrinsic and essential co-belonging. The great mystery is that emphasizing the unity without recognizing the difference is erroneous, and the same happens when stressing the difference without the unity. The balance between unity and diversity is key to understanding the divine nature and its manifestation in the three distinct persons. The paradox is indispensable to preserving the integrity of the theological mystery and avoiding simplifications that distort its essence.

In an attempt to explain the mystery, modalism has arisen, which asserts that there is one God who

---

20. Siecienski, Anthony Edward. *The Filioque: History of a Doctrinal Controversy* (Oxford University Press, 2010), 4–5.

Section II: Transcending the personal God

manifests in three distinct forms: first as the Father, then as the Son, and finally as the Holy Spirit. According to this doctrine, there would be three different modes of being of the same God, as if He had three different garments to reveal Himself. However, according to modalism, there are no three distinct persons but rather three modes of manifestation of a single divine person. Modalism, or Sabellianism, is considered a heresy by the Catholic Church. It should be clarified that heresy is any belief that is in marked disagreement with established customs or doctrines, especially those accepted by a religious organization. These doctrinal deviations are considered serious because they challenge religious orthodoxy and can lead to excommunication or other ecclesiastical sanctions.

From basic Christology, Jesus Christ is known as the Word Incarnate, which means He is a God-made man. He has existed as God from eternity, of the same essence and substance as the Father. According to the divine plan, He chose to become incarnate, assuming human nature. However, Christianity does not consider Him a man like us, as all human beings inherit the original sin of Adam. This sinful inheritance is transmitted through both parents, a father and a mother.

In contrast, Jesus does not inherit this sin because, although He was born of a human mother, Mary, He did not have a human father. In this way, He is exempt from the transmission of original sin and, therefore, remains pure and free from this original stain. This singularity underscores His divine nature and redemptive mission within the framework of the Christian faith.

Jesus is clearly human, but not only human. He is completely human and also completely divine. The problem lies in the relationship between the humanity and divinity of Jesus. If we say that Jesus is a true human being (*vero homo*) and a true God (*vero Deus*), we cannot claim that Jesus is two distinct persons. Jesus is a single person who possesses two natures: one human and the other divine. The union of both natures is known as the hypostatic union. The word *hypostasis* means that which underlies all natures. The noun hypostasis (ὑπόστασις) derives from the verb *hyphístēmi* (ὑφίστημι), or also *hypístēmi*: (ὑπίστημι), which intransitively means "to be beneath" and, in a more general sense, "to be present or to exist," and transitively means "to place, put beneath, or sustain." Thus, Jesus embodies a hypostatic union, which indicates that Mary is the mother of this hypostatic union, for she is not merely the mother of human nature nor solely of the divine one.

Mary is the mother of the complete person of Jesus, which justifies calling her Mary Theotokos, Mary Mother of God. The notion of Mary as the Mother of God is theologically grounded in a specific passage from the Gospel of Luke, where Mary is referred to as "Mother of God." In Luke, 1:43, specifically, Elizabeth addresses Mary with the words: "How is it that the mother of my Lord comes to me?" It is crucial to note that Kýrios is the Greek term reserved exclusively for

God, translating the ineffable name of God, Yahweh. Therefore, by referring to Mary as "the mother of my Lord," Elizabeth undoubtedly acknowledges her as "the mother of my God." Nestorius, considered a heretic, argued that Mary was the mother only of Jesus' human nature and not of his divine nature. In response, Athanasius argued that Mary is the mother of the complete person, not of a single nature.

The *communicatio idiomatum*, or "communication of properties," is an essential technical concept in the theology of the Incarnation. This principle holds that the properties inherent to the divine Word can be attributed to the man Christ, and reciprocally, the properties of the man Christ can be predicated on the divine Word. Such doctrine is legitimized through the language of the Scriptures and the Church Fathers, who clearly demonstrate the possibility and coherence of this mutual exchange of attributes. The communication of properties is of great importance in understanding the dual nature of Christ because it holds that all that belongs to one nature also belongs to the other.

In philosophy, nature is defined as the principle of operations. For example, Jesus performed divine actions, such as performing miracles and reading hearts. However, he also exhibited principles of human operations as he ate, drank, and slept. Since He is a single person possessing two natures, in this hypostatic communion, the properties are communicated, meaning the natures are shared. In the hypostatic union, by which the person is one and that

Chapter 7: The death of Christ

unity is substantial, all that belongs to one nature belongs, by transitive character, to the other. Consequently, Jesus Christ performed miracles both as God and as a human being since, due to the communication of properties, the properties of the divine nature were also attributed to human nature. Therefore, Jesus performed these actions divinely when he ate, drank, and slept like any human being. This doctrine presents a difficulty for non-Christians: if we accept the communication of properties, then not only did the human nature of Jesus die on the cross, but, in that act, it was God himself who was dying. The great paradox of Christianity lies in the assertion that God has died, an idea that resonates with Nietzsche's famous declaration: "God is dead on the cross."[21]

This "communication of properties," through which Christianity defends the exchange of human and divine attributes of Jesus, has a certain resonance in Carl Jung's conception of the human psyche. Jung divided the psyche into the individual consciousness, the individual unconscious, and the collective unconscious. These three dimensions can correlate with the human reality, the divine reality, and the fundamental unity of Being or the One. According to this perspective,

---

21. Nietzsche, Friedrich. *The Gay Science: With a Prelude in Rhymes and an Appendix of Songs*, trans. by Walter Kaufmann (Vintage-Random House, 1974), 167. Still in *The Gay Science*, the quote is stated through the voice of the "madman." Also, see Nietzsche, *The Gay Science*, Book III, Section 125, trans. Walter Kaufmann.

Section II: Transcending the personal God

the individual unconscious can only be fully known when the individual consciousness dissolves or dies. The individual consciousness, which represents our everyday human reality, makes way for the individual unconscious, which Jung associates with the divinity or the Christic aspect of our being. This transformation process suggests that a deeper and more transcendental reality is revealed in the death of human consciousness. Renouncing the Christic is imperative, as this concept still embodies individual spirituality. According to Christian mysticism, Christianity, in its essence, remains a religion centered on the individual. To transcend individuality, it is necessary that this individual Christ also dies.

The personal Christ must die for glory to be attributed to the Father, to the One. The true glory of the One cannot manifest as long as Christ has not died because Christ represents the religion of the "independent I," of individuated and individual consciousness, and relative duality. The transformation of individual consciousness involves a movement toward integration with the individual unconscious and, eventually, with the collective unconscious, which is the fundamental unity of Being. In this context, the symbolic death of the personal Christ reflects the transcendence of individual consciousness toward a more universal understanding of the Divine. Only when the personal Christ dissolves can the fullness of the One be experienced, where there is no longer duality nor separation between the individual and the Absolute. This process of integration

Chapter 7: The death of Christ

and transcendence is fundamental to achieving true union with the Divine, which is beyond the limitations of individual consciousness and the personal manifestations of spirituality.

From this perspective, what is Christic remains the exaltation of individual consciousness; therefore, it is essential that the human being dies so Christ may live. Likewise, it is indispensable for Christ to die for God to live fully. The death of Christ is necessary for God, the One Being, the One of Plato, the One of Plotinus, the absolute One, to live. This One is so transcendent that its name cannot be spoken and is beyond all image. However, Christ is still a name, an image, a person. This transition symbolizes the shift from individual spirituality to an experience of absolute unity with the Divine. In this sense, Christianity is a religion that leads to the end, because even the personal God must die for us to access absolute unity, the One. This is also expressed in the first letter of Paul to the Corinthians, where we read:

> But when all things are subjected to him, then the Son himself will also be subjected to him who put all things in subjection under him, that God may be all in all.
>
> (1 Corinthians, 15:28)

This verse from the New Testament teaches us that the Father has subjected all things to the Son, who is the perfect image of the personal God. However, this perfect

Section II: Transcending the personal God

image also submits to the absolute unmanifested God or pure consciousness, which allows the unmanifested God to be perceived as all in all. In its infinite wisdom, the impersonal absolute desires that all things and all people be subjected to the God Person. For this to happen, the personal God must first submit to the unmanifested God or pure consciousness. This process ensures that the Absolute can be recognized as, all in all, even encompassing the manifestation of the personal God. This teaching highlights the relationship and hierarchy between the personal manifestation of God and His unmanifested essence. Through the submission of the Son to the Father, a deeper truth is revealed: the unification of all things in God, who is all in all. This fusion underscores the transcendental nature of the Divine and the integrity of its presence in every aspect of reality, including in the figure of the God Person. This fusion, or reintegration as we have called it, must be understood as a process of negation and affirmation, of renunciation and overcoming, as described in the following passage from the Epistle to the Philippians:

> Have this mind among yourselves, which is yours in Christ Jesus, who, though he was in the form of God, did not count equality with God a thing to be grasped, but emptied himself, taking the form of a servant, being born in the likeness of men. And being found in human form, he humbled himself by becoming obedient to the

point of death, even death on a cross. Therefore, God has highly exalted him and bestowed on him the name that is above every name, so that at the name of Jesus every knee should bow, in heaven and on earth and under the earth, and every tongue confess that Jesus Christ is Lord, to the glory of God the Father.

(Philippians, 2:5–11)

To reach exaltation, Jesus must abase and humble himself. Individual consciousness becomes God through the personal God; the personal God must die to be glorified as the unmanifested God, or universal and pure consciousness. The absolute consciousness elevates the personal God only when He denies Himself, not when He asserts Himself. On the other hand, the unmanifested God does not need to deny Himself because He is the absolute unity. The affirmation of the impersonal God, or consciousness, is achieved through the denial of Christ, who represents the perfection of individual consciousness.

This is clearly established in the Gospels, where Christianity reveals itself as a path that guides us toward a unitary reality, using the interaction and contrast between the Son, which, as a direct path, leads to the Truth. In other words, only through the Son, that is, the personal God, is it possible to access the Father, who represents the absolute One, as shown in the following quotes:

SECTION II: TRANSCENDING THE PERSONAL GOD

> Jesus said to him, "I am the way, and the truth, and the life; no one comes to the Father except through me."
>
> (John, 14:6)

> For whoever has seen the Son has seen the Father:
>
> I and the Father are one.
>
> (John, 10:30)

And for further clarification, in the book of Peter, we find the following verse:

> For Christ also suffered once for sins, the righteous for the unrighteous, that he might bring us to God, being put to death in the flesh but made alive in the spirit.
>
> (1 Peter, 3:18)

Thus, through its teachings and practices, Christianity allows us to overcome the apparent separation and understand the essential unity underlying all existence. By correctly following the path of the personal God, it will eventually lead to the impersonal God.

This same movement we have described here with the terms of negation and affirmation, or renunciation and overcoming, is one of the key moments in Hegel's philosophy of history. Hegel himself describes the unfolding of the absolute spirit through a process

Chapter 7: The death of Christ

called *Aufhebung*, or "picking up by negating." *Aufheben* ('ʔaʊ̯fheb̩m), or *Aufhebung* ('ʔaʊ̯fhebʊŋ), is a German term that encompasses several seemingly opposite meanings, such as cancel, abolish, suspend, raise, transcend, and preserve. Specifically, Hegel used the term *Aufhebung* in his works on the concept of "dialectics," which has predominantly been translated as "sublimate." The use of the term *Aufhebung* implies a negation that assimilates and elevates, that is, transcends, rather than negating in order to discard what is negated. This is precisely the impersonal God's process with the personal God: it does not negate it to discard it, but to sublimate it.

The transcendence of divine personalization also appears in Zen Buddhism. Its *koans*, parables meant to break discursive thinking, aim to facilitate the approach to awakening. One of the most renowned *koans* is attributed to Linji: "If you meet the Buddha, kill him (逢佛殺佛)." The *koan* is usually accompanied by the phrase "on the path," resulting in the complete expression: "If you meet the Buddha on the path, kill him." This clarification indicates that the *koan* refers to encountering the Buddha conceived as an external and objectifiable figure, not as a representation of our true Buddhic nature. It is not surprising that many see this *koan* as heretical. Despite its abundant interpretive richness, it becomes evident if we consider the fundamental principle of Mahāyāna, as formulated in the third turn of the dharma: the Buddhic nature of all things, known as *tathāgatagarbha*. This principle is complemented by the doctrine of the second turn of the wheel of dharma, which establishes emptiness, meaning that all phenomena lack inherent existence. The Zen master Shunryu Suzuki, in his work *Zen Mind, Beginner's Mind*, offers an eloquent explanation:

> Kill the Buddha if the Buddha exists elsewhere. Kill the Buddha, because you must return to your own Buddhic nature.[22]

A similar movement occurs in the third turn of the dharma, where the Buddhic nature is emphasized as inherently present in all beings. This suggests that enlightenment is not obtained from the outside but revealed by dissipating the illusions and veils that conceal it. In contrast, the second turn of the dharma emphasizes that all things are empty and nothing has a fixed or independent essence. This teaching is crucial to understanding both the interdependence and impermanence of all phenomena. Shunryu Suzuki, in his famous exhortation to "kill the Buddha," does not propose a literal action; on the contrary, he uses a metaphor to encourage practitioners to free themselves from preconceived ideas and rigid images they may have formed about the Buddha. He emphasizes direct and intimate experience. Enlightenment and spiritual understanding are not found in the idolatry

---

22. Sheng-yen. *Hoofprint of the Ox: Principles of the Chan Buddhist Path as Taught by a Modern Chinese Master.* Translated by Dan Stevenson. (New York: Oxford University Press, 2002).

Chapter 7: The death of Christ

of religious figures but in recognizing our own essential nature. This perspective promotes a Zen practice that is dynamic and personal rather than static and dependent on external icons. Suzuki urges us to look beyond symbolic representations to find our intrinsic Buddhic nature.

The concept of Christ that we have paid special attention to in this chapter is in some ways equivalent to the Īśvara of Vedanta, which means that He represents the Absolute from the perspective of individual consciousness. This conception resonates both in Christian theology and in Vedantic philosophy. According to Vedanta, Īśvara, the Supreme Lord, is a personal manifestation of the Absolute in its relationship with the phenomenal world and individuals. Similarly, the *Bhāgavata Purana* narrates the death of Kṛṣṇa, which is another manifestation of the Absolute. The transition from an individual and personal understanding of the Divine to a realization of the Absolute that transcends any form or personal identity is emphasized. This moment of sublimation, which transcends individuated and personal form, is also detailed in the following quote:

मुषलावशेषाय:खण्डकृतेषुलुब्ध्को जरा ।
मृगास्याकारं तच्चरणं विव्याध मृगशङ्कया ॥

> *muṣalāvaśeṣāyaḥ-khaṇḍa-*
> *kṛteṣur lubdhako jarā*
> *mṛgāsyākāraṁ tac-caraṇaṁ*
> *vivyādha mṛga-śaṅkayā*

Section II: Transcending the Personal God

Just then a hunter named Jarā, who had approached the place, mistook the Lord's foot for a deer's face. Thinking he had found his prey, Jarā pierced the foot with his arrow, which he had fashioned from the remaining iron fragment of Sāmba's club.

(*Bhāgavata Purāṇa*, 11.30.33)

श्रीभगवानुवाच
मा भैर्जरे त्वमुत्तिष्ठ काम एष कृतो हि मे ।
याहि त्वं मदनुज्ञातः स्वर्गं सुकृतिनां पदम् ॥

*śrī-bhagavān uvāca
mā bhair jare tvam uttiṣṭha
kāma eṣa kṛto hi me
yāhi tvaṁ mad-anujñātaḥ
svargaṁ su-kṛtināṁ padam*

The Lord said: "My dear Jarā, do not fear. Please get up. What has been done is actually My own desire. With My permission, go now to the abode of the pious, the spiritual world."

(*Bhāgavata Purāṇa*, 11.30.39)

This passage from the *Bhāgavata Purāṇa* illustrates the significant moment in which Kṛṣṇa, as the incarnation of the Absolute, comforts the hunter Jarā, who unintentionally struck Him with a fatal wound. Kṛṣṇa's statement emphasizes that even events that may seem tragic or accidental are under divine control and form part of the cosmic plan. In this context, Kṛṣṇa's death symbolizes the transcendence of the Absolute's individual form, shifting toward a richer understanding of the Divine that transcends duality and individual consciousness. Both the death of Kṛṣṇa and Christ highlight that divinity must abandon its individualized form to reveal the absolute and transcendental unity. The Christian personal God is not a deity that proclaims that everything ends in Him; on the contrary, the personal God as such transcends toward the Absolute. Duality acquires meaning only when it is subordinated to unity. Thus, both in Christianity and in Vedanta, the importance of transcending individual consciousness to reach a direct and non-dual experience of the One, the Absolute, is emphasized.

Bibliography Section II

- Aquinas, Thomas. "*Chapter VII—That Evil is Not a Nature or Essence.*" In *Of God and His Creatures*. Accessed January 9, 2025.
- Nietzsche, Friedrich. *The Gay Science: With a Prelude in Rhymes and an Appendix of Songs*. Translated by Walter Kaufmann. New York: Vintage Books, 1974.
- Sheng-yen. *Hoofprint of the Ox: Principles of the Chan Buddhist Path as Taught by a Modern Chinese Master*. Translated by Dan Stevenson. New York: Oxford University Press, 2002.
- Siecienski, A. Edward. *The Filioque: History of a Doctrinal Controversy*. Oxford: Oxford University Press, 2010.

ולהביא על על השלישית ותרומת
הקודש ואת מעשר עדרם ובקרם
כתוב בו ליסד ממנו לכוהן ולדיא
ולעני ולשבת אשם היאה לחרוש
הארץ שנית וממשח הזית כי
הוא בא הארץ יאכלו לוא...
ואל יואכל איש אחר...
...שדה ויצהרו...
...כול...
...איש א...
...לוא יואכל אתה...
...המלאה ואדמעו...
אחר הקדישם הכוהנים
לוא יאכלו איש מ...

SECTION III
FROM PARTICIPATION TO EMANATION

CHAPTER 8

THE PATH OF PARTICIPATION: THE THOMIST DUALISM

In the previous section, we discussed the transcendence of individuation to the Absolute, defining it as a process of (re-)integration. That is, it is a movement that, even though it begins from unity, first separates, creating duality, only to reunify and converge back into unity.

To explain this movement of self-transcendence or sublimation in more detail, we will address a central concept to which both theology and philosophy have paid particular attention: participation. The concept of participation finds its foundations in the philosophies of Plato and Aristotle.[23] Later, St. Augustine left a significant mark on its development, as did Pseudo-Dionysius and Boethius. However, St. Thomas Aquinas consolidated its definitive theological version within the context of Christian theology. Since then, the concept of

---

23. Tollefsen, Torstein. T, "The Concept of Participation" in *The Christocentric Cosmology of St Maximus the Confessor* (Oxford University Press, Oxford 2008), 190–224.

SECTION III: FROM PARTICIPATION TO EMANATION

participation has maintained its continuity and continues to be a pillar of contemporary theological thought.

First, we should point out that participation is not related to either pantheism or nihilism. From a pantheistic perspective, if we begin with the axiom that God is everything, we are saying that there is nothing but God, which in itself denies the possibility of any participation.[24] That is, if God encompasses everything, then the being is nothing. In contrast, the concept of participation holds that there exists a Being whose essence is to be and other beings that exist by participation. This does not imply that beings exist outside of God. The essence of "participating" means that beings are in God but distinct from God.

On the other hand, participation differs from nihilism, which postulates that God is entirely separate from humanity. That is, if the human being is something, then God would be nothing. For nihilism, the foundation is nothing, which implies the negation of all metaphysics. This approach is somewhat similar to that of Plotinus, who states that the beings are, but God is not.[25] Both perspectives argue that either the Being is the beings and not God, or the Being is God and not the beings. The doctrine of participation, however, establishes a relationship in which beings exist in God but are distinct

---

24. Owen, H. P. *Concepts of Deity*. (London: Macmillan, 1971), 65.
25. Plotinus, *The Enneads*, vol. 5, Enneads V.1–9, trans. Arthur Hilary Armstrong, Loeb Classical Library no. 444 (Cambridge, MA: Harvard University Press, 1984), 59 (V.2.1).

Chapter 8: The path of participation: the Thomist dualism

from Him, allowing a coexistence that neither pantheism nor nihilism contemplates.

From a Christian perspective, God is the "Whole" in an essential way in Himself and God is in the beings in a participated way. In His own nature, God is by essence, while in the beings, He is through participation. Christian thought cannot deny metaphysical participation nor the reality of beings as something that exists. Indeed, every creature exists by participation. Every creature participates in the Being of God, but each does so according to its own nature. Therefore, there is a fundamental distinction: God is by essence, while beings are by participation. From the perspective of Christian theology, spiritual beings are immortal because what is spiritual does not get corrupted. Only matter is susceptible to corruption, while the soul is immortal.

To illustrate how beings participate in Being, let us take the example of a flower. A flower is a being that, in its way, participates in Being. The flower has parts that can be classified into two fundamental categories: those with a reproductive function and those without. The part of the flower without a reproductive function is called the perianth, consisting of several sterile structures such as sepals and petals. Other parts have a reproductive function. The first is the androecium, which is made up of the stamens, containing pollen grains, acting as the male reproductive organs. The second is the gynoecium, comprising the pistils containing the carpels, performing the role of female reproductive organs. The carpels, in

Section III: From participation to emanation

turn, are divided into three specific components: ovary, style, and stigma. Thus, the structure of the flower is organized in a combination of sterile and reproductive elements, each with its particular function in the process of reproduction and the development of the plant.

If we consider that a flower participates in the Being and recognize that it is composed of multiple parts, it is evident that each of those parts must also participate in the Being. There is nothing that does not participate in the Being; otherwise, it would not exist. Its petals are made of molecules and atoms, which, in turn, comprise subatomic particles like protons, neutrons, and electrons. Therefore, these atoms and molecules must also participate in the Being to exist. If we continue our analysis of the flower at the quantum level, we find quarks, leptons, gauge bosons, mesons, and baryons, among others. As a result, the entire flower and each of its parts participate in the Being. However, when we focus intensely on the flower, it seems to fade or dissolve into the Being. This happens because both the flower and each of its numerous and diverse parts exist as they participate in the Being.

To "participate" means that a part detaches from the Being, only to reintegrate into it again. In its fullness, Being draws something from itself that resides within it, though not identical to it. In this sense, beings were created to always be different from Being. It is an entity that remains in Being but without being Being itself. In this context, creation is distinct from the Creator but remains in Him. According to St. Thomas Aquinas,

CHAPTER 8: THE PATH OF PARTICIPATION: THE THOMIST DUALISM

creation, that is, the "other," remains as a distinct and independent entity from the Creator, Being. The "other" is precisely "other" because it differs from that from which it springs or proceeds. But it could not be "other" without a relationship of dependence, for it could not be "other" with regard to anything. This dependence already outlines a relationship, namely, of participation. In this sense, particular beings participate in Being in a limited and specific way, without merging entirely with the source of Being, and thus participating in God but being "other" with respect to Him. This viewpoint suggests that, while all creatures reflect the divine existence to some degree, they maintain their own identity and differentiation from the divine Creator from which they proceed.

The ontological distinction between the Creator and his creation is an essential principle in the philosophy of St. Thomas. This emphasizes the impossibility of a complete union or total integration with the original source of Being. In his interpretation of Christianity, though differently, the concept of Being encompasses the totality. Being is absolute in itself by its essence and manifests in particular beings through participation. This means that Being, in its most complete form, is identified with God, who possesses Being by His own nature. In contrast, created beings do not have Being in themselves, and only receive it to the extent that they participate in the divine Being. Thus, there is an essential distinction between Being in its highest

Section III: From participation to emanation

fullness, which is proper to God, and the participated Being, characteristic of creatures. This differentiation underscores the ontological dependence of created beings on the divine source of Being and establishes the foundations of Thomistic philosophy in general.

First, Thomistic philosophy is characterized by directly identifying between Being and God. Second, it also assigns a fully personal conception to God as Creator. And finally, it describes the relationship of the personal God with other beings and creatures through participation. These three premises led St. Thomas to present a dualist vision of existence, significantly influencing Western philosophy and the understanding of Christianity.[26] Therefore, Thomistic philosophy defines parameters that present God as a personalized and intelligible being, with whom we can relate rationally through thought. Moreover, for this to be possible, St. Thomas eventually inscribes faith within this same dualism. Furthermore, this rigid and robust structure confines God to these parameters, preventing humans from opening up to Him beyond those limits.

This problem has already been addressed in other religious beliefs. Some of these, however, have also recognized that the ultimate goal is not worshiping a personal God in itself, but transcending that limit in order to return to God or the absolute divinity. However,

---

26. Moreland, J. P. "The Origin of the Soul in Light of Twinning, Cloning, and Frozen Etnbryos" (PDF). *Journal of the International Society of Christian Apologetics*. (Volume 3, Number I, 2010), 4.

CHAPTER 8: THE PATH OF PARTICIPATION: THE THOMIST DUALISM

it is necessary to overcome any dualist approach that has given rise to or generated that personalized God to achieve this. Nevertheless, this transcendence requires approaches that surpass personal experience and guide us toward realizing the Absolute. Adopting these stances will allow us to establish a closer relationship with the unmanifested dimensions of spirituality and facilitate a more refined understanding of the Divine.

To surpass this stage and venture toward impersonal horizons, it is essential that we first experience a relationship with a personal God. In this sense, the limit imposed by dualist approaches can be considered a necessary stage in the journey, for without a clear understanding of this dualist structure and the personal God, it would be impossible to perceive the need for (re-)unification with the Absolute. In the terminology of the Gospels, the only way to the Father is through the Son, the dualist personal God who allows human beings to conceive of themselves as such in that relationship. Therefore, in this initial stage, it is crucial to advance to the limit of this duality through a devotional relationship with the personal God. This journey begins with the dual relationship between devotees who perceives themselves as "someone" and their personal deity; for one who considers themselves "someone," God will inevitably be seen as a divine individual. Ultimately, our conception of the Divine and how we relate to God will directly depend on our self-perception as participants of God, who is and is present in everything.

Section III: From participation to emanation

However, overcoming dualism requires "re-flection" and self-inquiry, thus opening a path to another form of "thinking" that we will describe later. For now, it is enough to note that the sublimation of the personal God into the Absolute and the reunification of the particular into Being is achieved through meditation and contemplation. In these paths, duality dissolves, and the Divine manifests clearly. The fading of the dualist structure will bring about the sublimation of both the personal God and the egoic phenomenon. It will overcome the rational subject that ontotheological and philosophical tradition has erected as the axis of all existence and truth.

The fading of the dualist structure does not imply the disappearance of Being; on the contrary, it marks the beginning of the first genuine manifestation of beingness. When the ego extinguishes, the true Being is experienced for the first time. The illusory dissipates, and the genuine reveals itself in all its magnitude. This process is part of God's will. God desires that we reach absolute liberation. At this moment, one experiences infinite gratitude toward God. Without His insistence, one would have remained in that pleasant but limited state. His final message is to transcend all attachment, which includes liberation from the image of God Himself.

> And you will know the Truth, and the Truth will set you free.
>
> (John, 8:32)

CHAPTER 9

EMANATION AND THE RETURN TO THE ONE IN PLOTINUS

So far, we have seen Christianity explained and understood through the philosophy of St. Thomas Aquinas. In the present chapter, we will offer an alternative reading that has impacted some interpretations within Christianity, but especially outside of it. This other path is the theory of emanationism in Plotinus' philosophy. Emanationism, the central doctrine of Neoplatonic philosophy, is primarily attributed to Proclus and Plotinus.[27] It was followed by numerous philosophers, including Avicenna, who played a significant role in Arab philosophy. In the Christian context, this doctrine also later influenced authors such as Pseudo-Dionysius and St. Augustine. Similarly, in various religious theologies, such as Jewish Kabbalah, the idea of a hierarchical, descending, and successive emanation of spiritual entities between the divine summit and the material world is also upheld.

---

27. Samuel Enoch Stumpf, *Philosophy: History and Problems* (New York: McGraw-Hill Inc., 1983), 122–123.

Section III: From participation to emanation

Plotinus is recognized as the founder of Neoplatonism in the history of modern philosophy. He establishes three essential principles in his writings: the One, the Intellect, and the Soul. For Plotinus, philosophy was not merely an abstract discipline but a way of life and a form of religion. There is little detailed information about his life, as the only reliable source is the preface written by his disciple Porphyry in *The Enneads*, a compilation of his master's works. Despite the scarcity of biographical data, Plotinus' influence spread widely and endured over time, from late antiquity to the Middle Ages and the Renaissance. His thought was fundamental in shaping the early developments of Christian theology while equally enlightening the path for many pagan, Gnostic, Jewish, and Islamic mystics over the centuries. Plotinus' philosophy, with its special emphasis on transcendence and unity, became a source of inspiration for various spiritual and philosophical traditions, leaving a lasting impact on the history of human thought.

More than a mere thinker, Plotinus was a master, one of those rare beings who form the final threshold on the path to Truth. He passed away in the summer of the year 270 at sixty-six. Only Eustochius, his physician and loyal disciple, managed to arrive just in time to hear the final words of the revered master:

Μέλλων δὲ τελευτᾶν, ὡς ὁ Εὐστόχιος ἡμῖν διηγεῖτο, ἐπειδὴ ἐν Ποτιόλοις κατοικῶν ὁ Εὐστόχιος βραδέως πρὸς αὐτὸν ἀφίκετο, εἰπὼν

CHAPTER 9: EMANATION AND THE RETURN TO THE ONE IN PLOTINUS

ὅτι σὲ ἔτι περιμένω καὶ φήσας πειρᾶσθαι τὸ ἐν ἡμῖν θεῖον ἀνάγειν πρὸς τὸ ἐν τῷ παντὶ θεῖον, δράκοντος ὑπὸ τὴν κλίνην διελθόντος ἐν ᾗ κατέκειτο καὶ εἰς ὀπὴν ἐν τῷ τοίχῳ ὑπάρχουσαν ὑποδεδυκότος ἀφῆκε τὸ πνεῦμα.

When (Plotinus) was about to die, as Eustochius told us, once Eustochius, who was then living in Puteoli, arrived late at his side, Plotinus said to him: "I was still waiting for you." And after recommending to him that he should strive to elevate what is divine in us toward what is divine in the universe, at the moment when a serpent slithered beneath the bed on which he lay and slipped into a crack in the wall, he exhaled his last breath.[28]

These last words, in nature, eminently exhortative, refer to the need to elevate the soul in an ascending movement and return to its origin. However, they can be interpreted broadly, applying to all of humanity. This is comparable to Hierocles' theory of concentric circles in relation to the doctrine of *oikeiosis* (οἰκείωσις). The reading of *The Enneads* encourages the practice of *anagogē* (ἀναγωγή), a term that translates as "elevation" and "return" of the soul to its original principles. This concept comprises two fundamental meanings of the

---

28. "Porphyry" *On the Life of Plotinus and the Arrangement of his Work* (The School of Athens, Raphael, 1509), 2.23–29 H-S1.

Section III: From participation to emanation

verb *anagō* (ἀνάγω): "to return or restore" and "to elevate or lift." In the Plotinian notion of *anagogē* (ἀναγωγή), both senses are integrated, representing a simultaneous ascent and return. That is, it involves both an elevation of the soul and its restoration or reconduction to its primordial source.

The significance of Plotinus in our study lies in his replacement of the notion of participation with the concept of emanation. In Greek thought, the terms translated as an emanation (*proeinai* or προεῖναι, *aporrein* or ἀπορρεῖν) evoke the idea of an "overflow." It is a causation where the effect inevitably arises from the cause but retains a continuity or gradation with it.

This concept, fundamental in Neoplatonic philosophy and thoroughly developed by Plotinus, describes a process by which the superior generates the inferior due to its intrinsic abundance, but without experiencing any loss in the process. This causation through emanation is based on the idea that every being, simply by existing, inevitably produces a reality that projects outward, acting as a manifestation of the archetypes from which it originates. This process is similar to how fire emits heat or how the sun, though it illuminates, does not diminish its energy. According to Plotinus, in emanation, the One remains substantially intact despite its generative capacity. That is, the innate generative capacity of the One, derived from its absolute perfection, allows for the generation of diversity without diminishing its essence. Thus, from the perfect Being emanates necessarily an eternal Being, but of lower ontological quality. This is because, although there is no diminution of essence, there is an ontological degradation, given that the beings emanated are always inferior to their original source. This same idea of emanation is also found in the invocation of the *Īśāvāsya Upanishad*:

ॐ पूर्णमदः पूर्णमिदं पूर्णात् पूर्णमुदच्यते ।
पूर्णस्य पूर्णमादाय पूर्णमेवावशिष्यते ॥
ॐ शान्तिः शान्तिः शान्तिः ॥

> *oṁ pūrṇam adaḥ pūrṇam idaṁ*
> *pūrṇāt pūrṇam udacyate*
> *pūrṇasya pūrṇam ādāya*
> *pūrṇam evāvaśiṣyate*
> *oṁ śāntiḥ śāntiḥ śāntiḥ*

That is the Whole, this is the Whole; from that Whole, this Whole is manifested. When this Whole is extracted, that Whole is still the Whole. *Oṁ* peace, peace, peace.

(*Īśāvāsya Upanishad*, invocation)

Emanationism holds that the entire universe, including individual souls, arises through emanation or flow from the divine totality,[29] the primordial One, either in a

---

29. Plotinus, *The Enneads*, vol. 5, Enneads V.1–9, trans. Arthur Hilary Armstrong, Loeb Classical Library no. 444 (Cambridge, MA: Harvard University Press, 1984), 61–63 (V.2.2).

Section III: From participation to emanation

mediated or immediate form. This perspective differs radically from the previously described creationism, as it does not refer to a temporal beginning of the world or creation *ex nihilo*. It is also not a theological or religious notion, although it has frequently been associated with creation. According to emanationism, God is conceived as the One, the absolute transcendent reality and the source of all that exists. From the One emanates the *Nous*, or 'intellect,' an entity that contains all the forms or ideas of the universe. In emanation, the beings emanated spring from the same origin as God, without separating from Him. The distinction between the One, God, or the Origin, and its emanations lies in their development and, in the case of human beings, in their lack of purity. It differs from creationism, in which there is a marked separation between the creature and the divinity, where the created is always Other in relation to the Creator.

In the emanationists' doctrine, the emphasis is not on the will of God but on the fact that, as descending parts of Him, our condition is derivative but not intentional. Moreover, the emanations of Being flow from its own essence. Since they are not essentially different from the Being from which they proceed, these emanations will ultimately return to Him. Although these emanations seem separated and show a clear ontological difference, they retain an essential connection to their origin, avoiding dualist duplicity. Being and what emanates from Being are one and the same.

Chapter 10

The three fundamental hypostases of Plotinus

Plotinian cosmology has three hypostases, or fundamental realities, namely The One, the Intellect, and the Soul.[30] At the apex, above Being and any idea, is the Absolute One, inspired by Platonic Good. The One is the first of the three divine hypostases and the source of the "procession" that generates the other two from its own superabundance: the Logos, also known as the Intellect or *Nous*, and the Soul of the World. From these three hypostases, the lower beings originate, ranging from individual souls to inert matter. Let us examine this closely.

The absolute One

In its natural tendency to expand, the One radiates its Being like a light or heat source. Existence implies

---

30. Lloyd P. Gerson and James Wilberding (eds.). *The New Cambridge Companion to Plotinus* (Cambridge University Press, Cambridge, 1996), 38–39.

Section III: From participation to emanation

determination; it is meant to be concrete, particular, and defined. Without this specificity, existence is not possible, since, for Plotinus, it is not viable to be nothing. What is nothing simply is not. Being implies being "a" something, and this something is "one" because it has existence and participates in unity. Therefore, the essence of Being lies in its specificity; "to be" is necessarily "to be something concrete and particular," and this concreteness causes the absolute transcendent to be identified as the One. It is by the One that Being is defined as something. The very existence of Being depends on the One. Hence, the One that confers identity to Being must be beyond Being itself, for without this transcendence, Being could not exist. If the One were not what it is, Being could not be something defined. Therefore, the unity of the One allows Being to manifest as something concrete and specific. This same idea appears in Judaism, as can be seen below.

שְׁמַע יִשְׂרָאֵל ה' אֱלֹהֵינוּ ה' אֶחָד:

(דברים ו', ד')

Hear, O Israel, the Lord is our God; the Lord is one.

(Deuteronomy, 6:4)

This implies:

וְהָיָה ה' לְמֶלֶךְ עַל־כָּל־הָאָרֶץ בַּיּוֹם הַהוּא יִהְיֶה ה' אֶחָד וּשְׁמוֹ אֶחָד:

(זכריה י"ה, ט')

Chapter 10: The three fundamental hypostases of Plotinus

> And the Lord shall become King over all the earth; on that day shall the Lord be one, and His name one.
>
> (Zechariah, 14:9)

Additionally, according to Plotinus, the One is not *per se*, meaning that this absolute One cannot be something or someone determined, for if it were, it would lose its quality of being absolute. Therefore, we must say that the One is nothing (concrete) at all. It is precisely because of its nature of being nothing (concrete), that is, of not being a determined something, that the One becomes the foundation of Being. Heidegger would later call this One that is nothing "the primordial nothing," which is the foundation of Being that, in turn, gives beings their foundation. Therefore, the root of Plotinus' teachings lies in the One, which transcends reality and thought. Its nature of unity makes it indescribable. Plotinus often refers to the One as the unique and infinite God. The One is the basis and foundation of everything and everyone, thus constituting the central axis of his philosophy.[31] Moreover, instead of engaging in debates or corrections, Plotinus preferred to remain silent when asked about the One. He adopted an introspective attitude, for the absolute transcendence of the One makes it difficult to find precise words to describe it. Since Plotinus's notion of the One transcends the

---

31. McInerny, Ralph. *A History of Western Philosophy, Volume I: From the Beginnings of Philosophy to Plotinus* (Chicago: Regnery, 1963), 342.

Section III: From participation to emanation

concept of Being, no positive definition can completely capture it. This absolute transcendence places the One beyond any category or description our cognitive abilities may formulate. Being beyond Being, substance, and person, the One becomes an entity that challenges any attempt to be defined or fully understood through human language or conventional logic. In other words, God is inconceivable and undefinable.

The ineffability and transcendence of the One make it impossible to define it positively, leading Plotinus to adopt the negative way. Therefore, instead of trying to define it through concrete statements, Plotinus emphasizes what the One is not. In this way, the limitation of definitions is avoided, and the integrity of the One as the supreme and incomprehensible entity is preserved. The One is the origin and the end of everything. The One is the principle and foundation of all reality, the source of an unlimited and eternal existence that transcends human understanding, identifying itself with the divine and eternal. Its indefinability is not a weakness but rather a sign of its perfect and transcendent nature and its essential role in the existence and order of the cosmos. This perspective invites us to contemplate the One with recognition of its infinite greatness and to accept the limitation of our cognitive capacities in the face of such a sublime reality.

Unlike the One, Being implies being something or someone determined and, therefore, must fundamentally be a notion, an idea fully defined when it

Chapter 10: The three fundamental hypostases of Plotinus

explains itself. We cannot understand the idea of Being without adding that it is one. For example, we could not explain beauty or goodness without the idea of being, because beauty and goodness *are*. At the same time, the idea of beauty is linked to the notion of the good because beauty is good. Likewise, the idea of good is related to the notion of Being, because the good *is*. Finally, the idea of Being is intrinsically tied to the idea of one because Being is one, and it is the One that determines it and gives it its own unity as something concrete. However, unlike Being, the One cannot be associated with any idea because it is neither beautiful nor ugly, neither good nor bad, neither being nor non-being. The One transcends all these qualities and determinations. To be the absolute One, it must be completely indeterminate. Therefore, Plotinus presents the One as the immediate indeterminate because it is present in everything, as if it is the unknown aspect of that thing. It is immediate because it is present in every emotion, thought, and experience. We can recognize that something is beautiful, ugly, unique, large, small, good, bad, and that it exists. All these predicates are understandable. However, while we understand the unity of a thing, that is, what makes a thing a thing, we do not understand the One that unifies everything. The One is what gives unity to the ideas of Being, beauty, and good. Essentially, and as we have seen, to be implies to be one, but nothing can be one without the intervention of the One.

Section III: From participation to emanation

It should be noted that, on one hand, the One is what confers Being, because to be is fundamentally to be one, while on the other hand, it is Being that provides existence. Therefore, the One uses Being for the idea of beauty to manifest, which means it is through Being that the One reveals itself. For its part, Being acquires its concreteness from the One, but it only manifests in the beings, for only the beings can be present.

At the same time, Plotinus insists that the One transcends the mere presence of the beings, for while Being represents the evident manifestation of presence, the One corresponds to its unmanifested aspect. One could argue that the One is neither present nor non-present in that it underlies everything as absolutely unmanifest due to its indeterminacy. This implies that nothing specific can be known about it. Therefore, it is impossible to qualify it as ugly or beautiful, bad or good. The concept of "Being," on the other hand, necessarily implies being something specific, which entails being determined, at least by two ideas: the idea of "being" and the idea of "something." Thus, "being" can manifest as beauty, goodness, intelligence, a chair, a person, Christ, or God. When we affirm that "the One" **is**, we assign it an ontological existence, even though "the One" transcends Being. This does not imply that "the One" does not exist but that it goes beyond the dichotomy of Being and non-being, as both are characteristics of the beings. In their essential nature, beings are necessarily defined as either existent or nonexistent. However, "the One" stands outside of this duality and cannot be categorized as either "is" or "is not" because it remains completely independent from both categories. Nothingness can affect or annul beings, but it can never reach or influence "the One," which always transcends the limitations that existence and nonexistence impose on Being, placing itself in a wholly different and unalterable sphere.

The *Nous* as the intellectual expression of the One

Within this philosophical system, the descending levels that emanate from the One are organized into three distinct degrees of perfection. The first emanation or reality that arises from the One is the *Nous*. Although there is no exact translation for it, some authors identify it with the spirit, while others prefer to describe it as pure intelligence, close to the One. To explain the *Nous*, Plotinus uses the analogy of the sun and its light: the One is like the sun, and the light is like the *Nous*. The function of the *Nous* is to allow the One to see itself, acting as an image of the One and the gateway through which we can perceive it. By thinking without separating itself from the One, the *Nous* produces the Soul of the World, from which individual souls derive. These souls manifest in the sensible world, where ideas can incarnate. In this context, matter is perceived as a shadow, weakening the original light.

SECTION III: FROM PARTICIPATION TO EMANATION

According to Plotinus, the *Nous* can be observed by directing the mind in the opposite direction of the senses, that is, in its internalization, which Patañjali and the *rāja-yoga* system refer to as *pratyāhāra* in Sanskrit. Therefore, the search for Truth must focus on the inner self, rejecting all mediation and objects, even the very "self," which leads to a mystical contemplation. Plotinus holds that the *Nous* arises from contact with the One. Before the *Nous* or spirit existed, it was simply an indeterminate idea. However, by being in the presence of the One, it became defined as spirit and adopted the idea of the forms of the existing beings. As we have seen earlier regarding the concept of emanation, the *Nous* does not emerge from the One by an act of will since the One is transcendental to any volitional act. Everything that proceeds from the One is a manner of "spreading out" in its act of self-generation. For this reason, the analogy of the sun and light should be seen simply as an illustrative image.

The Soul: immortality and fusion with the *Nous*

The soul constitutes the third hypostasis and possesses a dual nature. This duality is manifested in its connection with the *Nous* and sensory world, of which it acts as a shaping force. According to Plotinus, Nature is the result of a descending flow from the soul, which he considers the supreme authority of tangible and concrete reality, both in the realm of objects and thoughts. Since the mere

CHAPTER 10: THE THREE FUNDAMENTAL HYPOSTASES OF PLOTINUS

production of ideas and their execution is insufficient, generating matter is one of its main functions. Following the argument in Plato's *Phaedo*,[32] Plotinus asserts that the human soul is immortal.[33] However, his assertion does not stop at the mere immortality of the soul, as he emphasizes an inherent tendency within it: its fusion with the *Nous*. This integration process suggests that the soul ultimately loses its individuality by uniting with the *Nous* as the divine intellect in its search for the transcendental. Therefore, for Plotinus, immortality, rather than being equivalent to the continuation of personal identity, involves a return to a higher source in which individuality dissolves in favor of a higher and more unified existence.

Despite its apparent imperfection, in Plotinus' philosophy, matter must return to the One from where it emanates. However, to do so, it must undertake a regressive movement or reverse shift in search of reunification with its fundamental principle. In this retroprogressive process toward the One, staying alert to the illusion generated by the fascination with objective diversity is essential. To progress in the search for Truth,

---

32. Plato, *Phaedo* 73a. Version of this reference is found here Plato. *Plato in Twelve Volumes*, Vol. 1 translated by Harold North Fowler; Introduction by W.R.M. Lamb. (Cambridge, MA, Harvard University Press; London, William Heinemann Ltd. 1966).

33. Plotinus, *The Enneads*, vol. 4, Enneads IV.1–9, trans. Arthur Hilary Armstrong, Loeb Classical Library no. 443 (Cambridge, MA: Harvard University Press, 1984), IV.7.

Section III: From participation to emanation

we must focus on our reality's source and primordial origin. This requires conscious attention to the important, the unmanifest One in all things, thereby overcoming the superficial distractions that divert attention from the true and authentic. In the return to our origin, to the One of all, distinguishing between the apparent and the real becomes crucial in achieving a deeper and more unified understanding of existence. Following Plotinus' teachings, this process inevitably demands meditation as the path of ascension to the origin. Therefore, the soul's ultimate goal is to return to the One, the primal source of its emanation. Based on meditative introspection and contemplative self-knowledge, this spiritual quest leads the individual to a reconnection with their primordial essence, overcoming the illusions of diversity and achieving a higher unity.

This return to the origin, to the One of all, is a process that consists of several levels. This ascent's first level focuses on acquiring virtues and self-mastery. The second level involves intimate, intuitive communication with the Spirit. At the highest level, the soul reaches total integration with the One through ecstasy, culminating its spiritual journey in the fullness of its divine nature. This ascent is a complex process of liberation of the soul, which is initially trapped by material bonds and sensory illusions. Each phase of this spiritual journey represents a gradual advance toward complete unification, in which the soul transcends its limitations, progressively approaching a total symbiosis with the One.

The differences between emanation and participation

So far, the exposition of Thomas Aquinas and Plotinus provides a solid foundation for distinguishing clearly between emanation and participation. To delve deeper into this topic, Plotinus returns to the subject of unity in his work *The Enneads*, where he explains that emanation, unlike participation, involves the total surrender of Being. In the context of participation, created beings are not Being itself, but rather distinct products. However, in the process of emanation, everything we identify as beings is fundamentally Being itself. The concept of participation in Thomas Aquinas establishes a duality between Being and the created. In contrast, according to Plotinus, emanation allows us to overcome this duality, perceiving Being as an indivisible reality in all that is. Thus, the multiplicity of entities does not contradict the unity of Being.

This difference has significant consequences, especially for Christianity and, more specifically, for the idea of God. In this sense, the proposition of Thomistic participation is linked to the notion of a God Person, as we have seen earlier. Adherence to the faith in the personal God keeps us within a closed dualist structure whose framework, philosophically speaking, is impossible to transcend. The path of Thomas Aquinas will never lead to a non-dual reality. The conception of God as a person constitutes the final barrier in the

Section III: From participation to emanation

search for Truth. We may detach ourselves from all our possessions and relationships. But as long as we do not transcend the idea of the personal God, it will remain the foundation and root of the egoic phenomenon, or the separated, divided "I." Even if we renounce everything else, the presence of the personal God will maintain the base of the ego and the perception of duality, preventing complete transcendence toward realizing our authenticity. Through the doctrine of the Aquinate, it is possible to explore and understand duality to its limits. However, to transcend it and make the quantum leap toward the Absolute while remaining within Christianity, it is necessary to turn to philosophers such as Plotinus, whose texts allow us a transcendent understanding of Being. Therefore, although Thomistic theology provides a framework for exploration within duality, Plotinian philosophy is essential to transcend it.

Plotinus's non-dualist structure allows us to read the theses of Christianity from a different perspective. In summary, under Plotinus' framework, the One can be interpreted as the Father, Being as the Son, and the *Nous* or Soul as the Holy Spirit. From this viewpoint, Christianity offers a retroprogressive path of *teshuvah* (return) that progresses from the third (Holy Spirit) to the second (Son) and, through this, to the first (Father or the One). This progression, different from the Thomistic reading, shows us that the One unites two compounds, as is affirmed in Genesis:

Chapter 10: The three fundamental hypostases of Plotinus

וַיִּקְרָא אֱלֹהִים לָאוֹר יוֹם וְלַחֹשֶׁךְ קָרָא לָיְלָה וַיְהִי עֶרֶב וַיְהִי בֹקֶר יוֹם אֶחָד:

(בראשית א', ה')

And God called the light day, and the darkness He called night, and it was evening, and it was morning, one day.

(Genesis, 1:5)

However, this union of two compounds must be understood as a reunion or, better yet, a restoration of the unity that the One itself carries out through a conversion, an unfolding toward itself. This conversion, a term from the Latin *convertio* and includes the prefix *con* (together, united), does not equate to joining or transforming separate foreign units. On the contrary, it involves the reunification of the one with itself, which cannot be reduced to a structure of action. It does not arise from freedom or free will—the foundations of Thomistic dualism.

In this sense, conversion or turning inward, according to Plotinus, precedes freedom. It cannot be reduced to an act since it does not occur between distinct foreign entities. Conversion is more like a flow, like the transition from night to day and vice versa, as Genesis describes. From Plotinus' perspective, the "conversional" movement does not arise from a separating duality but from an overflowing that does not fragment. This allows us to reinterpret Christianity and God beyond

Section III: From participation to emanation

the Thomistic dualism. The emanationist thesis, with its implications, invites us to interpret the death of Christ as His conversion to the One, from which He emanates and to which He returns. Plotinus' philosophy explains how the dualism that sustains official Christianity hinders reunification with the Absolute. This dualism traps the Christian in an insurmountable dialectic between good and evil, creation and sin.

As mentioned earlier, to restore the unity of the Father, the One, the death of Christ is essential. While Christ lives, we operate within the framework of Thomas Aquinas, whose theology revolves around the living Christ. However, with Christ's death on the cross, God ceases to be a person. After completing the divine incarnation, we need to approach divinity from a different perspective.

In this new context, Plotinus' Neoplatonic notions offer an appropriate philosophical framework for understanding divine transcendence in the absence of the historical figure of Christ. Upon reaching the top of personal religion, we enter a phase where duality becomes how the person is purified to achieve perfection in Jesus Christ. From a strictly personal perspective, the connection with Christianity prevents the transcendence of Jesus from reaching the Father. Only by completing the path of personal religion toward perfection can Christ die, thereby allowing a quantum leap beyond individual existence.

Bibliography Section III

- Gerson, Lloyd P., and James Wilberding, eds. *The New Cambridge Companion to Plotinus*. Cambridge: Cambridge University Press, 2022.
- McInerny, Ralph. *A History of Western Philosophy, Volume I: From the Beginnings of Philosophy to Plotinus*. Chicago: Regnery, 1963.
- Owen, H. P. *Concepts of Deity*. London: Macmillan, 1971.
- Plato. *Plato in Twelve Volumes*, Vol. 1. Translated by Harold North Fowler. Introduction by W. R. M. Lamb. Cambridge, MA: Harvard University Press; London: William Heinemann Ltd., 1966.
- Plotinus. *The Enneads*. Vol. 4, *Enneads* IV.1–9 and Vol. 5, *Enneads* V.1–9. Translated by A. H. Armstrong. Loeb Classical Library 443. Cambridge, MA: Harvard University Press, 1984.
- Porphyry. *On the Life of Plotinus and the Arrangement of His Work*. The School of Athens, Raphael, 1509.
- Siecienski, Anthony Edward. *The Filioque: History of a Doctrinal Controversy*. New York: Oxford University Press, 2010.
- Stumpf, Samuel Enoch. *Philosophy: History and Problems*. Londres: McGraw-Hill Inc., 1971.

金剛般若波羅蜜經

是我聞一時佛在舍衛國祇樹給孤獨園與大比丘眾千二百五十人俱爾時世尊食時著衣持鉢入舍衛大城乞食於其城中次第乞已還至本處飯食訖收衣鉢洗足已敷座而坐時長老須菩提

奉請青除災金剛
奉請辟毒金剛
奉請黃隨求金剛
奉請白淨水金剛
奉請赤聲火金剛
奉請定除災金剛
奉請大神金剛

SECTION IV
THE FORGETTING AND BECOMING OF BEING

Chapter 11

The divorce
between being and thinking

In the previous sections of this study, we have explained the theological and philosophical foundations upon which Christianity has been built as ontotheology and consolidated as a religion. This has allowed us to sketch a small conceptual map that describes how Christianity has conceived of God and, by extension, the human being within the sphere of influence of the personal God. We have also introduced the figure of Plotinus, whose philosophy has opened the door to reconsidering Christianity from a philosophical perspective different from Thomism and scholastic theology. As we close the previous section and with the alternative vision of Plotinus, we aim to understand Christianity and the human being beyond a personal, anthropomorphized and ontified God, focusing instead on its sublimation and reunification with the absolute God.

The fourth part of this book begins precisely here, from the perspective of the philosophy of Martin Heidegger. Through it, we will detail how the coming

Section IV: The forgetting and becoming of Being

into being of Plotinus' One, or the absolute God that Heidegger has called the "Last God," can occur, and we will explore its implications for the human being. Before addressing this, we will examine a key issue in Heideggerian philosophy: "the forgetting of Being." We will see how this forgetting constitutes the core of the problem that has led us to the current crisis of meaning.

In his seminal work *Introduction to Metaphysics*, Martin Heidegger argues that the beginning of philosophical thought lies precisely in the Greeks' opening toward Being. This Being, the essence of all that exists, manifests itself as that which unfolds and opens itself in a continuous emergence that persists in its own essence.

According to Heidegger, Being is the Being of things and, as such, configures its destiny through its opening, consolidating and remaining in a self-unfolding that is not alien to the human being. This way of understanding Being begins in pre-Socratic philosophy, especially in the works of thinkers like Parmenides, Heraclitus, and Anaximander. Their teachings represent one of the foundations of Western philosophy. Heidegger warns that this first conception of Being, identified with Truth, faced a profound crisis with the emergence of philosophy as a discipline. Plato and Aristotle, in particular, through their epistemological approaches, generated an ontological confusion regarding Being and the thinking of Being. This confusion, we might say, is the root of what Heidegger later calls the "forgetting of Being." In his critique of Plato and Greek philosophy, he argues that philosophy, which was born to think about Being, paradoxically ended up forgetting it. In his work, *The History of Being*, Heidegger explains how this forgetting occurs:

> The first commencement is *physis* (φύσις). "Being" is not distinguished from truth. Both "are" the Same, which is also why the essential saying of Parmenides is immediately said: το γὰρ αὐτὸ νοεῖν ἐστίν τε καὶ εἶναι (*to gar auto noein estin te kai einai* - "for the same is to think and to be"). Being is not distinguished or differentiated from the "becoming" that is seen by Parmenides and Heraclitus in terms of the essence of physis (φύσις) and said in different ways. For both, *physis* (φύσις) is *logos* (λόγος).[34]

Pre-Socratic philosophical thought is based on a double fundamental premise. On one hand, to be is synonymous with to think, and on the other, to be is synonymous with truth. Therefore, being and truth are equivalent. From the pre-Socratic perspective, truth is intrinsically being itself, and this does not need to be thought to acquire veracity. What is, **is**, and insofar as it is, it is true. This same idea, although expressed differently, appears in the

---

34. Martin Heidegger, *The History of Beyng*, trans. William McNeill and Jeffrey Powell (Bloomington: Indiana University Press, 2015), section XI, "The Configuration of Saying [132–133]," §115, "The History of Beyng," 114.

Section IV: The forgetting and becoming of Being

New Testament, where we read:

> Jesus said to him: I am the way, and the Truth and the Life.
>
> (John, 14:6)

According to Heidegger, Parmenides' philosophy suggests that when we observe an object, such as a table, the essence is not the table as an object but the fact that it *is*. Similarly, when identifying ourselves as human beings, Chileans or Hindus, men or women, Christians or Jews, what is truly essential is the awareness that we *are*. Truth, therefore, resides in Being, which, according to Parmenides, is one, immutable, and indivisible.

The pre-Socratic philosophy emphasizes that what is fundamental is existence in its purest form—the simple fact of being. However, the emergence of Plato's and Aristotle's philosophy brought about significant transformations. According to them, Truth involves a correspondence between what is thought and what the thing is. Therefore, they open the first division between being and thinking and, consequently, between being and truth.

In Plato's case, Heidegger locates the origin of the problem in a double movement that unfolds in his philosophy, particularly in the dialogue *Phaedrus*. This movement involves a forgetting of the notion of *physis* (φύσις), understood by the pre-Socratics as nature in its totality, that is, the totality of beings. Furthermore,

Chapter 11: The divorce between being and thinking

for the pre-Socratic thinkers, there was a fundamental consensus regarding Being, which is that it revealed itself in everything. Being, as Being, was not meant to be actively thought through concepts or ideas, as if it were just another characteristic or object. Instead, Being was understood as the underlies of all thought and existence.

However, in the attempt to decipher Being as the foundation of all that is, philosophy begins to think of it as just another object of human knowledge. This approach leads to subjecting Being to specific structures of thought and reasoning, which hinder its understanding and turn it into a conceptual construct. Instead of allowing Being to manifest freely and spontaneously, philosophy reduces it to an idea produced by thought. In this way, thought becomes a productive activity, that is, the process that elaborates its own objects through a technique, or in Greek, *techne* (τέχνη). When this technical notion of thinking appears, Being is subsumed under the categories of production and objectification.

The philosophical emergence of Plato thus implies a first distinction between *physis* and *techne*. While *physis* would correspond to a notion of springing forth by itself, *techne* refers to the technique or art employed by humans to make something spring forth. The plant, for example, emerges naturally, while the table is produced by human intervention. What springs forth by itself corresponds to *physis*, while that which humans bring forth would be *techne*. Thus, for the pre-Socratic thinkers, Being would be *physis* itself, that is, that which springs forth by itself and manifests as such without any external intervention or need for conceptualization.

However, from this Platonic perspective, *physis* is no longer everything because philosophy itself has extracted Being from *physis* and turned it into an object of human conceptualization. This means that the notion of philosophy, specifically metaphysics, unfolds as a technique through which the humans attempt to make Being spring forth by defining it through concepts. Moreover, as a consequence of this rupture between *physis* (φύσις) and *techne* (τέχνη) brought about by the eruption of thought (*noein* - νοειν), Truth (*alétheia* - αληθεια) also ceases to be equivalent to Being and *physis*. Thus, it transforms into opinion or belief (*doxa* - δόξα), that is, into what only exists as something thought or believed.

Under this conception, only what appears before the eyes or the mind is accepted as Truth. This implies that, after this double separation, reality ceases to be Being (the pre-Socratic *physis*) and becomes a conceptual composition elaborated by reason. According to Heidegger, due to this separation between thought and Being, the original notion of Truth (*alétheia*) is reduced to merely the unveiling (*a-letheia*) of an idea. Heidegger's initial analysis suggests that this double separation, between *physis* and Being, and then between Being and *alétheia*—gives rise to the dualism that structures the philosophical thought of Plato, Aristotle, and the

Western tradition, which deeply influenced Thomas Aquinas. While Plato inaugurates the split between Being and thinking, Aristotle consolidates it by defining Truth as what would later be called in Latin *Adaequatio rei et intellectus*, that is, the correspondence between the known reality and the concept formulated by the intellect.

Truth becomes an adequation of thought to reality, ceasing to be equivalent to Being itself and instead becoming a relationship of adequation with Being. Thus, Truth becomes grounded in the concordance between thought and the thing, in a process that harmonizes thought with the object. Truth no longer resides in Being itself but in the precise correspondence between our conceptions and the ontological reality. This perspective suggests that Truth is based on the accuracy with which our concepts and judgments reflect the authentic nature of Being. Thus, it shifts from the ontological realm to the epistemological one, that is, from Being to knowing. It now depends on the human intellect's ability to capture and faithfully represent the essence of Being. This paradigm shift asserts that Truth is not Being, but rather resides and depends on the utterance of human thought. Aristotle confirms this by defining Truth as "to say of what is that it is, and of what is not that it is not,"[35] implicitly suggesting

---

35. Aristotle, *Metaphysics* (4.1011b). Ross, W. D. *Aristotle's Metaphysics*, a revised text with introduction and commentary. (Oxford: Clarendon Press, 1924).

that it lies in the precision of the language. This same argument is directly mentioned in *The History of Being*, where Heidegger says:

> *Noein* (νοεῖν) and *legein* (λέγειν) themselves are torn away from *physis* (φύςις) and made the responsibility of the human; the human being himself now receives his essence as *zōon logon echon* (ζώον λογον εχον).[36]

According to this quote, by extracting Being from *physis*, philosophy also empties *physis* of a presocratic notion of *noein* (νοεῖν), meaning "thought," and of *legein* (λέγειν), "to speak or say." This gives rise to the expression *zōon logon echon* (ζώον λογον εχον), which means "rational animal." Therefore, Platonic and Aristotelian philosophy redefine thinking and speaking, transforming them into "acts" whose structure allows Being to be objectified as if it were just another object or being.

The divorce between being and thinking is a cornerstone of Western philosophy for the coming centuries. This conception of Being, knowing, and the human being reaches its most radical culmination in Rudolph Hermann Lotze's neokantian theory of values. According to this theory, logical entities do not exist

---

36. Martin Heidegger, *The History of Beyng*, trans. William McNeill and Jeffrey Powell (Bloomington: Indiana University Press, 2015), section XI, "The Configuration of Saying [132–133]," §115, "The History of Beyng," 114.

but have value.[37] In other words, thought is no longer about Being itself but is reduced to using concepts. This conception is in direct conflict with the presocratic view. For example, Heraclitus believed that thought does not think of Being; instead, thought is of Being because it is Being who thinks. In contrast, Plato conceives of Being as what is thought, making it an object of the thought of a subject. This leads Lotze to argue that Being is nothing in itself, beyond being merely a value attributed to things. In his view, the world of Being transforms into the world of values. The question arises in this context: Where does the value of life lie? Life exists, but value is a different entity belonging to another reality order.

As we saw a few paragraphs earlier, Plato's philosophy introduces the concept of *techne* (technique) as a mode oriented toward uncovering through "machination" or "production." In *The History of Being*, Heidegger defines it as an insidious external calculative activity, or also merely frantic toward entanglement and destruction. What Platonic philosophy truly inaugurates, therefore, is the empowerment of the human being as a subject capable of creating categories that, since they cannot be fully explained, attempt to justify themselves using other categories. This process is repeated over and over again, generating new categories to explain the previous ones. Thus, philosophy becomes the creation of a hierarchical

---

37. Vagnetti, Michele. "Rudolph Hermann Lotze's philosophically informed psychology." *Journal of The History of the Behavioral Sciences* (Wiley Periodicals LLC, 2023), 1.

Section IV: The forgetting and becoming of Being

map of concepts intended to clarify other concepts that the same map includes.

This complex tangle arises because human beings have lost their belonging to Being, which they have turned into just another object of knowledge. Heidegger uses the word *machbarkeit*, which comes from *machen* (to make) and *bar* (capacity), to refer to the ability to introduce subjective logic into the ontological process of initial openness, similar to the concept of *Deus Ex Machina*. The term *Deus Ex Machina* referred, in Greek theater, to the intervention of an external character in the plot to resolve complicated situations and give meaning to the play. This technique introduced a divine or supernatural figure that unexpectedly solved the conflicts and provided a coherent conclusion to the narrative. This is precisely the calculative activity of Plato. Technique is *machbarkheit*, or "the creative activity" of the human being, now exalted as the "creator" or "producer" of Being. This human being bursts into the history of Being to grant it, or even impose upon it, a foreign coherence, for it does not belong to it.

For these reasons, Heidegger claims that the first appearance, still entirely concealed, was thereafter buried. In other words, the first manifestation of Being was hidden because human beings adhered to or clung to their own concepts of it and could only "see" Being through these concepts. By imposing an external coherence on Being, humans perceive themselves as

Chapter 11: The divorce between being and thinking

"doers." This is why Plato asserts that the human being is the sole guarantor of Truth and that Truth depends exclusively on philosophy. In *The Platonic Doctrine of Truth*, Heidegger delves into his critical analysis of the Platonic turn (*kehre*) and argues that it is Plato who inaugurates the subjectivation of Truth. This Platonic turn in philosophy involves establishing an epistemological structure based on the duality between subject and object, conceived as opposing poles, where the object is understood as "the other" in contrast to the subject. With this, a conception of knowledge is established that radically breaks with the pre-Socratic view of Being as that which reveals itself on its own.

This new epistemological perspective, introduced by Plato, was later developed in medieval philosophy, especially with Thomas Aquinas, and found a more marked emphasis in modern philosophy with Descartes. The consequence of this transformation is that Being, now "objectified" as "other" to the subject, no longer manifests in its own mode of being, but under the horizon of meaning projected by the subject through their cognitive capacities. In this framework, Truth ceases to be the manifestation of Being in its spontaneity and becomes a correlate of the subject's cognitive activity, thus subordinating Being to the structures of human thought. This shift, according to Heidegger, represents a turning point that defines the course of Western metaphysics, marking the beginning of the forgetting of Being.

Chapter 12

Truth as correction (*orthótes*) in Plato

This new horizon of meaning, grounded in the dual structure of the subject-object relationship, represents a paradigm shift that Heidegger analyzes through the terms *orthótes* (ορθοτης) and *alétheia* (αληθεια). As we mentioned earlier, introducing a conception of knowledge based on this duality removes Truth from Being, linking it to the subject's thought and completely transforming the meaning of Truth. For the Presocratics, Truth was understood as (*unconcealment*), intrinsically rooted in Being itself.[38] However, with the introduction of Platonic subject thought and its dual structure, a new conception of Truth arises as *orthótes*. This term can be translated as "correction or accuracy" of a representation. In this new framework, the thought of the subject, limited by its own structure of adequation of the object to the subject, confines Being within the

---

38. Most, Glenn W. "The poetics of early Greek philosophy." In A. A. Long (ed.). *The Cambridge Companion to Early Greek Philosophy* (Cambridge University Press, 1999), 332–362.

Section IV: The forgetting and becoming of Being

parameters of an object that, as such, is always for the subject. Within the parameters of the dual structure we have described, Being is "correct or accurate" when it aligns with what subjects expect to find in their Idea of Being. *Orthótes* therefore, implies that Being must express or reveal itself in a particular way. This perversion of Truth, which reduces the notion of *alétheia* to *orthótes*, causes Being to fade away. Truth ceases to be inherent in Being and instead depends on the representation formulated by the subject through their act of thinking.

Under this approach, which is consolidated in Cartesian and modern philosophy, Truth is no longer found in the Being of the object or in beings themselves but in the interpretation and declaration of the subject who perceives them.[39] This shift also emphasizes the subject's perspective, who becomes the axis and the main arbiter of all Truth. Therefore, we must avoid debating whether Truth belongs to the subject or the object. Heidegger argues that the essential philosophical debate does not lie in determining whether Truth belongs to the subject or the object but in recognizing that philosophy has established a dual epistemological structure that has distorted the original notion of Truth. The true philosophical problem is twofold. On the one hand, it lies in the fact that this duality has displaced Being as the central object of study, replacing

---

39. Descartes, René. *Meditations on First Philosophy*, translated by Elizabeth S. Haldane (Cambridge: Cambridge University Press, 1911), 10.

Chapter 12: Truth as correction (orthótes) in Plato

it with a "being" (in lowercase) ontologized, reduced to a mere object of thought that conforms to the cognitive structures of the subject. On the other hand, this process has led to the serious problem of forgetting Being since Truth, subordinated to the subjective perspective, has lost its essential connection with Being itself.

To speak of forgetting Being is to speak of concealing it, that is, leaving it outside the subject's field of vision. This terminology is not accidental, and its use reflects that this post-Socratic philosophical paradigm is structured through a visual schema of the world. In the philosophical tradition, knowing is seeing physically (perception) or intellectually (intuition). The subject sees what *is*, and what *is*, *is* because it is seen or understood. This epistemological structure of knowledge leads the subject to abandon seeing in order to believe, and is reduced only to the possibility of seeing in order to understand. According to post-Socratic philosophy, what cannot be perceived or understood through the subject's prism will never be considered true. Therefore, to be true, it must correspond correctly (*orthótes*) to the eye or mind that contemplates it. Because it does not conform to the parameters of thought, what is not seen or understood remains hidden. It is in this precise epistemological context where the subject emerges as the "separate I." With the egoic phenomenon, the machinery of the age of technology, established by the Athenians, emerges. They altered the fate of Being by granting humans the capacity to correct the presentation of Being, at

Section IV: The forgetting and becoming of Being

the expense of the very Being that, as such, faded and concealed itself beyond the perceptual and cognitive vision of the subject.

This notion of accuracy (*orthótes*) is closely linked to the subject of technique (*techne*), and this key connection now allows us to unravel the problem of this new philosophical structure in greater detail. According to Heidegger, this structure has alienated humans in the West from its own Being and God. In this context, *orthótes* (ορθοτης) presents itself as the ontological projection of *techne* in the ethical realm, constituting a manifestation of *alétheia* (αληθεια). As we have observed, *orthótes* is a form of Truth through which the human being corrects the representation of Being. By becoming the controller of reality, of what is, of Being, and Truth, now understood in terms of accuracy, the human being personifies technique (*techne*). Therefore, technique controls beings for practical purposes while also extending into the domain of Being. Technique also reveals what is hidden, what does not produce itself and is not yet present, allowing it to appear in various ways. Technique seeks to extract from Being what it (still) does not show. For example, when building a house, a boat, or forging a sacrificial cup, the human being brings to light "that-which-must-be-brought-to-the-front." However, this process is not limited to technical making or the practical knowledge of the artisan but extends to art in its highest sense and to the fine arts. *Techne*, therefore, belongs to the realm of "bringing-to-the-

Chapter 12: Truth as Correction (Orthótes) in Plato

front," of *poiesis* (ποίησις), which refers to what is made or produced. Therefore, while *physis* blooms on its own, *techne* represents the subjective intervention that makes what it is directed at bloom or appear.

To delve into this relationship between technique and Truth, and to further clarify the impact of this ontological shift, we will analyze in detail this important passage from Heidegger:

> The change from correctness (*orthótes* ὀρθότης) to *certitudo* brings the determination of the essence of being as *repraesentatio* ("subjectivity"). All that now remains is: The unfolding of representation into the unconditional character of "thinking" (as absolute Spirit) and/or the unfolding of the human into the "over-man." In each instance an ultimate refuge is taken in "activity," be it that of reason thinking itself or that of the will as will to power.[40]

Let's analyze this passage in parts:

---

40. Martin Heidegger, *The History of Beyng*, trans. William McNeill and Jeffrey Powell (Bloomington: Indiana University Press, 2015), section XI, "The Configuration of Saying [132–133]," §115, "The History of Beyng," 115.

Section IV: The forgetting and becoming of Being

The change from correctness (*orthótes* ὀρθότης) to *certitudo* brings the determination of the essence of being as *repraesentatio* ("subjectivity").

Converting the manifestation of Being into subjective certainty, called *orthótes* (ὀρθότης), involves positioning the human being as the new guarantor of Being, establishing a framework through which Being is revealed. Truth no longer resides outside individual consciousness but is created and represented in the mind. By positioning itself as the guarantor and foundation of the appearance of Being, this human becomes an overman. With his reason, he knows all reality (in Hegel's terms), and with his will, he aspires to all power (as Nietzsche would later say). Objectifying reality, Being, means placing something before consciousness and making it its object. However, this operation has consequences because, by objectifying it, Being escapes this machination and hides. In other words, by attempting to think of reality (what is) through the epistemological structures proposed by Plato, Western philosophy itself has actively contributed to the concealment of the Being of all reality. By trying to think of it as an object of thought, of consciousness, we hide its true essence, left only with what consciousness sees, which is no more than an Idea, a form, but not Being itself. Consciousness remains with the "Idea of Being." The subject's technified thought perceives the Being as an entity and causes the withdrawal of the Being. In this regard, Heidegger continues by saying:

> **All that now remains is: The unfolding of representation into the unconditional character of "thinking" […].**

Because of this, Heidegger argues that this objectifying thought with which Plato inaugurates Western philosophy as a discipline no longer has any other condition than the very act of thinking. In other words, it is the self-referentiality of human thought, the solipsism of the mind. The human mind, enclosed within itself, reflects only on what it creates and sees and what it places before itself. The mind only gathers what it has previously projected. It is no longer that all human beings do not inhabit the same world, but rather that we move within our own mental universe, which, though it can be shared, remains a reality created in our solitude. That is, the subject only knows what the subject itself constructs. In Heidegger's own words:

> **In each instance an ultimate refuge is taken in "activity," be it that of reason thinking itself or that of the will as will to power.**

The consequence of objectifying, which means placing something before consciousness, is that Being transforms and is confused with an ontic object. In this confusion, Being itself escapes the thought that seeks to envelop it and hides beyond the technical powers of the subject. In their attempts to resolve this problem, Hegel first represented the subject as reason thinking of itself, while Nietzsche later embodied the subject as the will to power. However, for Heidegger, both Hegel and Nietzsche represent the culmination of immanence, which starts from subjective certainty and returns to it, from which thought, as a technique (techne), cannot escape. Therefore, we can consider these thinkers the last philosophers of technique. Despite reversing Plato's postulations, Nietzsche remains Platonic because, at the bottom, he perpetuates the separation between being and thought, granting will the guardianship of human dignity. In this way, the rational, volitional subject extracts power from Being and transfers it to itself, establishing that power now resides in the human being as the subject about which all reality predicates.

Moreover, according to Heidegger, the process of ontification of Being through representative correction (*orthótes*) consolidates the stabilization of beingness (*ousía* - ουςια) as presence (*parousía* - παρουσία). That is to say, in an attempt to understand Being from within their own horizons, philosophical subjects assign to Being a temporality that corresponds to a "presenting coming-forth that is continuously having been" in constant formation. However, this temporality is alien to Being.

Chapter 12: Truth as correction (orthótes) in Plato

In trying to enclose Being within a concept in order to possess it and comprehend it, the philosophical subject dislocates both Being and Time.

In other words, an ontified temporality is ascribed to Being, which is a linear temporality that proceeds from the past and moves into the future passing through the present. This had stripped Being of its own Time, substituting the Time of Being for the temporality of the thinking subject. As a result of this, Being manifests itself and is conceived as an entity within the temporality framework created by the human being. This axial subject rises now as the center around which everything revolves and acquires meaning. "Being" without Time becomes the "being" (with a lowercase "b") of the subject—namely, an entity—conceived in terms of its everyday, empirical temporality, whose reality is to show itself as present before the subject who thinks it. Said differently, the entity is everything that Being can fit within the presentability (temporality) in which objects can be thought of in consciousness.

Human beings, as controllers of the world, transform God into an entity to dominate it. Being, ontified and hidden, can only communicate what humans can perceive in the realm of the objective, that is, the ontic. The ontification of Being leads us, ultimately, to the ontotheologization of God. The ontotheological God is literally a human creation and possession, that gives rise to idolatry.

Section IV: The forgetting and becoming of Being

In essence, Platonic philosophy and much of Western philosophy generally identify Being with thinking or individual consciousness, although they are treated as two distinct entities here. The concealment to which Being is subjected, which occurs within the parameters of knowledge in the philosophy of Plato and Aristotle, happens through human perception, correcting what is not perceived clearly. Subjects hold the power and the technique to determine, by means of their method, whether the representation is correct or incorrect. Everything that corresponds to beings is considered true insofar as it is accurate or correct, while what does not correspond to beings is considered false. In other words, and as science has perfectly assimilated, the determination of all truth has, and can only have an empirical basis.

In this regard, Heidegger's philosophy is devastating and calls into question the Western philosophical tradition that originates in Plato's dialogues, which he ultimately attributes to the forgetting of Being. This is a crucial point that calls for reconsidering philosophy as a whole. This critique constitutes an invitation to rethink philosophy from its foundations, exploring the possibility of an "other-thinking" that does not replicate traditional epistemological and metaphysical structures or their errors. The ultimate purpose of this rethinking is to recover the ability to attend to Being and understand what it means to be human, transcending the subject-object structure. As will be addressed in the book's final section, this return to Being is the path that allows for a renewed approach to God.

Chapter 13

THE OPENING TO BEING:
A NEW BEGINNING

Heidegger proposes a new beginning, in contrast to the Platonic structure, where Being is concealed behind the shadows of the entity-object of human thought. This opening of the human being to Being is not based on the action of a powerful subject who foresees and designs reality according to its own structures and horizons of meaning. On the contrary, the opening to Being is based on a passivity that allows Being to show itself as it is, on its own terms. Any human attempt to actively intervene in this process will create a new machination (*machenschaft*).

Heidegger's invitation, therefore, proposes suspending objectifying thought and adopting an attitude of passivity and calm that allows what we might call "simply waiting." This waiting involves a meditative attitude, as opposed to that of the traditional subject, which allows human beings to observe without the intervention of objectifying thought. Meditating is not about replacing one activity with another. On the

Section IV: The forgetting and becoming of Being

contrary, it means precisely the absence of all activity. It is about suspending our own subjectivity, our own eagerness to define. To meditate is to wait without expecting anything specific. It is letting Being to be and listen passively without anticipating any communication.

The greatest benefit of meditation, understood in this way, is in freeing oneself both from the objectifying mind and from the temptation to view it as a technique to reach a goal. Authentic meditation is the opposite of technique because it involves liberating oneself from our cognitive practices. Also, those who tend to cling tenaciously to meditation as a practice end up becoming slaves to the meditation itself. This practice becomes their most valuable possession and a source of personal pride, though all it accomplishes is transferring dependency from one object to another. The problem remains the same in both cases: thinking or meditating as a methodology pointing to a goal will only continue to conceal Being. Therefore, meditation cannot be a technique, a method, or a correction. Meditation must be a "way of being," an attunement that seeks nothing more than to let Being manifest in its fullest expression. Heidegger's proposal ultimately invites us to suspend our cognitive abilities to discover Being as primordial reality. In philosophical terms, it is to suspend epistemology and opt for ontology as *prima philosophia*. Prior to being thinking humans, we are Being. Understanding philosophy as ontology, and not merely as epistemology, means focusing on Being

Chapter 13: The opening to Being: a new beginning

to allow its unveiling as Being, and not as an object of our knowledge.

From the perspective of Heideggerian ontology, only when humans allow themselves to be engulfed by their contemplative passivity can they become open to Being and repatriate themselves to access a state of authentic peace and silence. Because only in that state, which is more primordial than thought and objectification, does the subject itself vanishes as "someone." This means that, by transcending the cognitive powers of our mind, a fundamental part of our identity is left behind, and a different dimension of the human being emerges. With the fading of the mind, our worldly ego dissipates, and we free ourselves from our cognitive, religious, or spiritual egos. Without technical-corrective thought, we cease to be a mind, a soul (psyché) in the Aristotelian and philosophical sense.

Furthermore, by transcending thought and meditation as a technique, we renounce all structure and order, surrendering ourselves to the unknown. We are called to exile from ourselves. This letting go allows us to transcend all structural duality. Freed from the limitations imposed by the dual structures of thought, we can be absorbed by the authentic plenitude of Being.

In this philosophical framework, the notion of *Dasein* is understood as the starting point. *Dasein*, that is, the human being understood as being-there-in-the-world, with its facticity and entire Being, presents itself stripped of the historically attributed conditions by epistemological

Section IV: The forgetting and becoming of Being

philosophy: consciousness, transcendental ego, or even subject. What remains of the human being when these attributes imposed by philosophy are abolished? What or who is this being-there-in-the-world? Heidegger defines *Dasein* more by what it is not than by what it is, mainly when he writes:

> *Da-sein* is not νοῦς (*Nous*), and is not ψυχή (*psyche*), is not the human being and is not "consciousness," is not "Subject," and is not Spirit, and is not "practical life." Da-sein is the essencing of revealing and demands an inceptual finding of the essence of the human being in terms of his relation to the truth of being [...].[41]

Heidegger points out that there is a being in which Being can be held: the human being. However, he does not conceive of the human being as a transcendental ego but as *Dasein*—that is, as being-there-in-the-world. There is indeed an ontological relationship between Being and the "I," for Being fully resides in the "I," granting it a triple preeminence: ontic, ontological, and ontic-ontological. To explain this triple preeminence, Heidegger draws on Aristotle, who held that the soul is, in a sense, all things. Heidegger will revisit this assertion in *Being and Time*,

---

41. Martin Heidegger, *The History of Beyng*, trans. William McNeill and Jeffrey Powell (Bloomington: Indiana University Press, 2015), section XI, "The Configuration of Saying [132–133]," §115, "The History of Beyng," 115.

Chapter 13: The opening to Being: a new beginning

positing that in order to access Being, it is necessary to identify the being that holds preeminence over other beings, thereby enabling it to inquire into Being. On one hand, *Dasein*'s preeminence is ontic because, unlike other entities, it possesses a "relation of being with its Being." On the other hand, its ontological preeminence is evident in its capacity to question and systematically develop an ontology of its Being. This ontic-ontological preeminence is grounded in the fact that all entities are implicitly contained within the Being of *Dasein*.

In this brief quote, Heidegger critically reviews some of the previous conceptions of human essence formulated by the fields of philosophy and psychology. Plato defined the human being as a soul, while Descartes conceived it as thought and Marx as matter. However, Heidegger asserts that the human being is not essentially consciousness, matter, or soul in the Platonic sense. Being-there (*Dasein*), individuated but desubjectivized, is characterized more by negation, by what it is not, than by what it is.

In this sense, Sartre aligns with this tradition by postulating that the human being is precisely everything that it is not. Negatively defining this allows for exploring human essence from a perspective that challenges simplistic categorizations. This facilitates an understanding of existence that, in our context, will better explain the authentic relationship of meditation, waiting, and listening to Being. Therefore, by asserting that "the human being is everything that it

Section IV: The Forgetting and Becoming of Being

is not," Jean-Paul Sartre refers to his interpretation of existence and freedom in his existentialist philosophy. Although this assertion is complex, it can be broken down to facilitate understanding.

In his existentialism, it is essential to distinguish between being-in-itself (*l'être-en-soi*) and being-for-itself (*l'être-pour-soi*). Being-in-itself corresponds to inanimate objects that exist without consciousness or the capacity for change; these objects are completely determined, being exactly what they are. On the other hand, being-for-itself refers to human beings who possess consciousness and the ability to reflect on their own existence. This self-consciousness involves freedom and the ability to transcend their current state. For Sartre, human beings do not have a predetermined essence; no "being" is fixed at the center of their existence. Instead, human beings are projects that are constantly developing and being transformed.

However, this project begins with the question of nothingness, that is, with what is not. According to Sartre, unlike objects, human beings are born with the freedom to define themselves through their actions and decisions. This freedom implies that we are always immersed in becoming what we are not yet, continually surpassing our current condition. The "nothingness," in Sartre's philosophy, symbolizes the absence of a fixed essence in human beings while also enabling freedom and change, making the human being an emptiness that can be filled with infinite possibilities. In this sense, we are what we are not because we are always in the process of becoming something new.

For example, let us think of someone currently working as an office employee but aspiring to be a musician. According to Sartre, this person is not defined solely by their current job; they are also all the possibilities they have not yet realized, such as becoming a musician, writer, or traveler. Their current being includes all the potentialities not realized in the present but that may be fulfilled in the future. When Sartre states that "the human being is everything that it is not," he refers to the capacity of human beings to define themselves through their actions and choices. Therefore, by using Sartre's notion of nothingness,[42] we can imagine a human being open to what is not, to what they do not perceive or understand. A human being who lives as a witness to their existence can hear the call of Being without prejudices or machinations.

What is relevant in this argument is that it posits that the capacity of the egoic subject to transcend itself lies in its nature, in its original openness to what is still not. In other words, this transcendence is only viable from the ontological question that the subject can pose. Proposing ontology as *prima philosophia* ("first philosophy") therefore implies a retreat that allows for a new beginning. This starting point offers the human

---

42. Jean-Paul Sartre, *Being and Nothingness: A Phenomenological Essay on Ontology*, trans. Hazel E. Barnes (New York: Pocket Books, 1966), Part 1.

being the possibility of making an existential leap into openness to Being. This movement brings them closer to a deeper understanding of themselves beyond their "own" epistemological structures.

Chapter 14:

Existential Analytics, Poetry, and the Manifestation of Being

As presented in the previous chapter, Heidegger proposes a new beginning through ontology, which he calls the "existential analytic"[43] of the *Dasein* itself. His ontology directs attention to the most fundamental dimension of the human being, being-there, moving away from an epistemological investigation that assumes a dual subject-object structure to study our cognitive capacities. His analysis relied on the factual and concrete experience of the human being as a finite and situated being. In this context, Heidegger faces the limitations inherent in using traditional concepts. Although he does not entirely abandon these concepts, he recognizes their inadequacy in fully capturing the richness of human experience. This drives him to explore alternative forms of understanding that transcend mere abstraction. He argues that abstract categories, no matter how precise

---

43. Heidegger, Martin. *Being and Time*, translated by John Macquarrie and Edward Robinson, (Blackwell Publishers Ltd, 1962), 67.

(*orthótes*) they may be, fail to capture the specificity of the *Dasein*.

A clear example of this tension is categorizing the human being as a "rational and political animal," which is indiscriminately applied to all contexts when assumed to be universal and necessary. However, this universality detaches human beings from the particularity of individual existence. As we have shown earlier, even as a rational, social, and political being, human beings are not only that. It ceases to be relevant for any particular individual when valid for all. In this context, more than a method, Heidegger's "existential analytic" is a philosophical, specifically ontological effort to show the singular existence, which cannot be subsumed under an abstract category like "rational animal." The concrete *Dasein*, with its fears and sorrows, is the true concern because it is in this intimate vulnerability where the human being begins to show itself as *Dasein*, as being-there, and less as an object of abstract knowledge.

Recognizing the limitations of abstract concepts does not mean rejecting philosophical rigor, but it does require redefining what it means to be rigorous. For Heidegger, rigor does not consist in creating clear and distinct concepts. On the contrary, his rigor is expressed in pursuing a deep and authentic understanding of human life, which avoids dissolving into abstractions and remains faithful to the complexity and contingency of existence. In this sense, and in his endeavor to transcend the limitations of traditional philosophical categories,

Chapter 14 :: Existential Analytics, Poetry, and the Manifestation of Being

Heidegger seeks to create categories that are valid for *Dasein*'s concrete and finite experience. These categories, known as "existentials," seek to address human life in a factual way and not only abstractly.

Therefore, Heidegger introduces terms such as being-there, being-there-in-the-world, being-with-others, and being-toward-death, among others. They attempt to capture human existence's specific and intimate nature in its most singular dimension. It is important to note that, in advancing this task, Heidegger himself faces an intrinsic limitation. Concrete experience resists being fully understood, even through what he calls "existentiary categories." In other words, Heidegger's existential analytic, as an ontological approach, faces the contradiction of trying to describe a particular reality, or haecceity, as Duns Scotus called it, through structures that are ultimately still formal.

This evolution becomes evident in *Being and Time*, where Heidegger continues to work within the traditional frameworks of Western philosophy, using abstract concepts to analyze the concrete human being. Despite introducing the "existentiary categories," he acknowledges that the problem does not lie in the concepts themselves but in the impossibility of conceptualizing the unconceptualizable. The concepts, no matter how novel they may seem, remain limited by their universal and abstract nature, which makes them inadequate to capture the singularity of human existence.

SECTION IV: THE FORGETTING AND BECOMING OF BEING

Due to this problem, Heidegger himself begins to consider the possibility of introducing poetry as a *modus operandi* of the existential analytic. Unlike philosophy and formal logic, poetry is not limited by the need for conceptual precision. This makes it an open and personal interpretation of existence, which is precisely what makes it a richer medium to express the ontological singularity of human experience. In its ability to be "charged with content" by each reader, poetry provides a more flexible and adaptable means of access to human experiences than rigid philosophical concepts. In this way, Heidegger does not reject philosophy *per se*, but he acknowledges that its limits become evident when attempting to address the particularity of *Dasein*. Thanks to its ambiguity and capacity to resonate with factual experience, poetry becomes a more effective vehicle to express what philosophy cannot fully capture.

In this context, centered on ontology and poetry, Heidegger is particularly drawn to poets such as Hölderlin. The language of his works can recover what Heidegger calls the "existential analytic," that is, the study of the fundamental structures of finite existence. Poetry, being non-conceptual in the sense that it does not adhere to structures governed by formal logic, allows Heidegger to address the "ontological difference" and preserve the peculiarity of *Dasein* without falling into abstraction.

Specifically, Heidegger finds in poetry a reflection capable of avoiding traditional categories of metaphysics, such as act, potency, substance, and accident. Such reflection consists of pure observation devoid of intellectual intervention. However, poetry is not simply the creation of verses with a specific meter and norms, but the expression of authentic meditation, testimony, language, and what Heidegger calls the "house of Being." One of the key points of Heidegger's later thought is his proposal that poetic language inaugurates new ways of understanding, displacing formal concepts. In this sense, poetry transcends its merely artistic character to become a privileged means of revelation of Being, allowing us to uncover aspects of reality that typically remain hidden. For Heidegger, language is the house of Being.[44] However, it is through poetic language that Being manifests itself, overcoming the limitations of everyday and technical language and opening up new forms of understanding. The essence of poetry lies in its ability to name and make present, without abstracting or caricaturing, what allows things to be perceived in their true reality.

At this point, Heidegger takes up the Greek term *alétheia* (unconcealment), which was mentioned earlier, and associates it with poetry. He attributes to it the ability to reveal a profound truth of Being and existence, which goes beyond the mere transmission of information. The poet plays a crucial role as the guardian of Being. The poet protects and reveals the essence of things, resisting the

---

44. Martin Heidegger, "Letter on Humanism," in *Basic Writings*, ed. David Farrell Krell (New York: Harper Perennial Modern Thought, 2008).

trends of modernity that lead to their forgetfulness and concealment. Ultimately, poetry allows for intertwining the past, present, and future in a non-linear horizon. In this space, Being unfolds as time rather than being placed within time or the temporality of the subject. This allows for a deeper and fuller understanding of Being as such, without reducing it to an ontic being.

For Heidegger, poetry allows thinking beyond the technological structure of epistemological thought, which has permeated philosophy, Western culture, the sciences, and even religion. Thinking through poetry is resisting the tendency to reduce everything to mere resources, disconnecting us from Being. In this sense, poetry provides a way to recover this connection and resist the objectification and domination of nature (*physis*). This is equivalent or tantamount to establishing itself as an essential means for the revelation of Being as *physis*, enabling us to experience and understand the world more authentically and fully.

From Heidegger's perspective, this "other-thinking,"[45] or poetic thinking, corresponds to the contemplative attitude of the poet, which allows one to think without the objectifying structures of the intellect. Poetic thinking makes authentic meditation possible, free from the abstract conceptualizations typical of the realm of technique. This is possible because, as we mentioned earlier, poetry does not try to extract Being from *physis*.

---

45. Heidegger, Martin. *What Is Called Thinking?*, trans. Fred D. Wieck and J. Glenn Gray (Harper & Row, 1968).

Chapter 14 :: Existential analytics, poetry, and the manifestation of Being

In this way, it recovers the word, the *logos*, which pre-Socratic philosophy understood as inseparable from *physis* and Being.

As Heidegger reminds us in his seminar on Heraclitus, the more initial thinking is, the more its reflection is tied to the word. This initial connection between thought and word indicates an essential unity in the early developments of philosophy when it had not yet been transformed into a discipline. According to Heidegger, the authentic act of thinking, therefore, arises from the word, and it is through it that the most fundamental reflections on Being are expressed. In this context, the word is not limited to being a mere instrument of communication. However, it becomes the channel through which Being manifests itself in its purest and most original form. This is why Heidegger speaks of language, of the word, as the house of Being. Through its existential analytic and poetic expression, Heidegger's ontology invites us to return to the notion of "word," of *logos*, intimately linked to *physis*. In this way, it seeks to embrace us with the profound or deepest meaning of Being.

CHAPTER 15

A FIRST APPROACH TO GOD

Letting ourselves be embraced by Being in its full meaning—as we mentioned at the end of the previous chapter—means letting ourselves be expressed or spoken by Being itself. However, this involves the manifestation of an original lack that Heidegger associates with the notion of "poverty." As being-there (*Dasein*), humans do not possess anything by themselves, for everything they have is given to them. Heidegger expresses this when he writes:

> Poverty is the inexhaustibility of bestowal, abyssally decided from out of itself.[46]

To be poor means not owning anything by one's own merit. Many individuals, through various religions, seek spiritual fulfillment through renunciation and

---

46. Martin Heidegger, *The History of Beyng*, trans. William McNeill and Jeffrey Powell (Bloomington: Indiana University Press, 2015), section VIII, "Beyng and the Last God," §99, "Poverty [109–110]," 93.

Section IV: The forgetting and becoming of Being

the acceptance of vows of poverty. However, true renunciation lies in understanding that, in essence, we own nothing to which we can truly renounce. True renunciation involves recognizing our original poverty and being aware of the inherent lack of material possessions from the very beginning. This understanding leads us to a more genuine and complete realization that transcends mere external actions of renunciation and focuses on an attitude and acceptance of our fundamental nature. There is an inherent poverty since everything given to us is donated; therefore, since we receive everything from Being, we lack a personal reserve. Through this state of original poverty, Heidegger begins to redefine the human relationship with Being.

It is asserted in theology that there is no synergy, that is, no joint labor (*ergos*) between Being and man. Instead, there is talk of monergism, a work exclusively of Being. This theological concept suggests that our capacity for action and creation depends entirely on Being, rather than being autonomous. That is, before we become subjects endowed with free will and freedom, we already are-there. Therefore, our apparent lack of our own resources is because everything we have and we are, has been granted to us by Being. This way of understanding the relationship highlights humanity's fundamental dependence on Being, underscoring the absence of collaboration and the predominance of the unilateral nature of Being in human existence. The openness to Being is not synergistic but monergistic. That is, Being and human beings do not originally collaborate actively in the process of realization and existence (synergism). On the contrary, all action and creation emanate exclusively from Being, without human intervention (monergism). As explained in the terms used so far in this section: it is Being that tells us and expresses itself in us, not the other way around, as traditional philosophy had thought. This theological debate presents two approaches to the relationship between Being and man, raising profound questions about the autonomy and dependence of human existence. Through these issues, Heidegger begins to connect the problem of Being and *Dasein* with the question of God.

Heidegger expresses it as follows:

> Yet ask *beyng*, and in it the god responds as the word, that is to say: in the word "of" *beyng*, godship comes [...].[47]

Heidegger says that the answer to the call of God is the openness to Being through the word and meditative serenity, from the stillness of a waiting that foresees nothing and no one, as a witness and not as a subject. Instead of speaking to Being through concepts, *Dasein* allows itself to be spoken to and expressed, and the

---

47. Martin Heidegger, *The History of Beyng*, trans. William McNeill and Jeffrey Powell (Bloomington: Indiana University Press, 2015), section III, "Passage. The History of Beyng [30–31]," §31, "The History of Beyng," 28.

Section IV: The forgetting and becoming of Being

Last God is revealed as absolutely transcendent and incomprehensible. It is only from the most authentic poverty, from a state of *Dasein* that precedes all freedom and will, that it is possible to re-establish a primordial connection between humanity and the transcendental divine. Therefore, the revelation of God as such cannot be the result of an active action by a subject but an experience of passive reception and listening in a state of stillness and contemplation. Before Being, we were poor and did not possess the subjective will to open ourselves to it.

All techniques become unfeasible in the openness to Being through meditative passivity because Being possesses absolute freedom. Any action that attempts to objectify it is destined to fail. Heidegger emphasizes that from Plato onward, traditional philosophy, by renouncing Being has limited its scope to the ontic world, thus denying any possibility of relation to the truly transcendental, that is, to the sacred. Countering this trend and restoring a constant relationship of openness to Being, ontology proposes a return to a state of maximum stillness. In this state, *Dasein* fully accepts its original poverty, recognizing its absolute inability to influence or control the manifestation of Being. The freedom of Being surpasses any human attempt at domination or technique, highlighting the essential limitation of our actions in the face of the immensity of Being. This "awareness" or "acceptance" of our impotence before Being allows us to recognize that

Chapter 15: A first approach to God

true openness to Being lies beyond our intervention and control. In adopting this attitude of humility, the Divine, the purely transcendental, opens before us as merely ineffable.

From this point, Heidegger starts to delve further into this relationship based on humility and acceptance of our incapacity to comprehend the ineffable. For this, he introduces another theme, that of the earth and the human relationship with it, and writes:

> Beyng that is asked about, from which the last god answers in his time, attunes, however, into confidence in the bestowal of the most silent relation to the earth of a world, which, contesting their essence, open out into the site of a history of the countering of human beings and the last god. This confidence is not chained to what is at hand, nor built upon any being. It is appropriated from beyng as the ever inceptual serenity, never collapsing into habituation, of an extended courage to watch over the preparing for the event.[48]

For Heidegger, the relationship with the earth is essential. The quadrature composed of God, sky, earth, and man requires perfect harmony, which allows Being

---

48. Martin Heidegger, *The History of Beyng*, trans. William McNeill and Jeffrey Powell (Bloomington: Indiana University Press, 2015), "Draft for Koinón. On the History of Beyng," §213, 179.

Section IV: The forgetting and becoming of Being

to manifest fully. It is indispensable for human beings to maintain a balanced connection with the sky, with Divinity, and with the earth. We cannot fall into the illusion that we can exploit the earth without consequences, neglect our fellow humans, or be negligent or manipulative with meditation, which represents our relationship with the sky. Focusing solely on Being without considering these other vital aspects leads to an incomplete and fragmented understanding of our existence and drives us to resort to technique. The integrity of Being emerges only when all these components are in balance and resonance with each other.

This reveals the existence of a conflict, a fundamental dispute over the essence of the world. This disagreement arises from the two ways in which the world can be defined: on the one hand, in relation to being, as technology does; and on the other hand, in relation to Being, as Heideggerian ontology intends. Heidegger affirms that by aligning with technique, human beings no longer live on the earth but in a technical realm that has devastated the natural environment (*physis*). In this sense, the technique (*techne*) with which human beings approach the world reflects both the domination over entities and the forgetting of Being. In their eagerness to know and detail the empiricism of reality, *physis*, and Being, human beings have reduced that reality to an object of conquest and manipulation, stripping it of its essence. However, the world can also find its identity in relation to Being, rejecting the supremacy of technique.

Chapter 15: A first approach to God

These two positions, however, are mutually exclusive. The world cannot be simultaneously defined by Being and by technique. This is the core of the conflict over the essence of the world and why the relationship between human beings and the world depends primarily on the relationship between human beings and Being.

Moreover, the essence of the world has a decisive influence, for it defined the course of human history and the arrival of the Last God. This highlights that openness to Being is not a whim or an option but an intrinsic necessity for human beings. This openness allows one to understand oneself in relation to Being and, from this, understand one's own historical becoming in the world.

Heidegger describes this meditative attitude of openness to Being through terms such as passivity, serenity, or waiting. Firstly, in relation to trust, he says in the cited passage:

This confidence is not chained to what is at hand, nor built upon any being.

Opening to Being, according to Heidegger, implies placing absolute trust in it, transcending any foresight, calculation, or conceptualization that could objectify it. This act of trust does not focus on any particular being; rather, it involves a receptive openness and attentive listening to Being, allowing it to reveal itself in its absolutely transcendent and ineffable character.

Section IV: The forgetting and becoming of Being

As we will see later, trust, in this sense, is not exhausted in the relationship of openness to Being, but instead rocks us before the revelation of what Heidegger calls the Last God. This act of trust transcends the rational and ontologizing thought characteristic of traditional epistemology. It opens the possibility for a more intimate relationship with Being and with the divinity that manifests through listening. Furthermore, Heidegger points out that this trust issue inaugurates a new relational horizon. After the emergence of epistemological philosophy, the human being's relationship with Being was reduced to reflection on a concrete being. This limitation also affected religion, where God came to be understood as a particular entity within the same dualist philosophical parameters.

In contrast, Heideggerian ontology's openness avoids this conceptualist structure and promotes a relationship of trust that radically transforms our understanding of reality. In this rethinking, God is no longer conceived as a specific, concrete, or personal entity, as was the case in ontotheology, but as a more primordial reality accessible only through the trusted openness to Being. Returning trust to Being allows us to access a more authentic and transcendent experience of the Divine.

Heidegger grounds trust and the meditative attitude in the notion of serenity, about which he says:

IIt is appropriated from beyng as the ever inceptual serenity, never collapsing into habituation [...]

CHAPTER 15: A FIRST APPROACH TO GOD

According to him, the fundamental characteristic of the experience of trust in Being resides, thus, in serenity, that is, in that perpetual calmness that the ancient Greeks knew as *ataraxia*. This original serenity is a serenity of the spirit that entails an imperturbability in the face of the vicissitudes and challenges of existence, and that, as such, stands as the highest ideal of classical philosophy. More than simply denoting the absence of emotional turmoil, *ataraxia* also suggests an inner balance, a mental state in which peace and stability remain unshaken by external circumstances. This state of calm and serenity, highly valued by Hellenic thinkers, is essential in the quest for integral well-being and the authentic understanding of the nature of Being. In other words, without serenity, no trust is possible, and without trust, there is no meditation. The ability to maintain this tranquility or serenity in the face of external events constitutes a central element in the philosophical aspiration for a full and balanced life, as well as for openness to Being.

Trust and serenity are fundamental elements of what Heidegger calls authentic passivity, a disposition devoid of corrective techniques or interventions. In this attitude, it is Being that calls upon the human being, and the human responds from their most radical vulnerability and honesty. The essence of this relationship lies in the summons of Being, a call that orients us toward its encounter without imposing prior conditions or mediating expectations. Being speaks to the human

Section IV: The forgetting and becoming of Being

being because it is Being that calls and summons them. That is the crucial moment: in the face of the call, human beings respond, whether through technical or corrective activity or through serenity and trust that open them to Being.

An essential change occurs when "the human," understood as an agent subject and master of technique, transforms into "what is human," into *Dasein*. When we respond to that call from serenity and trust, we cease being "doers" to become passive witnesses. Then, *techne* dissolves, allowing *physis* to emerge once again by itself.

However, instead of merely denying the cognitive capacity of the human being, Heidegger reorients its primordial[49] nature, defining the human being as being-there and not as a cognitive and epistemological subject. *Dasein* represents the primordial foundation of human existence: being human is not about objectifying but about being-there, and being-there means being-there-in-the-world-with-others (*Mitsein*). Heidegger can affirm that being means being affected by Being. This approach suggests that what is truly crucial is to be found in the openness of Being. Therefore, rather than conceiving *Dasein* as a new subject, we must understand it as an openness to Being. That is, *being-there* is not simply *being-there*, but *being-in-the-there*, being affected by Being.

---

49. Heidegger, Martin. *Being and Time*, translated by John Macquarrie and Edward Robinson, (Blackwell Publishers Ltd, 1962), §13, 31–34.

Chapter 15: A first approach to God

In this sense, Heidegger's proposal represents an authentic philosophical revolution. It seeks for human beings to penetrate their own Being, not by an egoic decision to reconquer the hidden, but as a response to the call of Being itself. The human being will only be able to hear once they have shed their egoic garments and show a passive predisposition toward pure transcendence, toward that which they do not see, do not know, and cannot even comprehend.

Chapter 16

The unity of humanity in Being

The previous chapter has led us to establish a crucial connection between the technologization of thought and the forgetting of Being, as well as between this forgetting and the absence of a shared history. In other words, the forgetting of Being and the lack of Being as a homeland have led us to the absence of a shared history. The evident problem is that technologization stems from a scientific approach that reduces reality to a set of empirical beings, configuring a nature alienated and stripped of Being. This technological perspective, rooted in traditional epistemological philosophy, has fostered the forgetting of Being in various fields. First, as we have already pointed out, that is, in the philosophical and religious realms. Second, in the historical realm, humans are denied the ability to understand their historical existence on earth and in the world beyond a mere collection of dates and objectified events.

For Heidegger, all knowledge is inevitably "thrown" into a particular situation of understanding. This means there is no neutral point of view from which to access

Section IV: The forgetting and becoming of Being

a universal truth. In other words, there is no single and true objective history of the human being. When we assert that we know the authentic history, we forget that this reading is merely an interpretation, a vision of the facts, but not the truth itself.

Although science is an effective and powerful method for understanding empirical reality, it remains an interpretative construction rooted in a specific openness of meaning, grounded in the pre-scientific structures of being-in-the-world. In light of this reading, Heidegger describes this condition as a "crisis" that permeates the totality of Western thought. By becoming the predominant way of understanding the world, science ignores its foundation in concrete human existence. Science transforms into a "worldview" that considers its method the only legitimate way to access reality. However, it ignores that its perspective is only one of many possible ways to relate to Being and the world.

Despite all this, Heidegger does not reject the validity of science; instead, he reinscribes it as a particular modality of "unveiling" Being (*alétheia*), which should not be assumed as definitive or exclusive. Therefore, Heidegger's hermeneutic ontology[50] concludes that all knowledge—including scientific knowledge—is a form of interpretation dependent on a pre-understanding of Being. Consequently, skepticism and relativism

---

50. Heidegger, Martin. Ontology. *The Hermeneutics of Facticity*, translated by John van Buren, (Indiana University Press, 1999), 11–14.

CHAPTER 16: THE UNITY OF HUMANITY IN BEING

are not merely epistemological obstacles to overcome but fundamental challenges that require a radical reconsideration of what Truth and knowledge mean.

The situation of our current society is reflected in the famous maxim by Thomas Hobbes, author of *Leviathan*: "Man is a wolf to man."[51] This expression refers to the innate cruelty in human nature, highlighting how, frequently, our worst enemies are our own fellow human beings. With his insightful understanding of the human condition, Hobbes emphasizes that competition, hostility, and aggression can arise even in our most intimate interactions. This observation, far from losing its relevance over time, remains a disturbing reflection of contemporary reality, where rivalry and conflict between individuals are constant. For his part, Heidegger holds that human beings will only truly achieve brotherhood when they open to Being, and they will become aware that they share a common homeland. According to his perspective, this profound and shared understanding will allow humanity to overcome the divisions and fragmentations that so deeply affect us. The recognition that we all belong to the same homeland, which is Being, gives us the possibility of harmonious and supportive coexistence. This idea underscores the importance of a common and collective identity that transcends individual and cultural differences, fostering a more authentic union among people.

---

51. Höffe, Otfried. *Thomas Hobbes*, trans. Nicholas Walker (Albany: State University of New York Press, 2015), 126.

Section IV: The forgetting and becoming of Being

For Heidegger, we can only forge lasting and meaningful bonds of brotherhood through this awakening to our shared homeland, which is Being. That is, it is not from politics alone, nor ethics as a discipline, that human beings can create coexistence based on respect for diversity. For this, it is necessary first to rethink the origin of the forgetfulness of Being and rethink the human being as *Dasein*. This similar idea already resonates strongly in the Old Testament, specifically in the "Prayer for Liberation." In the tenth blessing of the prayer of the "Eighteen Blessings," which was compiled by the sages of the Great Assembly and precedes the *Tana'im* and the *Zuggot* in time, we read:

תְּקַע בְּשׁוֹפָר גָּדוֹל לְחֵרוּתֵנוּ וְשָׂא נֵס לְקַבֵּץ גָּלֻיּוֹתֵינוּ וְקַבְּצֵנוּ יַחַד מְהֵרָה מֵאַרְבַּע כַּנְפוֹת הָאָרֶץ לְאַרְצֵנוּ: בָּרוּךְ אַתָּה ה' מְקַבֵּץ נִדְחֵי עַמּוֹ יִשְׂרָאֵל.

(תפילת שמונה עשרה, ברכת קיבוץ גלויות)

Sound the great *shofar* (ram's horn) for our liberty, and raise a banner to gather our exiles, and gather us together quickly from the four corners of the earth into our Land. Blessed are You, Lord, Gatherer of the dispersed of His people Israel.

(The "Eighteen blessings prayer," the
"Prayer for deliverance" blessing)

Chapter 16: The unity of humanity in Being

This blessing is based on a verse from Isaiah.

וְהָיָה בַּיּוֹם הַהוּא יִתָּקַע בְּשׁוֹפָר גָּדוֹל וּבָאוּ הָאֹבְדִים בְּאֶרֶץ אַשּׁוּר וְהַנִּדָּחִים בְּאֶרֶץ מִצְרָיִם וְהִשְׁתַּחֲווּ לַה' בְּהַר הַקֹּדֶשׁ בִּירוּשָׁלָםִ:
(ישעיהו כ"ז, י"ג)

And in that day, a great *shofar* (ram's horn) shall be sounded; and those who are lost in the land of Assyria and the expelled who are in the land of Egypt shall come and bow down to the Lord on the holy mount, in Jerusalem.

(Isaiah, 27:13)

In other words, the force that used to unite us around Being has faded, as each individual now creates their own religion or philosophy. This fragmentation has led to the loss of a shared congregation that would unify us. The absence of God equates to humanity's deprivation of a unifying factor.

Similarly, the proliferation of religions demonstrates the absence of a true God, whose existence would imply precisely the nonexistence of multiple religions. In Heidegger's view, the more religions multiply, the less divine presence we have. It is for this reason that, for Heidegger, as for Nietzsche before him, the most encouraging news is the death of God and the subsequent gradual disappearance of religions, one by one. In other words, Moses was neither orthodox, conservative, nor reformist, just as Jesus was not Anglican, Protestant,

Section IV: The forgetting and becoming of Being

Catholic, or Jehovah's Witness. The death of the personified, ontotheologized God signifies the end of the God of religion, paving the way for the emergence of the Last God—a God who is neither personified nor conceptualized.

Heidegger turns to the work of Rilke to explore this very idea. In fact, from the 20th century to the present, Rilke's work has captured the attention of many philosophers due to the richness of his poetry. In his essay *And What Are Poets For?*, Heidegger explores the connection between Rilke's poetry and the scarcity of our time, stating, "Not only have the gods and God fled, but in universal history, the splendor of divinity has faded." With the extinction of the splendor of divinity, humanity finds itself immersed in the darkness of obscurity, wandering, confused, and continually colliding with its fellow beings. This decline of the divine brightness has plunged individuals into disorientation, where confusion and bewilderment have replaced clarity and understanding. The ability to discern and authentically connect with others has been severely affected in this darkness, resulting in a constant clash and conflict. The loss of that radiance, which once illuminated human existence, has led to a situation where coexistence becomes difficult and mutual understanding is scarce.

The eminently political responses that have emerged are varied. Communism, for example, has not represented a solution. On the contrary, it has worsened the situation. As Heidegger mentions in the *Letter on*

Chapter 16: The unity of humanity in Being

Humanism, Marxism transforms being into mere material for labor, keeping it within the realm of *techne*. The state cannot impose unity on the human race through a system of laws that dictates that individuality should be abandoned to become a collective or forcefully shift from the "I" to the "we." Those who sought unity, as Karl Marx did with his famous call "workers of the world, unite"[52] failed to achieve authentic cohesion. Heidegger argues that true unity and communion cannot emerge from an ideology like communism. Instead, he holds that the genuine path to unity lies in humans recognizing and understanding their common homeland in Being. Rather than seeking unity imposed by political or legal structures that lead to the forgetfulness of Being, we must find our deep connection in Being itself. This understanding of Being as a common foundation can foster authentic communion and cohesion among people beyond state borders or ideological impositions.

Heidegger agrees with Marx's diagnosis, as both consider it necessary to overcome selfish individualism. However, they disagree on the proposed solution. While Marx advocates for the unification of workers in a social struggle, Heidegger does not believe this path will lead to authentic human communion. Ideologies may promote a certain cohesion and cooperation in the social and political sphere. However, these forms of

---

52. Karl Marx and Friedrich Engels, *The Communist Manifesto*, trans. Samuel Moore, rev. Friedrich Engels, with an introduction by David Harvey (London: Pluto Press, 2008), 84.

unity are often superficial and temporary and are always devoured by the same technologization that generated them. True unity transcends ideological constructs and is based on a shared understanding of our essence as human beings. We can establish genuine and lasting communion only by recognizing and experiencing this essential unity in Being.

BIBLIOGRAPHY SECTION IV

- Descartes, René. *Meditations on First Philosophy*. Translated by Elizabeth S. Haldane. Cambridge: Cambridge University Press, 1911.
- Heidegger, Martin. *Being and Time*. Translated by John Macquarrie and Edward Robinson. Oxford: Blackwell Publishers, 1962.
- Heidegger, Martin. *Contributions to Philosophy: From Enowning*. Translated by Parvis Emad and Kenneth Maly. Bloomington: Indiana University Press, 1999.
- Heidegger, Martin. *The Fundamental Concepts of Metaphysics: World, Finitude, Solitude*. Translated by William McNeill and Nicholas Walker. Bloomington: Indiana University Press, 1995.
- Heidegger, Martin. *The History of Beyng*. Translated by William McNeill and Jeffrey Powell. Bloomington: Indiana University Press, 2015.
- Heidegger, Martin. *Introduction to Metaphysics*. Translated by Gregory Fried and Richard Polt. New Haven: Yale University Press, 2000.
- Heidegger, Martin. "*Letter on Humanism*." In *Basic Writings*, edited by David Farrell Krell, 213–265. New York: Harper Perennial Modern Thought, 2008.
- Heidegger, Martin. *Ontology: The Hermeneutics of Facticity*. Translated by John van Buren. Bloomington: Indiana University Press, 1999.

SECTION IV: THE FORGETTING AND BECOMING OF BEING

- Heidegger, Martin. *What is Called Thinking?* Translated by Fred D. Wieck and J. Glenn Gray. New York: Harper & Row, 1968.
- Heidegger, Martin. "*The Origin of the Work of Art.*" In *Off the Beaten Track*, translated by Julian Young and Kenneth Haynes, 1–56. Cambridge: Cambridge University Press, 2002.
- Höffe, Otfried. *Thomas Hobbes*. Translated by Nicholas Walker. Albany: State University of New York Press, 2015.
- Marx, Karl, and Friedrich Engels. *The Communist Manifesto*. Translated by Samuel Moore. Revised by Friedrich Engels. With an introduction by David Harvey. London: Pluto Press, 2008.
- Most, Glenn W. "*The Poetics of Early Greek Philosophy.*" In The Cambridge Companion to Early Greek Philosophy, edited by A. A. Long, 332–362. Cambridge: Cambridge University Press, 1999.
- Prior, Arthur N. "*Correspondence Theory of Truth.*" In *Encyclopedia of Philosophy*, Vol. 2, edited by Paul Edwards, 223–226. New York: Macmillan, 1969.
- Ross, W. D. *Aristotle's Metaphysics: A Revised Text with Introduction and Commentary*. Oxford: Clarendon Press, 1924.
- Sartre, Jean-Paul. *Being and Nothingness: A Phenomenological Essay on Ontology*. Translated by Hazel E. Barnes. New York: Pocket Books, 1966.
- Vagnetti, Michele. "*Rudolph Hermann Lotze's Philosophically Informed Psychology.*" Journal of the History of the Behavioral Sciences 59, no. 1 (2023).

SECTION V
FROM ONTOTHEOLOGY TO THE UNKNOWN GOD

CHAPTER 17

THE UNKNOWN GOD

In Section I of this study, we have analyzed the historical evolution of the concepts from Plato and Aristotle to medieval scholasticism. Western philosophy has applied this conceptualization to Being, which caused it to fall into an ontological crisis. Ontotheology has attempted to transform God into an object of study, reducing the Divine to a conceptual being. As we saw in Section II, this perspective influenced the human search for God. In Christianity, for example, the absolute and ineffable God is reduced to a personal, ontotheologized God, which was adapted to the parameters of human thought.

In Section III, we analyze how the dualist structure of Thomas Aquinas led Christianity into a dead-end. God, now created in the image and likeness of the human being, becomes an identifiable, definable, and understandable concept. This produces a double impoverishment: on the one hand, it limits God as a figure of the Divine; on the other hand, it restricts the human capacity to open up and approach the ineffable. Thus, both God and the human being are trapped

Section V: From ontotheology to the unknown God

within the epistemological limits imposed by philosophy and theology.

Finally, in Section IV, we address Heidegger's critique of Western philosophy for having forgotten Being. The conceptualization has caused a disconnection from the essential. Heidegger proposes a return to Being through passivity and meditation.

The present section explains the need to transcend the traditional categories of metaphysics and religion. It suggests reconsidering the Divine and the human being as an openness to a realm that transcends the epistemological, enriching their experience and meaning. We will begin by distinguishing between the personal, ontified God and God as purely transcendent. In the book of Acts, we read:

> For as I passed by and observed the objects of your worship, I also found an altar with this inscription: TO THE UNKNOWN GOD. What therefore you worship as unknown, this I proclaim to you.
>
> (Acts, 17:23)

The personal God mentioned so far represents the known God, a product of human thought, in contrast to the impersonal or unknown God alluded to in this passage from the book of Acts. This difference can be better understood through the concepts of form and image, to which we have already paid attention.

Chapter 17: The unknown God

Therefore, in order for human beings to know, they need to create an image that allows them to think about that which they wish to know. That is to say, in terms of the parameters of Platonic philosophy, knowledge (*epistēmē*), as a product of thought, emerges from the creation of an image,[53] a Greek term closely related to the concept of "idea" (*eidos*). It is worth noting that eidos, which also means "image," comes from *éidōlon* (εἴδωλον), which is translated as "figure." Therefore, to think as the basis of knowledge means to elaborate, or present before oneself, an image or figure as the idea that shapes what is thought. This establishes the dualist relationship we have analyzed earlier. Furthermore, as the Old Testament reveals, the problem is not merely in the act of thinking but in the human difficulty of relating to that which transcends and exceeds their cognitive capacities. Specifically, the book of Exodus refers to the creation of idols, from the Latin *īdōlum*, a term once again directly related to *éidōlon* and *eidos* (idolatry).

---

53. In Plato's *Phaedo* 72e, Cebes declares that Socrates is accustomed to always mentioning "the theory that learning is recollection" often, which reflects the Platonic notion of "image" as a symbol of abstract ideas, which he called *Forms*. Plato. *Phaedo, Plato in Twelve Volumes*, Vol. 1 translated by Harold North Fowler; Introduction by W.R.M. Lamb (Cambridge, MA, Harvard University Press; London, William Heinemann Ltd. 1966), 72e.

Section V: From ontotheology to the unknown God

לֹא־תַעֲשֶׂה־לְךָ פֶסֶל וְכָל־תְּמוּנָה אֲשֶׁר בַּשָּׁמַיִם מִמַּעַל וַאֲשֶׁר בָּאָרֶץ מִתָּחַת וַאֲשֶׁר בַּמַּיִם מִתַּחַת לָאָרֶץ: לֹא־תִשְׁתַּחֲוֶה לָהֶם וְלֹא תָעָבְדֵם כִּי אָנֹכִי ה' אֱלֹהֶיךָ אֵל קַנָּא פֹּקֵד עֲוֹן אָבֹת עַל־בָּנִים עַל־שִׁלֵּשִׁים וְעַל־רִבֵּעִים לְשֹׂנְאָי:

(שמות כ', ד'–ה')

You shall not make for yourself a graven image or any likeness which is in the heavens above, which is on the earth below, or which is in the water beneath the earth. You shall not bow down to them or worship them, for I, the Lord, your God, am a zealous God, Who remembers the sin of the fathers upon (the) sons, upon the third and the fourth (generation) of those who hate Me.

(Exodus, 20:4–5)

The commandment not to make an image of the unknown God suggests that God cannot, and should not, be conceived through thought, that is, as an idea or as a separate, shaped figure. As we mentioned earlier, image and thought are interconnected. We can only think about what we are able to visualize, that is, that which we can form a limited mental image. Therefore, the commandment seems to be saying that the human relationship with God cannot be reduced to an idyllic relationship and, consequently, an epistemological one. This is because God, as unknown, cannot be known as just another object of human thought. Moreover, if

Chapter 17: The unknown God

we create an image of God, we will only have an idea of Him, but God will have concealed Himself behind the horizon of that idea. This leads us to conclude that human beings must explore other relational paths with God to avoid confining Him to an image that satisfies the desire to know Him. This other relationship can or should respect God in His beingness and do justice to Him without violating Him by attributing to Him a reality that, as God, is foreign to Him.

To analyze the relationship that human beings can or should have with the "unknown God" beyond all imagination, ideas, or thoughts, we will turn to the Old and New Testaments. Additionally, we will explore how Heidegger approached the topic of God in his later writings, one of the most controversial subjects in his thought. However, his view is interesting because it focuses on the appearance of a Last God on the horizon of what he calls "the other beginning."[54] This vision offers a new dimension for understanding the Divine under different parameters. The Last God represents a return to a beginning prior to the philosophical turn of Plato and Aristotle, whose philosophies established epistemological parameters. This beginning demands, first of all, a return to Being, which has been buried in oblivion and replaced by an entity through epistemology and metaphysics.

---

54. Martin Heidegger, *The History of Beyng*, trans. William McNeill and Jeffrey Powell (Bloomington: Indiana University Press, 2015), section VI, "The Sustainment. The Essence of Power. The Necessary," §49, "The Decision [55–56]," 49.

Section V: From ontotheology to the unknown God

At the same time, this recovery cannot be initiated from a thought that merely replicates the same epistemological structures we wish to transcend. On the contrary, and this is Heidegger's proposal, it must begin with an ontological turn aimed at providing us with foundations that will allow us to present the issue of the Last God. From this fundamental ontology, as he calls it, we can begin this new direction. This requires, first, an analysis of *Dasein* that restores a foundation for the human being to reopen to Being. In other texts, Heidegger explains this shift from subject to pre-subject, from a merely thinking subject to *Dasein*. This is achieved through the adoption of serenity and authentic meditation, addressed in Section IV, which are the path to reopening to Being and, with it, to the reinstatement of the sacred.

To this end, the state of serenity suspends reasoning, imagination, and the will to know. This allows one to fully surrender to the passivity of silence, established in the "*páthos* of listening." For Heidegger, adopting this serenity and passivity involves preparing the human being for a reopening to Being. This requires rethinking the human being not as a subject but as *Dasein* (being-there-in-the-world), investigating its beingness to uncover its most primordial and authentic existence. From there, it can open to an essential Truth without resorting to machinations. This process first involves the fading of the human being as an egoic phenomenon and transcendental subject. Then, it gives way to the advent of that which underlies all subjectivity: the human being as being-in-the-world, as a being that lives. Then it disappears as a conceptualized organism and returns to exist in a world that is more than a set of resources.

The introduction of *Dasein* implies that the human being is not reduced to its epistemological existence. Before being a thinking being, it is in a permanent disposition toward the world and other humans, living the world with them through experiences. Heidegger's central philosophical turn proposes, therefore, that ontology as prior to all epistemology. In other words, thinking is preceded by the fact of being, which implies that "being" is not a construct or a simple image created by our intellectual faculties but the condition of possibility for all thinking. Furthermore, this argument posits that this new direction is not an idealization of his philosophy but is grounded in an ontological reality that precedes everything else.

This notion of Being was already present in history through three fundamental authors: Heraclitus, Parmenides, and Anaximander. Their approaches to the manifestation of Being mark the beginning of Western history. Heidegger calls them "the shepherds of Being." Western civilization is founded precisely with the advent of Being. However, as we have seen in detail, Plato and Aristotle intervene, and instead of receiving Being with reverence, they introduce categories to determine it. Plato formulates the ideas, and Aristotle establishes the categories. This act of creating molds, that is, forms,

Section V: From ontotheology to the unknown God

which give rise to images to define Being, threatens its inherent freedom as Being.

Moreover, the idealization and categorization of Being leads to that of God Himself or, in biblical terms, to idolatry. By creating concepts and categories of Being to make it understandable, Being withdraws and hides. In the face of this void, the human being, instead of remaining open, expectant, and receptive to the manifestations of Being, builds a substitute god: the God of ontotheology, which replaces the true God. This very idea is already exposed in the Old Testament, where we read:

וַיְדַבֵּר ה' אֶל מֹשֶׁה לֶךְ רֵד כִּי שִׁחֵת עַמְּךָ אֲשֶׁר הֶעֱלֵיתָ מֵאֶרֶץ מִצְרָיִם: סָרוּ מַהֵר מִן הַדֶּרֶךְ אֲשֶׁר צִוִּיתִם עָשׂוּ לָהֶם עֵגֶל מַסֵּכָה וַיִּשְׁתַּחֲווּ לוֹ וַיִּזְבְּחוּ לוֹ וַיֹּאמְרוּ אֵלֶּה אֱלֹהֶיךָ יִשְׂרָאֵל אֲשֶׁר הֶעֱלוּךָ מֵאֶרֶץ מִצְרָיִם:

(שמות ל"ב, ז'-ח')

And the Lord said to Moses: Go, descend, for your people that you have brought up from the land of Egypt have acted corruptly. They have quickly turned aside from the way that I have enjoined upon them; they have made themselves a molten calf and bowed to it and sacrificed to it, and said: "These are your gods, O Israel, who have brought you up from the land of Egypt."

(Exodus, 32:7–8)

Chapter 17: The unknown God

Heidegger and Hölderlin describe the phenomenon of the ontologization of Being and the subsequent idolatrous worship of humanity as "the flight of the gods."[55] This explains that the forgetfulness of Being and the creation of idols on the one hand and the fading of God on the other are not isolated phenomena. According to Heidegger, idolatry would be nothing more than the direct consequence of the forgetting of Being. This occurs because, when Being withdraws, it does not do so as an ontic object that hides behind another but ceases its manifestation. Being, in its manifestation, responds to the radically transcendent, which, as such, always exceeds the boundaries and limits of all forms and ideas. When Being does not manifest as absolute, that is, as sacred, as radically Other—as Levinas would say—the human being is confronted with a void or deathly silence. This void drives humanity to create gods-idols, always forged in its image and likeness, as substitutes for the absolutely transcendental. Heidegger calls this deathly silence "the resonance," comparing it to the silent and overwhelming echo that remains after the violent closing of a door when someone leaves a room in a fit of rage.

According to him, various religions arise precisely to make sense of that overwhelming and deafening void left by the withdrawal of Being. This withdrawal implies, by definition, the absence of all manifestations of Being

---

55. Heidegger, Martin. *Companion to Heidegger's Contributions to Philosophy* (Indiana University Press, 2001), 204.

Section V: From ontotheology to the unknown God

and transcendence. This passage from the withdrawal of Being to the emergence of idols has implications that transcend both religion and philosophy. In the absence of a purely transcendental God, who can only manifest from Being, humanity organizes and institutionalizes its religions. Thus, it grants power and control to their leaders over the masses, both socially and politically, with all the consequences this entails.

However, at a certain point, the very institutionalized religion, as a substitute for the Absolute, ceases to inspire humanity. Corrupt institutions and selfish leaders, promoters of beliefs, lose the ability to attract the public because their idols cannot fill the void or calm the vertigo caused by the flight of the ineffable.

That is to say, the God of ontotheology is devalued when humanity itself abandons its beliefs. The truths of organized religions are ignored until, eventually, humanity reaches a point where it ends up believing in nothing. In other words, the God of ontotheology from a metaphysical perspective and the personal God from a religious approach have transformed into the antechamber of nihilism, the most absolute of vacuities.

In the face of this situation, Heidegger introduces hermeneutics and *Dasein*. He does not do so merely to show that both are more primordial than epistemology or the transcendental subject, respectively, but as a path to allow the manifestation of Being. This approach seeks to attend to its sacred revelation with the divine character it possesses. Through this, humanity

Chapter 17: The unknown God

can rediscover meaning in its existence beyond the knowledge of forms and images and overcome nihilism. According to the early Heidegger, humanity itself must liberate God. It is *Dasein* who must break the conceptual chains imposed by philosophy and metaphysics that have transformed Being into an entity. This has reduced God to an ontified object, that is, another idol. To put it more radically, humanity must detach themselves from their objectifying subjectivity and immerse themselves in its pre-subjective existence. They must stop thinking and start meditating. In Heidegger's philosophy, this means that fundamental ontology is not a theory nor an imposition but emerges from the desolation in which idolatry and institutionalized religion have subsumed the subject. It is the subject itself that has overcome the fascination for manufacturing idols and has lost the allure of creating golden calves.

Being aware of its disillusionment, *Dasein* transforms into the openness necessary for Being to manifest in its truth. In other words, the subject suspends its own rationality—as in a phenomenological reduction—to discover itself as being-there-in-the-world-with-others. Moreover, Heidegger seems to suggest that the nihilism into which humanity has been dragged is almost a necessity. That void, that nothing (*nihil*), before which subjects bow, drives them to abandon their rationalization of the world. In doing so, they also renounce the personalized God they had created as a substitute for the authentically sacred.

Section V: From ontotheology to the unknown God

The renunciation of superficial subjectivity is authentic meditation. It is not a practice but a way of being characterized by contemplative passivity and serenity. Heidegger associates this state with a posture of vulnerability and silence, which emerges precisely when humanity can no longer find words to express its disbelief. The sermons and preachings from institutionalized religions no longer inspire them; they provide no teaching nor offer meaning or purpose to their existence. This void of inspiration and meaning leads the individual to adopt an attitude of reverent silence, anchored in the serenity that arises as a response to disillusionment with traditional religious structures. The attitude of the sacred, therefore, arises from the deep silence that humanity is capable of expressing. Then, desolated by the very religion, humanity no longer seeks to conceptualize or define God in any way and begins to look infinity in the eyes. When we stop believing in the idolized god promoted by the propagandists' beliefs, the Last God can communicate once again from beyond all religions. That unknown God from the book of Acts ultimately transcends religion itself.

CHAPTER 18

THE ONTOLOGICAL DEATH OF *DASEIN*

The advent of this Last God, the impersonal, inconceptualizable, and unimaginable God, the God without form or figure, without *Eidos*,[56] is already somewhat outlined in the New Testament when the abandonment of Jesus on the cross is described:

> And about the ninth hour, Jesus cried out with a loud voice, saying, "*Eli, Eli, lama sabachthani?*" That is, "My God, my God, why have you forsaken me?"
>
> (Matthew, 27:46)

And then He gives Himself over to the Last God:

> And Jesus, crying out with a loud voice, said, "Father, into Your hands I commit my spirit." Having said this, He breathed His last.
>
> (Luke, 23:46)

---

56. *Eidos* is a Greek term for "form, essence, type, or species."

Section V: From ontotheology to the unknown God

On the cross, Christ is abandoned by the God of ontotheology and entrusted to the Last God. He dies as a personal God—conceptualized and religionalized God, only to rise again as Plotinus' One, the primordial source of authentic religion.

It is impossible to eliminate Buddha, Kṛṣṇa, Christ, or any personal God without having fully traversed one's relationship with Him. The devotee cannot dispense with the figure of the personal God without first having loved Him, served Him, and undergone an inner death. One must first live the religious practice in its fullness and walk its path. Only by bringing personal religion to its most refined expression can one transcend duality, dissolve individuality, and access the absolute unity of Being. The passage into the unity of Being is attainable only through the death of God.

> For God so loved the world that He gave His only Son, that whoever believes in Him should not perish but have eternal life.
>
> (John 3:16)

The death of the devotee or the independent "I" is not physical but through love because to love implies dying. To the extent we love, our being diminishes because the beloved occupies the central role. Love aspires to a union so profound that both the lover and the beloved disappear in a complete fusion. It is, therefore, a death

Chapter 18: The ontological death of Dasein

of both the devotee and the personal God in which both reveal themselves as a unity.

For Heidegger, death is a horizon defining the totality of our existence, and not merely the biological end we share with other living beings. "Being-toward-death" challenges traditional conceptions of human finitude. We must first understand that *Dasein* does not refer only to the human being as a biological entity but to the Being that reflects on its existence, questions its purpose, and examines its relationship with the world. In this context, Heidegger highlights a unique characteristic: its ability to project itself into the future. While a rock or a tree are simply present, *Dasein* lives in constant relation to what it can become. In this sense, *Dasein* does not just "is," but it continuously "becomes." This projection toward the future includes an inescapable possibility: death. Therefore, for Heidegger, death is not a distant event at the end of life. It is a possibility always present. This perspective transforms our understanding of time and Being. The recognition of our mortality generates anxiety (*angst*). Unlike fear, which is directed at a concrete object, anxiety arises when we confront nothingness, the void that reveals our finitude. Although it may seem overwhelming, Heidegger considers this experience to have a revealing character.

Routines and conventions keep us trapped in the "one" (*das Man*). In that state of inauthenticity, we live according to social expectations, following patterns

Section V: From ontotheology to the unknown God

without questioning their meaning. But anxiety strips us of everyday distractions and forces us to confront the essentials: our finitude and the limits of our existence. This analysis leads us to a key distinction in Heidegger's thought: the difference between authentic and inauthentic life. Inauthentic existence occurs when *Dasein* avoids confronting its death, living as if it were something distant that only affects others. This avoidance leads to a superficial life, guided by what "is said" or "is done," but without reflection.

In contrast, an authentic life mainly arises when we accept death as a personal and intransferable possibility. It does not imply an obsessive fixation on the end, but it does mean recognizing that death is what gives meaning to our finitude. By accepting our condition of "being-toward-death," we stop living according to external expectations and begin to live according to our most proper being.

Heidegger distinguishes between two types of death: biological and ontological. Biological death, experienced by all living beings, is the cessation of vital functions. In contrast, only *Dasein* faces ontological death, which involves the possibility of ceasing to be as "Being" in the world. This distinction is essential because while biological death is a fact that occurs in time, ontological death is a possibility that always accompanies us. Ontological death is the ultimate horizon that defines our existence and invites us to make conscious decisions aligned with our most

Chapter 18: The ontological death of Dasein

authentic being. In Heidegger's thought, ontological death is related to the concept of *ereignis*, translated as "event or appropriation." This term refers to a fundamental event in which *Dasein* takes possession of its own being, abandoning the masks imposed by the "one." From this perspective, death is more than just an end; it is the culmination, the moment, in which *Dasein* frees itself from the limitations of its concrete existence. This is the death that *Dasein* is aware of in its authentic version.

For its part, *ereignis* is not a temporal event but a continuous process that shapes our relationship with Being. In this sense, death transforms into the ultimate horizon of authenticity. Therefore, Heidegger's "being-toward-death" is not just a reminder of our biological finitude but an invitation to rethink our existence. By accepting death as an ontological possibility, we live authentically, recognizing that more than limiting life, it is finitude that gives life meaning. In this vision of death, Heidegger provides us with a perspective that transforms our relationship with life. In our ontological finitude, the potential for a full existence is found, where each moment becomes unique and unrepeatable.

ای خنک آن را که پیش از مرگ مرد
یعنی او از اصل این رز بوی برد

Section V: From ontotheology to the unknown God

Oh, happy is the one who died before death, that is, the one who managed to smell the origin of This Vineyard.[57]

(Rumi, Masnavi, IV)

For whoever wants to save their life will lose it; but whoever loses their life for my sake will find it.
(Matthew, 16:25)

וַיֹּאמֶר לֹא תוּכַל לִרְאֹת אֶת־פָּנָי כִּי לֹא־יִרְאַנִי הָאָדָם וָחָי׃
(שמות ל"ג, כ')

And He said, "You will not be able to see My face, for man shall not see Me and live."
(Exodus, 33:20)

---

57. *On the Heart*. Rumi, Mevlâna. The Threshold Society (n.d.).

CHAPTER 19

HEIDEGGER'S ONTOLOGICAL-HERMENEUTIC TURN *(KEHRE)*

In *Being and Time* and other texts from early Heidegger, fundamental ontology is built on an exhaustive analysis of *Dasein*. *Dasein*'s possibility for understanding the essence of Being opens up from its own capacity to question its own existence and reveal itself as *Dasein*. In general terms, as a de-subjectivized subject, *Dasein* becomes the essential starting and ending point for exploring Being in its most profound and meaningful sense.

However, we could say that a second turn seems to take place in Heidegger's later works. This second turn which we could call "post-ontological," marks a significant shift in his philosophical approach. Contrary to what has sometimes been stated, this second *kehre* should be understood as a radicalization of the first turn, not as a correction, contradiction, or change of direction. In this second turn, Heidegger's focus gradually shifts from *Dasein* to Being itself (*Sein*). Instead of focusing exclusively on *Dasein* as the origin of the revelation of Being and the manifestation of the Last

Section V: From ontotheology to the unknown God

God, Heidegger begins to investigate and prioritize the history of Being (*Seinsgeschichte*). At this stage, *Dasein* is no longer the exclusive center but becomes a witness and participant in the historical unfolding of Being.

In this sense, *kehre* represents a crucial transition from existential phenomenology to hermeneutic ontology, where the main concern is understanding Being in its historical becoming and manifestation. The focus shifts from an anthropological-existential concern to a broader and deeper inquiry into Being and its historical development. In other words, this turn implies that *Dasein* loses its central role and is no longer the axis of all understanding. Instead, it is the history of Being that generates meaning. Let us examine this in more detail. As previously outlined, from the perspective of the existential analytical of *Dasein*, human beings, confronted with the void, reject personal idols and surrender to calmness and passivity. This allows them to suspend their reasoning and begin to meditate. By overcoming their epistemological structures, they open themselves up to a contemplation of Being that transcends the duality of subjects and objects.

This authentic meditation is intertwined with the calmness and passivity that prepare *Dasein* to become the event (*ereignis*) of Being. The passivity of silence means that humans have not only ceased to speak and create gods, synagogues, churches, and temples. More importantly, by doing so, they have implicitly renounced their subjectivity in order to reveal themselves as *Dasein*, as being-there. "There" is a "where" from which they can overcome the nihilism that had dragged them. However, *Dasein*, and more concretely the "there" (*da*) of "being-there," is not a static place (*topos*) where the event occurs. On the contrary, *Dasein* itself, in all its complexity, becomes the event (*ereignis*) of Being. For this reason, the term *Dasein*, which can be interpreted as "being-there" or "the there of Being," rather than being conceived as a delimited *topos*, must always be understood as a dynamic event in which Being can reveal itself again. One of the central elements of Heidegger's second turn is precisely this dynamic or historizing conception of the "there" (*Da*) of *Dasein*.

This suggests that from the perspective of the later Heidegger, the revelation of Being is, and necessarily must be, dynamic. In *Being and Time* (*Sein und Zeit*), Heidegger focused on the meaning of Being. Later, specifically in *Vom Ereignis* and in some writings from his *Collected Works* (volumes 65 and 71), he shifts his focus to the truth of Being. Truth of Being must now be understood as that truth that manifests but also gestates and unfolds throughout history, that is, dynamically. The truth of Being resides in its clearing, revealing, or uncovering, namely, that which is known as *aletheia*. To understand or attend to Being means to attend to the history of Being. This, in turn, implies understanding the history of philosophy, to which Heidegger pays so much attention throughout his work. In this context, it is no longer *Dasein*, as in *Being and Time*, with its fundamental

Section V: From ontotheology to the unknown God

ontology, that prepares the way for the encounter with Being. As Heidegger explains in his *Letter on Humanism* (1946), now it is Being itself, as *ereignis*, that configures its own dynamic-fundamental structure as it gradually reveals itself all along history.

To explain the dynamic character of the revelation of Being in more detail, Heidegger turns to the concepts *Grund* and *Abgrund*. In German, *Grund* is translated as "ground" or "foundation." In this sense, for Heidegger, *Grund* refers to the ontological base upon which the understanding of Being is built. It is the primordial ground from which entities and their Being emerge. The term "foundation," used similarly to *Grund* in Heidegger's philosophy, is not static or immutable, but dynamic and permanently open to interpretation. This dynamic character allows Heidegger to question the traditional concept of foundation and argue that Being lacks an absolute foundation. This suggests that insofar as Being is dynamic, it is then in a constant process of becoming, making it impossible to categorize or define as something fixed.

On the other hand, *Abgrund* means "abyss," which, for Heidegger, does not simply denote the lack or absence of a foundation, but rather the existence of a fundamental void. This abyss represents the dark and deep background of Being. It is a void that defies any attempt to establish a definitive and solid foundation. It suggests that Being is always at risk of falling into nothingness, and that our understanding of Being is always provisional and incomplete, though not necessarily deficient. That is, (1) *Grund* and the term "foundation" designate the base or ground from which Being and its understanding emerge, while (2) *Abgrund* represents the lack of a solid foundation, an abyss that questions the stability of any ontological foundation. These concepts illustrate Heidegger's view of the dynamic and open nature of Being, together with the constant tension between Being and nothingness.

This "new" dynamic and abyssal reading of Being suggests that to access the *Abgrund*—that which is radically transcendental and elusive to knowledge—, all foundation (*Grund*) must be transcended in the first place. In other words, to access the *Abgrund* implies transcending or "killing" the personal God of organized beliefs, the ontotheological God, and his rigid epistemological structures. Accessing the *Abgrund* would be equivalent to accessing the One of Plotinus—the Last God. This access is only possible for a predisposed human being, a *Dasein* that lives authentically. For this, *Dasein* must remain open, recognize that its finitude gives meaning to its existence, and be able to listen even in the deepest silence. At the same time, this is now a *Dasein* that surrenders itself to Being as its witness, while the unveiling of Being itself configures its own essence and internal coherence, transcending the epistemological structures of a subject that is now merely presumable.

For this reason, Heidegger's philosophical purpose is no longer to carry out an existential analysis of the finite

Section V: From ontotheology to the unknown God

essence of *Dasein* itself, as was the case in *Being and Time*. Rather, the aim is now to investigate *Dasein* as a witness to a more genuine history: the history of Being (*Die Geschichte Des Seyns*). The goal is no longer to understand history from the horizon of *Dasein*'s own meaning. With this second turn, Heidegger seeks, through *Dasein*, to trace the history of Being. In other words, this ontology is not solely a philosophical anthropology but a purely metaphysical question. It should be noted that the *Kehre*, or hermeneutic radicalization of Heidegger's ontology, does not appear in 1946 with the *Letter on Humanism*, as has sometimes been claimed. In short, this second turn is foreshadowed a decade earlier in *Contributions to Philosophy*. This confirms that Heidegger's philosophical approach does not undergo a self-correction but a radicalization within itself. That is, there would be no hermeneutic ontology without a prior fundamental ontology. Or, in other words, there would be no metaphysics without a preparatory philosophical anthropology. And although it is true that in this second *Kehre* (turn or twist), Heidegger abandons one approach for another, it is also important to say that both approaches are inseparable, with the second emerging from the depths of the first.

This transition from the analysis of *Dasein* to the history of Being illustrates the search for a more holistic and comprehensive understanding of Being, transcending individual existence to encompass its historical and temporal dimensions. Surprisingly, Heidegger himself

Chapter 19: Heidegger's Ontological-Hermeneutic Turn (Kehre)

classified his work *Being and Time* as the last great book of the era of technology and the God of ontotheology. This suggests that fundamental ontology, understood as philosophical anthropology, remains anchored in a subject. Even though it is *Dasein*, it still, in some way, acts as a subject through which Being finds its meaning. However, after the second turn, Heidegger's central issue is no longer *Dasein*, but Being itself. Before the *Kehre*, the human being, whether as traditional transcendental subject or as *Dasein* in phenomenological ontology, is conceived as the one that paved the way for the manifestation of Being. After this second turn, it is Being that begins to prepare its own becoming through *Dasein*.

This turn is also reflected in how Heidegger writes and understands certain terms. Let's begin with the term "Being." Writing the term as *Sein*, that is, with "i," specifically refers to the concrete and particular existence of something, meaning, to the Being of whatever is. *Dasein* is also written with "i" because it contains the same term (*Sein*). Hence, the *Sein* (Being) of *Dasein* denotes the Being of "being-there," which refers to the human being in its singularity and capacity to be conscious of its own existence. In contrast, when Heidegger changes the "i" to "y" (i.e. *Sein* to *Seyn*), he is evoking the idea of pure Being, that is, Being as independent of or not relative to *Dasein*. This concept refers to Being in its most abstract and fundamental essence, a notion that transcends the existence of any specific entity. In this sense, *Seyn* indicates a Being detached from any entity and from all

Section V: From ontotheology to the unknown God

the characteristics and limitations of individual entities, while *Sein* refers to the Being of a specific, concrete entity. We will revisit this issue in the following paragraphs.

At the same time, this notion of Being as *Seyn* has a significant structural impact on the relationship with the human being, which, after this second turn, Heidegger begins to define with the term *Wächter*, or "shepherd." Speaking of the human being in terms of "shepherd" implies that Being resides in language. From this idea arises the importance of sacred texts or Holy Scriptures. This sacred language must be preserved, cared for, and protected from the influence of the technique. The responsibility of the human being (*Dasein*) is to act as its guardian, shepherding and safeguarding its integrity. It is essential to remember that, in this new approach where the human being ceases to be the central axis, *Dasein* no longer orders or directs Being. Now, *Dasein* is simply its shepherd, its guardian, the dynamic "there" where Being becomes. In the language of the *Dasein*, *Seyn* can express itself without being shaped in the image of anything or anyone. The shepherd remains open and receptive to the sacred, that is, to what is incomprehensible through ideas, concepts, forms, or categories.

In Heidegger's philosophy, this openness to the sacred, described in the *Letter on Humanism*, can be interpreted as a "dawning." This awakening to the dawn occurs only when "Being (*Sein*) itself is unveiled." At that precise moment, the human being can recover their authentic "homeland," their intimate closeness with the cleared

Chapter 19: Heidegger's Ontological-Hermeneutic Turn (Kehre)

Being (*Seyn*). This proximity happens when the individual, as the "clearing" of Being, experiences the process of "unveiling." According to Heidegger, the Divine can only manifest when Being (*Sein*) is unveiled, freeing itself from the concepts imposed by traditional metaphysics and radically emancipating itself from its structures. In this clearing, Being reveals itself in its authenticity, that is, as *Seyn*, enabling the true experience of the Divine. The process of unveiling involves the removal of all concepts that have accumulated as layers over Being, covering and hiding its true essence.

However, as addressed in a central passage of the *Letter on Humanism*, there is a link between the sacred and God that, while paradoxical, also allows them to be differentiated and understood in their respective essence. First, Heidegger affirms that without the presence of God, the advent of the sacred is not possible, which suggests that God is the prior condition for the sacred. At the same time, he maintains that the sacred constitutes the necessary space for the divinity to manifest without appearing, implying that the sacred is, in turn, a condition for the appearance of God.

As we have seen, for human beings to abandon the use of traditional metaphysics, it is essential that Being be revealed. However, this process of the opening of Being cannot occur if the human being continues to use metaphysical concepts rooted in traditional epistemology. In some way, we are trapped in a vicious circle: Being will not reveal itself as long as the individual continues to cling to metaphysical categories, but these categories will continue to be used while Being remains concealed. Therefore, overcoming metaphysics requires a disposition of the human being so that Being can manifest in its authentic essence, free from such concepts. In reality, both processes unfold simultaneously. The revelation of Being and the abandonment of metaphysical categories are interdependent phenomena that, from Heidegger's perspective, happen together and reciprocally.

The same paradox occurs between the *versagen von Gott* and the *ereignis*. Both assemble simultaneously and interdependently. The "decision" in Heidegger must be understood as an articulation of the assembly in which the *Geviert*, or "quadrature," unfolds together in its fullest expression. This interpretation reveals an intrinsic complexity in which each component unfolds in coordination with the others, creating a coherent and unified whole. Therefore, either sacred space is the necessary condition for the manifestation of God, or the sacred occurs only if God so desires. In reality, these assemblies happen simultaneously.

In this paradox, Heidegger asserts that the authentic homeland of the human being is Being, a place where Being itself unveils as *Sein* and reveals itself in its true essence as *Seyn*. Without positioning oneself in *Seyn*, the individual experiences a constant diaspora, living as a stateless person. This allows for a more explicit understanding of the motives behind the second turn.

CHAPTER 19: HEIDEGGER'S ONTOLOGICAL-HERMENEUTIC TURN (KEHRE)

From this perspective, the *Dasein* that emerges within the realm of fundamental ontology is still a human being. Its relationship with Being, mediated by meditation and passivity, retains Being as *Sein*, that is, as relational to *Dasein*. Through this same relationship with Being (*Sein*), the human being remains in exile. This situation, where the *Sein* of *Dasein* does not truly emancipate, and *Dasein* remains estranged from itself, demands the second turn described in this chapter. This turn seeks to reframe the relationship between them, overcoming this limitation. It is the condition necessary for the Last God to reveal itself without appearing, that is, to manifest beyond any understanding. This idea is expressed in the Old Testament, where it is said:

אֵיךְ נָשִׁיר אֶת־שִׁיר־ה' עַל אַדְמַת נֵכָר:
אִם־אֶשְׁכָּחֵךְ יְרוּשָׁלָָם תִּשְׁכַּח יְמִינִי:
תִּדְבַּק־לְשׁוֹנִי לְחִכִּי אִם־לֹא אֶזְכְּרֵכִי אִם־לֹא אַעֲלֶה אֶת־יְרוּשָׁלַָם
עַל רֹאשׁ שִׂמְחָתִי:

(תהילים קל"ז, ד'-ו')

How can we sing a song of the Lord on alien soil? If I forget you, O Jerusalem, let my right hand forget her cunning; Let my tongue stick to my palate if I do not remember you, if I do not set Jerusalem above my highest joy.
(Psalms, 137:4–6)

Section V: From ontotheology to the unknown God

Only in its homeland, where Being (*Sein*) is stripped of metaphysical concepts and reveals itself in its purity (*Seyn*), is it possible to live the experience of the sacred. To reside in the homeland means not to live in the realm of beings or technique (*techné*). To be situated in the homeland means not remaining in the ontic but inhabiting the radicality of the ontological instead. The *Letter on Humanism* establishes that the human being finds its identity only in relation to Being. This implies that the essence of our existence is intrinsically connected to the understanding of Being. Above all, we are human beings; this is our identity, founded on this intrinsic and essential connection to Being. That is, instead of referring to a physical territory, our true "homeland" or place of belonging is an existential dimension rooted in Being (*Seyn*). In this way, the relationship with Being defines and constitutes our beingness, establishing a bond that transcends conventional notions of nationality and belonging.

To put it differently, prior to being a political or rational animal, before belonging to an ethnicity, race, culture, sex, or gender, what identifies us as human beings is this existential relationship with Being. More specifically, it is in the paradoxical opening moment, like a clearing in a thick forest, when Being frees itself from all conceptualization and expresses itself in us as *Seyn* beyond any category, image, idea, or form.

Thus, although the second turn has not eliminated *Dasein*, it has positioned it as the shepherd or guardian

Chapter 19: Heidegger's Ontological-Hermeneutic Turn (Kehre)

of Being (*Sein*). Moreover, it is the guardian of the process in which Being (*Sein*) unveils from within itself to get manifested in its purity (*Seyn*). Therefore, unveiling is a process that emanates from Being itself and not from human action or agency. As such, it demands an intervention that transcends human capacity. However, for this revelation to occur fully, prolonged preparation is essential to enable the human being to comprehend the "Truth" that is manifested, which unfolds with the unveiling of Being.

As we have already seen, this preparation involves the progressive abandonment of the metaphysical and epistemological categories established by the philosophy of Plato and Aristotle, which have gradually lost their relevance. This prolonged preparation process requires the human being to immerse themselves in profound introspection and contemplation. One must surrender to a state of passivity that allows for the essence of the Truth revealed by Being (*Seyn*) to be grasped. Preparation is not merely temporal but also existential, demanding a thorough commitment and an open disposition to receive what Being (*Seyn*) has to offer in its revelation.

Being clears itself by its own initiative when it sheds the conceptualizations that have veiled it. In doing so, it seeks to un-cover (*a-letheia*) its authenticity as *physis*. The revelation requires extensive and careful repair. Being guides the individual toward a progressive disillusionment with preconceived concepts during this process. Gradually, these conceptualizations become exhausted, lose their value, and dissolve into a deep and dreadful void. In other words, the second turn shows us that it is not the subject, nor even *Dasein*, who decides to suspend its subjective rationality to contemplate Being. Being itself, present in the *Sein* of *Dasein*, drives human beings to abandon their subjectivization, thus allowing Being to unveil in all its purity. In this sense, Heidegger's second turn seeks to establish itself as the end of all subjectivist philosophy and the dawn of the reemergence of the uncategorized Being, as was understood before Socrates: *alétheia*, *physis*, and logos simultaneously. For this reason, as Levinas will point out, it manifests as radical otherness, the origin of all existence, meaning, and possible "understanding."

Thanks to this second turn, meaning is no longer a product or elaboration (*techne*) of a subject, not even of *Dasein*. On the contrary, meaning emerges in the unconcealing of Being, through which *Sein* reveals itself as *Seyn* in all its purity, that is, as meaningfulness. In other words, returning to the subject of dynamicity and history mentioned earlier, the meaning of Being, of the pre-Socratic *physis*, is revealed to the human being in the historical process of the becoming of Being itself. Heidegger asserts that Being is, ultimately, its own history and becoming. Being is the transition from *Sein* to *Seyn*. It is the liberation from any concealment.

It is in this context that the term *Abgrund* shows its true relevance. For insofar as Being is its own becoming —just as Heraclitus wisely noted—then Being

Chapter 19: Heidegger's Ontological-Hermeneutic Turn (Kehre)

must be understood as "Being and not-yet-Being" simultaneously, which prevents us from mistaken it for a *Grund*, namely, a static foundation. When Heraclitus wrote *panta rhei* (everything flows), what he was actually saying is not just that we do not bathe twice in the same river, but that we do not bathe even once in the same river. For since the water is never the same, neither can be the river. In this sense, Being is its history, and its history is its own becoming and constant flow, its incessant un-hiding. Being is this very process in which Being itself is generated as a continuous flow, never becoming a final foundation (*Grund*) but rather remaining instead as the abyss (*Abgrund*) that underlies everything.

The notion of Being as a flow of continuous unveiling understood as historicity, is key in Heidegger's thought. It allows us to understand his explanations of technique (*techne*), the resulting nihilism, and his ontology as a way back to Being. Heidegger integrates his two philosophical turns into the becoming of Being. Each stage, period, and turn is presented as an essential part of this process. This is important because Heidegger points out that his philosophy should not be interpreted as a new Platonism. With his ontological and hermeneutic turns, he clarifies that he is not proposing a new metaphysics that repeats the mistake of conceiving Being as an object external to thought.

In Heidegger's philosophy, Being is not the simple object of ontology and hermeneutics. On the contrary,

Section V: From ontotheology to the unknown God

it is ontology and hermeneutics which emerge from the process of the becoming of Being. Moreover, they are necessary moments, just like Platonic philosophy and the 2,500-year-old philosophical tradition. That is, if Being had not been concealed, it would not have become from oblivion to its non-apparent manifestation. Very close to Hegel, Heidegger seems to attribute a sense of necessity to everything that happens. Although he does not express it in those terms, he suggests that everything that is—including having thought and concealed Being as has occurred in philosophy and religion—is necessary for Being to be and become as it is. In this framework, Heidegger understands not only his own philosophy but also pre-Socratic thought, Platonic philosophy, Thomism, religion, and Christian metaphysics as necessary moments leading us to the forgetting Being.

More specifically, for Heidegger, technique (*techne*) should be understood as the attempt to capture Being within the confines of metaphysical concepts in an effort to appropriate Being. Under these parameters, and as we have seen in detail, to understand is to know, and to know is to possess. However, this colonization of Being—if we can call it that—is part of an extensive process in which technique emerges, develops, reaches its peak, and eventually begins to deteriorate and decline. This cycle of rise and fall of technique culminates in what Heidegger and Nietzsche before him called "nihilism," which is essential for the unveiling of Being. Only through this process can human beings free themselves

Chapter 19: Heidegger's Ontological-Hermeneutic Turn (Kehre)

from the limitations imposed by metaphysics and come closer to Being, that is, to the unveiling of Being in its purity (*Seyn*).

The final decline of technique is also addressed in the philosophies of Hegel and Nietzsche, and perhaps in a more resolutive way in *Being and Time* by Heidegger. The problem of the technique (*techne*), intrinsically linked to the metaphysical apparatus of the West, places human beings in a position they cannot escape alone. For this reason, Being finally frees itself from the constraints of the conceptual dictionaries that human beings imposed upon it with their concepts and definitions. In doing so, Being itself unveils and, in turn, frees the human being from their own dehumanization. This instance in which Being becomes, and the human being (*Dasein*) can approach it, must be understood as an *ereignis* (event). However, instead of simply responding to a structure of cause and effect, or action and reaction, this event shows us the dynamic historicity of Being that defines its own relationship with *Dasein*.

To explain the history of Being from the perspective of *ereignis*, we must not conceive it as a pre-written history or a teleology leading linearly to a final truth. On the contrary, the history of Being is a process in which Being itself, by veiling and unveiling itself, through the human being, assembles what Heidegger calls *Fügung* (assemblages). These are parts of the becoming of Being that, far from integrating immediately, present themselves as dispersed and fragmented. *Being itself gradually* unites

Section V: From ontotheology to the unknown God

them, folding them to build a coherent puzzle. This is what we had indicated with *Sein* becoming *Seyn*. By veiling and unveiling itself, Being acquires meaning and cohesion as the pieces are assembled gradually and articulated meaningfully. In other words, the history of Being is a process of assembly in which that history acquires meaning as it is configured. The history of humanity and its meaning was not written; history is written by Being in its process of hiding and unveiling through the human being. In other words, history is hermeneutic because it is, essentially, the pure generation of meaning. History enables both the unveiling of Being and the liberation of the human being from their metaphysical chains.

A few paragraphs earlier, citing the central section of the *Letter on Humanism*, we spoke of the link between the sacred and God, which, as we have presented, appears initially as contradictory. On the one hand, it is stated that if God "is denied," the day of the sacred does not arrive, suggesting that God is a necessary condition for the sacred. On the other hand, it is upheld that the sacred is the condition, as the event and appearance of God. In this apparent paradox, we could ask ourselves which precedes which: the sacred or the manifestation of the Last God? Heidegger links these questions by understanding that the assemblages happen simultaneously. That is why Heidegger's "decision" is conceived as a fold of the assemblage in which the quadrature (*Geviert*) unfolds together. It is not a decision that is solely divine or exclusively human but a mutual opening. There is, therefore, no causality between both, but a relationship of concomitance. After the decline of technological society and organized religion around a personal God, the human being has chosen silence, in which God has chosen to reveal himself. In the next section, we will examine in more detail the issue of the assemblages as pieces of the becoming of Being as *Seyn*.

Bibliography Section V

- Heidegger, Martin. *Contributions to Philosophy: From Enowning*. Translated by Parvis Emad and Kenneth Maly. Bloomington: Indiana University Press, 1999.
- Plato. *Phaedo*. In *Plato in Twelve Volumes*, Vol. 1. Translated by Harold North Fowler. Introduction by W. R. M. Lamb. Cambridge, MA: Harvard University Press; London: William Heinemann Ltd., 1966.
- Rumi, Mevlâna Jalāl al-Dīn. "*On the Heart.*" The Threshold Society. Accessed May 5, 2025.

SECTION VI
THE JOURNEY TOWARD THE LAST GOD

Chapter 20

The six assemblies toward the last God

In the first stage of his writings between 1936 and 1937, Heidegger outlined the six fundamental assemblages that constitute the central structure of his work, specifically around the phenomenon of *ereignis*. These assemblages, moments in the history of Being, can also be compared to the three stages mentioned by Plotinus in the *Return to the One*. They represent six levels through which every seeker passes on their path toward Being. This new "thought" is based on the necessary silence to listen to Being and the proper temperament. This temperament understood as passivity and authentic meditation as a state rather than a practice, allows human beings to be interpellated by Being.

Those who transition from metaphysics toward a new way of thinking about Being must, therefore, pass through these six stages, which ultimately open us to the title of this book: to discover the Last God. Heidegger names these six stages as follows:

Section VI: The journey toward the Last God

1. The resonance (*Der Anklang*).
2. The pass (*Das Zuspiel*).
3. The leap (*Der Sprung*).
4. The foundation (*Die Gründung*).
5. The future ones (*Die Zu-künftigen*).
6. The Last God (*Der letzte Gott*).

In addition to these assemblages, there is an extensive section called *Vorblick* (prospective or prior look), where Heidegger presents his work's general guidelines and articulation. Later, in 1938, he completed the final part of his work, titled *Seyn*, in which he integrates and revisits what was previously developed, thus offering a more holistic and unified vision. We will now analyze these assemblages and attempt to articulate their meaning and relationship to the purpose of this book.

(1) The resonance (*Der Anklang*) is the echo that Being leaves after withdrawing. Each time Being attempts to manifest itself fully and is hindered by the constraints imposed by technology, an intrinsic demand for justice arises. This demand implies that the circumstances must be oriented toward the necessary and just outcome, that what must happen will happen. When discussing the concept of "resonance," Heidegger highlights how the reactive character of "machination" becomes evident. Machination appears as a reaction, responding to the call of Being. In the face of this call, we have two possible responses. The first manifests as the *páthos* of listening, marked by the serenity that

emanates from the sacred. This necessarily involves the suspension of all egoism, already present in some way in pre-Socratic thought. The second response materializes in technological machination, which is the manifestation of the egoic phenomenon emerging with post-Socratic philosophy. According to Heidegger, these two alternatives symbolize two possible responses to the call of Being. This same idea appears in the Gospel of Luke, where we read:

> It happened that as they went on their way, he entered a village; and a woman named Martha welcomed him into her house. She had a sister called Mary, who sat at the Lord's feet and listened to his word. But Martha was distracted with much serving, and she came to him and said, "Lord, do you not care that my sister has left me to serve alone? Tell her then to help me." But the Lord answered her, "Martha, Martha, you are anxious and troubled about many things. But one thing is necessary. Mary has chosen the good portion, which will not be taken away from her."
>
> (Luke, 10:38–42)

Mary, adopting a receptive attitude and full attention to Being, listens with patience and serenity. In contrast, Martha complains, convinced that Mary is not doing her part. However, Jesus asserts that Mary has made the

Section VI: The Journey toward the Last God

better choice. Thus, we observe the *páthos* of listening to the call of Being in Mary and the technological machination in Martha.

In a moment of "self-consciousness," the human being can recognize the disconnection from Being and feel the need to attend to the call. The more the idea is promoted that everything is possible, especially in situations of "emergency" that deny the existence of real problems, the more prominent a genuine problem becomes, marking the decline of the first beginning. Authentic problems do not lie in metaphysics, poverty, relationships, indigence, or capital. The fundamental problem is the disconnection from Being. When human beings understand that this disconnection is their true and only problem, the other conflicts lose their importance and fade away.

This emergence is the "resonance" of the other beginning, which machination seeks to conceal through its epistemological structures. Despite the constant murmur that tries to silence it, it remains passively audible. It manifests with tenacity in the background of human consciousness. Resonance is a noise that emerges from the disturbing silence that machination tries to suppress because it cannot tolerate the deafening silence that reveals the true problem it faces.

(2) The pass (*Das Zuspiel*), for its part and following Heidegger, is the beginning of the history of the essentialization of beings in their totality, a process which, in turn, is divided into three phases or levels.

Chapter 20: The six assemblies toward the last God

First, the technique emerged, as exemplified by Plato and Aristotle. Then, a significant turn toward consciousness occurs, as evidenced by the philosophies of Descartes and Leibniz. Finally, this process culminates with the turn toward the Absolute, as articulated by Hegel and Nietzsche, although from opposing perspectives. The pass consists of experiencing the original situation and moving toward a new beginning, encompassing everything from Plato and Aristotle to Nietzsche. While Descartes and Leibniz focus their attention on the subject, they do so within the framework of ontotheology. This term describes the horizon where the forgetting of Being occurs. To return to attending to Being, we must surrender, listen to the call, and open ourselves to the Absolute, beyond the ego and individual consciousness.

(3) The leap (*Der Sprung*) later originates in the impulse to find oneself thrown from *Dasein* through *ereignis*, or the "appropriating event" in which Being pulsates within *Dasein*. Each of these leaps makes overcoming the trace left by the initial history of ontotheology possible. There are two fundamental beginnings: the first, linked to the teachings of pre-Socratic thought from Heraclitus, Parmenides, and Anaximander; and the second, which marks the beginning of Western history and ontotheology. In this second beginning, after Heidegger's first *kehre* (ontological turn) occurs, the death of the God of ontotheology manifests, symbolized by the death of Kṛṣṇa or the crucifixion of Jesus. This leap represents the passage from Thomas Aquinas to

SECTION VI: THE JOURNEY TOWARD THE LAST GOD

the One of Plotinus, as outlined in the third section of this book. Thus, in this third disposition, the transition from the first beginning to the other ceases to be merely a "resonance" or a "pass," and becomes the "leap," a definitive decision in favor of the other beginning. This leap is made, even at the cost of sacrificing all the securities acquired, because only then can *Dasein* involve itself from the excess or abundance of Being and reach its full realization. In other words, this leap represents renouncing the security offered by a life of slavery to seek a promise. This is illustrated in the books of Exodus and Numbers, where we read:

הֲלֹא־זֶה הַדָּבָר אֲשֶׁר דִּבַּרְנוּ אֵלֶיךָ בְמִצְרַיִם לֵאמֹר חֲדַל מִמֶּנּוּ וְנַעַבְדָה אֶת־מִצְרָיִם כִּי טוֹב לָנוּ עֲבֹד אֶת־מִצְרַיִם מִמֻּתֵנוּ בַּמִּדְבָּר:
(שמות י"ד, י"ב)

Is this not the thing which we spoke to you in Egypt, saying: "let us be, that we may serve the Egyptians, for we would rather serve the Egyptians than die in the desert"?

(Exodus, 14:12)

זָכַרְנוּ אֶת־הַדָּגָה אֲשֶׁר־נֹאכַל בְּמִצְרַיִם חִנָּם אֵת הַקִּשֻּׁאִים וְאֵת הָאֲבַטִּחִים וְאֶת־הֶחָצִיר וְאֶת־הַבְּצָלִים וְאֶת־הַשּׁוּמִים: וְעַתָּה נַפְשֵׁנוּ יְבֵשָׁה אֵין כֹּל בִּלְתִּי אֶל־הַמָּן עֵינֵינוּ: וְהַמָּן כִּזְרַע־גַּד הוּא וְעֵינוֹ כְּעֵין הַבְּדֹלַח:
(במדבר י"א, ה'-ז')

Chapter 20: The six assemblies toward the last God

> We remember the fish which we ate in Egypt freely, the cucumbers, the melons, the leeks, the onions, and the garlic. But now our soul is dry: there is nothing at all, besides this manna, before our eyes. And the manna was like coriander seed, and its color was like the color of crystal.
>
> (Numbers, 11:5–7)

To return to the first beginning, it is necessary to abandon all the certainties provided by metaphysics and technique. It is essential to renounce the comforts offered by institutionalized religion, organized belief, and tradition. The pass (*das Zuspiel*) involves a transition from one level to another without denying the previous one, whereas in the leap (*der Sprung*), the previous one is indeed denied. The leap involves completely abandoning one assemblage to enter the next, constituting a rupture or break in history.

(4) The foundation (*die Gründung*) refers to the abyss of "meanwhile" understood as the truth of Being (*Seyn*) to which we have previously referred. This "meanwhile" stands as the God of ontotheology: a supplementary, ephemeral, and transitory god that, nevertheless, has allowed us to transit up to the point where we needed to go. It is comparable to the golden calf that the people of Israel worship while Moses descends from Mount Sinai with the Tablets of the Law.

Section VI: The journey toward the Last God

וַיְדַבֵּר ה' אֶל־מֹשֶׁה לֶךְ־רֵד כִּי שִׁחֵת עַמְּךָ אֲשֶׁר הֶעֱלֵיתָ מֵאֶרֶץ מִצְרָיִם: סָרוּ מַהֵר מִן־הַדֶּרֶךְ אֲשֶׁר צִוִּיתִם עָשׂוּ לָהֶם עֵגֶל מַסֵּכָה וַיִּשְׁתַּחֲווּ־לוֹ וַיִּזְבְּחוּ־לוֹ וַיֹּאמְרוּ אֵלֶּה אֱלֹהֶיךָ יִשְׂרָאֵל אֲשֶׁר הֶעֱלוּךָ מֵאֶרֶץ מִצְרָיִם:

(שמות ל"ב, ז'-ח')

And the Lord said to Moses: Go, descend, for your people that you have brought up from the land of Egypt have acted corruptly. They have quickly turned aside from the way that I have commanded them; they have made themselves a molten calf and bowed to it and sacrificed to it, and said: "These are your gods, O Israel, who have brought you up from the land of Egypt."

(Exodus 32:7–8)

This fourth moment of the foundation describes how being-there (*Dasein*) reaches its full realization in the "appropriating event," in the *Da* (there), which is temporal—not merely spatial (*topos*). After manifesting itself following its withdrawal, this is where Being unveils itself before *Dasein*, incorporating and integrating it into its essence. It is a complex process where Being manifests and is grounded in its deepest truth, involving a dynamic of appropriation that reveals its authentic nature. Through this foundation, an intrinsic bond is established between Being and being-there, showing how Being is rooted in the truth of the event that appropriates and defines it.

Chapter 20: The six assemblies toward the last God

Some understand that merely moving from one assemblage to another while negating the previous one is ineffective and that it is necessary to turn toward the foundation. In other words, it is essential to delve into the underlying base of each structure without completely rejecting the previous one. This approach requires deeper reflection and understanding of the foundations supporting each level. Only in this way can one progress meaningfully and authentically, integrating past knowledge into the new context rather than discarding it entirely. The foundation is the return to the source and involves allowing oneself to be appropriated by the foundation established in the origin. However, the challenge lies in the fact that this foundation is not definitive; there is "something" beyond it. As we have explained earlier, behind the *Grund* lies an *Abgrund*, an abyss. Yet, to access it, one must first reach and understand the initial foundation. This process of deepening is essential to unveil the underlying layers of reality, leading to a more complete understanding of Being. In other words, the Last God can only be revealed after the human renounces the golden calf.

(5) The future ones (*Die Zu-künftigen*) are those who bear witness to the action of the Last God. They are also called the devoted ones, the ones to come, the poets, and the shepherds (*Wachter*) of Being. These poets are named "the coming ones" because they are the prophets who announce the arrival. Knowing what is to come, the prophets ensure that an authentic future

is always available to all humanity. What they proclaim transcends individual benefits. Among them is Hölderlin, considered by Heidegger as "the most coming among the coming ones." They are the first guardians of being-there, although they are not its founders. The creation of the guardians of art refers to all of humanity, avoiding reducing their work to a mere technical analysis. On the contrary, they transmit the Truth in a way that is unattainable for scientific systematization. Only those rooted in Being can fully understand what their works communicate. An inadequate methodology would be established if the guardians of the Truth were to transmit it like a newspaper or a trivial talk. This would provoke the withdrawal of Being, for Being cannot be expressed in any way. The existence of these shepherds of Being demonstrates that the possibility of an authentic and meaningful future is always open, facilitated by those who understand and express divine action. The poets, with their ability to listen, contemplate, and allow Being to manifest, play a crucial role as custodians of this Truth, even though they do not originate it. These artists are the shepherds of Being, preparing the path for Being.

For example, in the Hebrew tradition, we find numerous references that characterize revealing literature as a form of poetry in a sense similar to what Heidegger conveys to us:

וְעַתָּה כִּתְבוּ לָכֶם אֶת הַשִּׁירָה הַזֹּאת וְלַמְּדָהּ אֶת בְּנֵי יִשְׂרָאֵל שִׂימָהּ בְּפִיהֶם לְמַעַן תִּהְיֶה לִּי הַשִּׁירָה הַזֹּאת לְעֵד בִּבְנֵי יִשְׂרָאֵל:
(דברים ל"א, י"ט)

Chapter 20: The six assemblies toward the last God

And now, write for yourselves this song and teach it to the children of Israel, place it in their mouths, so that this song be a witness for Me with the children of Israel.

(Deuteronomy, 31:19)

[...]שֶׁצִּוָּנוּ שֶׁיִּהְיֶה לְכָל אִישׁ מִמֶּנּוּ סֵפֶר תּוֹרָה לְעַצְמוֹ[...] וְהוּא אָמְרוֹ יִתְעַלֶּה: "כִּתְבוּ לָכֶם אֶת הַשִּׁירָה הַזֹּאת"[...] (דברים ל"א, י"ט) כִּי אָמְנָם רָצָה בְּאָמְרוֹ "אֶת הַשִּׁירָה" כָּל הַתּוֹרָה הַכּוֹלֶלֶת זֹאת הַשִּׁירָה. וּלְשׁוֹן גְּמָרָא סַנְהֶדְרִין (כ"א): "אָמַר רַבָּה: 'אַף עַל פִּי שֶׁהִנִּיחוּ לוֹ לָאָדָם אֲבוֹתָיו סֵפֶר תּוֹרָה מִצְוָה לוֹ לִכְתֹּב מִשֶּׁלּוֹ שֶׁנֶּאֱמַר: וְעַתָּה כִּתְבוּ לָכֶם אֶת הַשִּׁירָה'".

(רמב"ם, ספר המצוות, מצות עשה י"ח)

That He commanded us that every man among us should have a Torah scroll for himself [...] And this is His saying, "Write for yourselves this song" (Deuteronomy, 31:19) [...] For when He said, "this song," He intended the whole Torah, which includes this song (of *Ha'azinu*). And the language of the *Gemara* (*Sanhedrin*, 21b) is: "Rabbah said: 'Even if his ancestors left him a Torah scroll, it is a commandment for him to write a scroll of his own, as it is stated: and now write for yourselves this song'."

(Maimonides, *Sefer HaMitzvot*, "Positive Commandments," 18.1)

Section VI: The journey toward the Last God

אָמַר רֵישׁ לָקִישׁ: "כָּל הָעוֹסֵק בְּתוֹרָה בַּלַּיְלָה הַקָּדוֹשׁ בָּרוּךְ הוּא מוֹשֵׁךְ עָלָיו חוּט שֶׁל חֶסֶד בַּיּוֹם, שֶׁנֶּאֱמַר: 'יוֹמָם יְצַוֶּה ה' חַסְדּוֹ'. וּמָה טַעַם 'יוֹמָם יְצַוֶּה ה' חַסְדּוֹ'? מִשּׁוּם 'וּבַלַּיְלָה שִׁירֹה עִמִּי'".

(תלמוד בבלי, חגיגה, י"ב, ב')

Reish Lakish said: "Whoever occupies himself with Torah at night, the Holy One, Blessed be He, extends a thread of kindness over him by day, as it is stated: 'By day, the Lord will command His kindness,' and what is the reason that 'by day, the Lord will command His kindness'? Because 'and in the night His song is with me'."

(*Babylonian Talmud*, "Ḥagigah," 12b)

וְכָל מַחֲלֹקוֹת הַתַּנָּאִים וְהָאָמוֹרָאִים, וְהַגְּאוֹנִים וְהַפּוֹסְקִים בֶּאֱמֶת — לַמֵּבִין דָּבָר לַאֲשׁוּרוֹ — דִּבְרֵי אֱלֹקִים חַיִּים הֵמָּה, וּלְכֻלָּם יֵשׁ פָּנִים בַּהֲלָכָה. וְאַדְרַבָּה: זֹאת הִיא תִּפְאֶרֶת תּוֹרָתֵנוּ הַקְּדוֹשָׁה וְהַטְּהוֹרָה. וְכָל הַתּוֹרָה כֻּלָּהּ נִקְרֵאת "שִׁירָה", וְתִפְאֶרֶת הַשִּׁיר הִיא כְּשֶׁהַקּוֹלוֹת מְשֻׁנִּים זֶה מִזֶּה, וְזֶהוּ עִקַּר הַנְּעִימוֹת. וּמִי שֶׁמְּשׁוֹטֵט בְּיָם הַתַּלְמוּד – יִרְאֶה נְעִימוֹת מְשֻׁנּוֹת בְּכָל הַקּוֹלוֹת הַמְשֻׁנּוֹת זֶה מִזֶּה.

(הרב יחיאל מיכל הלוי אפשטיין, הקדמה לספר ערוך השולחן)

And those who precisely understand, know that all the disputes of the *Tana'im* and the *Amora'im*, the *Ge'onim*, and the *Poskim*, are the words of the living God, and they all are legitimate aspects of the *Halachah* (law). As a matter of fact, this is the glory of our holy and pure Torah. And the entire Torah is called *shirah* (song, poetry, tune),

Chapter 20: The six assemblies toward the last God

and the glory of the song is when the sounds [the tune is composed of] are different, and this is a fundamental principle in composing. And those who travel the Talmudic Ocean will notice different tunes with so many different sounds.

(Rabbi Yeḥi'el Michel HaLevi Epstein, *Aruch HaShulḥan* introduction)

הָא מִיהָא יֵשׁ לְהָבִין הֵיאַךְ נִקְרָא כָּל הַתּוֹרָה שִׁירָה? וַהֲרֵי לֹא נִכְתְּבָה בְּלָשׁוֹן שֶׁל שִׁירָה? אֶלָּא עַל כִּי יֵשׁ בָּהּ טֶבַע וְסִגְלַת הַשִּׁירָה, שֶׁהוּא דִּבּוּר בְּלָשׁוֹן מְלִיצָה. דְּיָדוּעַ לְכָל מֵבִין עַם תַּלְמוּדוֹ, דִּמְשָׁנֶּה לָשׁוֹן הַ'מְּלִיצָה' מִסִּפּוּר 'פְּרָזִי' [פרוזה] בִּשְׁנֵי עִנְיָנִים: בְּטֶבַע וּבִסְגֻלָּה.

א) דְּבַשִּׁיר אֵין הָעִנְיָן מְבֹאָר יָפֶה כְּמוֹ בְּסִפּוּר פְּרָזִי. וְצָרִיךְ לַעֲשׂוֹת הֶעָרוֹת מִן הַצַּד, דְּזֶה הֶחָרוּז וְזֶה לָזֶה הַסִּפּוּר וְזֶה הֶחָרוּז כֵּוֵּן לָזֶה... כָּךְ הוּא טֶבַע כָּל הַתּוֹרָה שֶׁאֵין הַסִּפּוּר שֶׁבָּהּ מְבֹאָר יָפֶה. אֶלָּא יֵשׁ לַעֲשׂוֹת הֶעָרוֹת וּפֵרוּשִׁים לְדִקְדּוּקֵי הַלָּשׁוֹן וְלֹא נִקְרָא דְּרוּשׁ, אֶלָּא כָּךְ הוּא פְּשַׁט הַמִּקְרָא.

ב) דְּבַשִּׁיר יֵשׁ סְגֻלָּה לְפָאֲרָהּ בִּרְמָזִים מַה שֶּׁאֵינוּ מֵעִנְיָן הַשִּׁיר, כְּמוֹ שֶׁנָּהוּג לַעֲשׂוֹת רָאשֵׁי הַחֲרוּזִים בְּדֶרֶךְ א"ב אוֹ שֵׁם הַמְחַבֵּר..וְדָבָר זֶה מַמָּשׁ הִיא בְּכָל הַתּוֹרָה כֻּלָּהּ, שֶׁמְּלֻבָּד הָעִנְיָן הַמְדֻבָּר בִּפְשַׁט הַמִּקְרָא, עוֹד יֵשׁ בְּכָל דָּבָר הַרְבֵּה סוֹדוֹת וְעִנְיָנִים נֶעֱלָמִים, אֲשֶׁר מֵחֲמַת זֶה בָּא כַּמָּה פְּעָמִים הַמִּקְרָא בְּלָשׁוֹן שֶׁאֵינוּ מְדֻיָּק כָּל כָּךְ. וְכָל זֶה אֵינוֹ בַּתּוֹרָה הַקְּדוֹשָׁה לְבַד אֶלָּא בְּכָל מִקְרָאֵי קֹדֶשׁ...

(הנצי"ב מוולוז'ין בהקדמה לספרו 'העמק דבר')

Section VI: The Journey toward the Last God

However, we should understand how is it that the entire Torah is called *shirah* ("poetry" or "song"), while it is not written in poetic verse form. The answer is that it has the quality and nature of poetry, meaning it is spoken in a way of poetic phrasing. For it is known to the learned that poetry differs from prose in two ways: nature and quality:

1. In poetry the topic is not properly explained, like it is in prose, and it requires some commentary by its side, to explain that this rhyme meant this, and this rhyme meant this. So is the nature of the entire Torah, that the story in it is not clearly explained but it requires commentaries and grammatical analysis, and this is not expansive exegesis (*drash*), but [for understanding] the simple meaning of the Torah (*pshat*).

2. Another quality of poetry is that it can be decorated with hints that are not related to the content, such as ordering the first letter of each line in an alphabetical order, or in the order of the author's name [...] and we can observe this quality in the entire Torah, that far beyond the simple meaning, it contains many secrets and concealed topics, which results in apparently inaccurate language at

times. And this is the case not only with the Holy Torah, but with all of the Holy scripture.
(*The Netziv of Vollozhin*, introduction to his Torah commentary *Ha'amek Davar*)

Unlike philosophers or scientists, poets allow themselves to be embraced by Being, permitting it to express and manifest itself as Being. With the emergence of poetic language or art, Being shines with its own significance. When poetry infuses all sciences or becomes the only mode of expression, the significance of the Last God will deeply resonate in the human heart. This Last God can only reveal itself when the human being allows Being to manifest, "think," and "encounter" itself exclusively in artistic expression, transcending all formal logic.

The future ones (*die Zu-künftigen*) represent a form of existence intimately linked to the idea of authentic time. They are not limited to a linear projection toward the future as a mere anticipation of events yet to come. On the contrary, they inhabit a complex temporal dimension where past, present, and future intertwine, generating an experience of time that is qualitatively different and transformative.

The uniqueness of the ones to come lies in their ability to position themselves at an ontological threshold, where the present and the forthcoming converge. This mode of existence involves an openness toward future possibilities and the ability to reconfigure the present from these potentialities. In this sense, they establish new horizons of meaning and existence, consolidating themselves as agents of transformation who transcend the inertia of ordinary chronology.

In Heidegger's philosophy, authentic time opposes the predominant linear and cumulative conception of time in everyday experience. Instead, he introduces a unified and dynamic temporality characterized by the non-sequential intertwining of the dimensions of past, present, and future, a phenomenon he describes with the concept of "ecstaticity." In this framework, the future ones represent how humans can inhabit this authentic temporality, freeing themselves from the constraints of a purely chronological historical understanding.

The German term *Zu-künftigen* illustrates this idea clearly. It is translated as "those who come toward" (*Zu-künft*); it emphasizes an active movement that does not simply involve the arrival of something in the future but an eruption into the present, capable of radically transforming it. This disruptive character highlights the capacity of the future ones to generate new orders of meaning from the present toward the possible.

The future ones open themselves to the *ereignis*, the appropriating event that redefines the connection between human beings and Being. They are not passive observers of becoming; rather, they shape a more authentic existence. This role demands overcoming the abandonment of Being (*Seinsverlassenheit*), a condition that Heidegger identifies as the ontological distance separating human beings from their essential foundation. They find

Chapter 20: The Six Assemblies Toward the Last God

themselves in a guiding attunement (*Leitstimmung*) that combines trembling (*Schrecken*) and reverential awe (*Scheu*). This emotional disposition should not be understood as a sign of despair nor as a reaction of paralyzing fear. Rather, it constitutes a response rooted in the mystery and magnitude of the *ereignis*. In it, reverence for the possibility of a radical transformation of Being in its very essence manifests itself.

Ultimately, the future ones are those who can transform the present from the future by fully inhabiting authentic temporality. They do not simply conform to existing historical or cultural circumstances; they actively contribute to the foundation of a horizon of uncharted meaning. This horizon redefines the relationship between the human and the Divine, enabling the eruption of the new. The future ones, therefore, are the heralds of change and the architects of a becoming that is still to be configured.

(6) The Last God (*Der letzte Gott*), which we can identify with the One of Plotinus, is finally revealed within the framework of the economy of salvation. This manifestation occurs because Being manages salvation and its appearance throughout history. Being has been managing and unfolding revelation through the ages, culminating in the supreme and final. In this journey, a meaning and understanding will emerge that transcend what was offered by traditional philosophy, from Plato to postmodernity, understood as an extension of modernity itself. More concretely, this appearance

Section VI: The Journey toward the Last God

marks the continuation of a hidden path initially traced by Plato, which is related to the origin of Being (*Seyn*) and whose manifestation occurs without consideration of the human being. The original event did not position humans as the center of everything. Rather, they were subordinated to the event, which was the true focal point. This God, in its aspiration to rise above Being, but still based on Being, becomes the very source and cause of Being, encompassing more than just the simple entity. The Last God is not a God in the traditional sense, nor can it be categorized as such. While it can only be revealed in the manifestation of Being, it transcends Being itself. This implies that there is a transition from Being to the Last God, a journey that the human being must undertake.

CHAPTER 21

A NEW PHILOSOPHICAL FRAMEWORK

The becoming of Being in its essence as *Seyn*, explained in the previous section, constitutes the starting point for understanding what Heidegger calls "the Last God." However, given the problems and errors into which metaphysics and organized religion have repeatedly fallen, it might be necessary first to ask how we should approach the question of this Last God. Or should we even ask about Him?

At this point, it is evident that it is impossible to inquire about the Last God through a "what," that is, within traditional philosophy. Based on epistemological structures, this approach would again reduce Him to the category of a being, to another lowercase god. Essentially, it would be a new version of the golden calf forged in the desert of Sinai, whose idea has persisted to this day in all organized religions, supported by their respective philosophical and theological foundations.

In this sense, we are dealing with a God completely different from the one conceived by ontotheology. His nature is radically distinct and transcends the traditional

Section VI: The Journey toward the Last God

categories of the theology of Being. In fact, Heidegger refers to this Last God as "The totally other over against gods who have been, especially over against the Christian God" (*Der ganz Andere gegen die Gewesenen, zumal gegen den christlichen*),[58] a definition with which he opens the seventh chapter of his *Contributions to Philosophy*. The Last God is an absolutely Other compared to all known gods, as we have shown earlier by quoting the book of Acts. That is to say, on one hand, He is unknown because He is unknowable, which makes Him a totally Other, beyond the reach of the institutionalized concept of God. However, He is the true God of all religions. By observing the intellectual trajectory followed by the author, we can discern that this Last God, characteristic of post-metaphysical thought, is defined exclusively by His negative characteristics. That is to say, He is anonymous, detached from any religion, synagogue, temple, mosque, or church, and transcends what is calculable and finite.

Furthermore, as God, He is completely foreign to the qualities with which metaphysics traditionally described God. In this sense, the Last God is not a supreme entity, a first cause, or an infinite creator. Moreover, He is not "last" in the sense of a chronological succession. On the contrary, He is Last in the sense of finality, for being absolutely undetermined, He is neither something nor

---

58. Heidegger, Martin. *Contributions to Philosophy (From Enowning)*, translated by Parvis Emad and Kenneth Maly (Bloomington: Indiana University Press, 1999), Section VII: "The Last God", 283.

someone. He lies in the background, constituting the foundation of all determinations without Himself being determined. In this sense, He is pure poverty because He lacks essence, name, or identity.

Heidegger has stated that the last is, in reality, the first because in the search, one arrives at the last, which is truly the first and original, as already preached in the Gospel of Matthew when it says:

> Thus, the last will be first, and the first, last.
> (Matthew, 20:16)

In other words, what is found first in the order of Being turns out to be the last in the order of thought. The primordial, which constitutes the essence of Being, only reveals itself at the end of a profound process of reflection. Therefore, the original foundation, which is the first in ontological reality, is reached by concluding the philosophical inquiry. This paradox highlights the inherent complexity in thinking and the very nature of Being, where the most elementary and fundamental is discovered only after a long, arduous, and necessary analysis. For this reason, Heidegger argues in *Contributions to Philosophy* that the advancement of Being as an idea is the end of the Divine; in other words, the greater the understanding, the greater the distance from God. Humanity can only approach God again when it abandons the idea of treating Him as an object of thought.

Section VI: The journey toward the Last God

הִנֵּה יָמִים בָּאִים נְאֻם ה' אֱלֹהִים וְהִשְׁלַחְתִּי רָעָב בָּאָרֶץ לֹא רָעָב לַלֶּחֶם וְלֹא צָמָא לַמַּיִם כִּי אִם לִשְׁמֹעַ אֵת דִּבְרֵי ה':
(עמוס ח', י"א)

Behold, days are coming, says the Lord God, and I will send famine upon the land, not a famine for bread nor a thirst for water, but for hearing the words of the Lord.

(Amos, 8:11)

It is perhaps for this reason that Heidegger does not ask about the Last God using any of these terms and instead attempts to define it through what it is not:

> The last god is not an end (*Ende*) but rather the beginning as it resonates unto and in-itself and thus the highest shape of not-granting (*Verweigerung*), since the inceptual withdraws from all holding-fast and holds sway (*west*) only in towering over (*Überragen*) all of that which as what is to come is already seized within the inceptual—and is delivered up to its [the inceptual's] determining power. The end is only where a being has torn itself away from the truth of be-ing and has denied every question-worthiness (*Fragwürdigkeit*), and that means every differentiating, in order to comport itself in endless time within endless possibilities of what is thus torn away. The end is the unceasing

etcetera from which from the beginning and long since the last (*das Letzte*) as the most inceptual has withdrawn. The end never sees itself; it takes itself instead to be completion and will therefore be least of all ready and prepared either to await the last or to experience it.[59]

Let us analyze this complex, and even strange, passage part by part:

The last god is not an end (*Ende*) but rather the beginning [...].

The beginning that took place with pre-Socratic thought, which was later diverted by the *orthótes* of Platonic philosophy, is recovered deeper since this beginning still belonged to Being. However, this new beginning or return to the origin is understood as *Abgrund*, not as *Grund* or "foundation." That is to say, it is understood as what lies beyond the foundation or beyond Being, a place where the Last God "resides," transcending any ontotheological basis. This primordial return is a gaze into the roots, revealing a deeper understanding. In this context, the principle or Being constitutes only one half of the whole, while the

---

59. Heidegger, Martin. *Contributions to Philosophy (From Enowning)*, translated by Parvis Emad and Kenneth Maly (Bloomington: Indiana University Press, 1999), section VII, "The Last God," §256, 293.

Section VI: The Journey toward the Last God

Last God would represent the other half, devoid of foundation.

> **[...] and thus the highest shape of not-granting(*Verweigerung*), since the inceptual withdraws from all holding-fast and holds sway (*west*) only in towering over (*Überragen*) [...].**

The Last God is not limited by the historical determinations of Being, such as essence, substance, accident, act, power, idea, matter, mind, or consciousness. It transcends all these categories, distancing itself from each of these fixations. The Last God withdraws from any form of definition or limitation. Its action is essential and guided by its own nature. From this perspective, the aim is no longer to gather Being in its historical forms. It is necessary to understand it in an absolute and superior dimension that transcends all specific determinations. In the beginning of metaphysics, although Being reveals itself or seems to reveal itself, it is susceptible to being controlled through technique. However, for the sacred history to unfold in its ultimacy, Being itself no longer manifests as such. The Last God reveals itself, remaining foreign to any attempt at technical domination. This change marks a crucial transition: while we could attempt to understand Being through technical methods, the Last God is unreachable by human capabilities. That is why:

CHAPTER 21: A NEW PHILOSOPHICAL FRAMEWORK

> **[...] only in towering over (*Überragen*) all of that which as what is to come is already seized within the inceptual—and is delivered up to its [the inceptual's] determining power.**

Being nothing in itself, for it is merely an abyss (*Abgrund*), the Last God can make everything else be. Being devoid of any specific determination, it has the faculty to determine everything without being a logical cause. Furthermore, this absence of defined qualities bestows upon it an absolute and universal power, allowing it to be the source of all existence. Therefore, in its vacuity, the Last God becomes the origin of diversity and multiplicity, establishing a parallel with the Neoplatonic concept of the One, which generates all realities by its supreme simplicity. The absence of determination becomes a universal determinative capacity. This paradox highlights a profound idea in metaphysics: the ultimate source of all Being transcends limitations or definitions. This same principle is already present in the Supreme Lord, as mentioned in one of the main Puranas:

राजन् परस्य तनुभृज्जनननाप्ययेहा
मायाविडम्बनमवेहि यथा नटस्य ।
सृष्ट्वात्मनेदमनुविश्य विहृत्य चान्ते
संहृत्य चात्ममहिनोपरत: स आस्ते ॥

Section VI: The journey toward the Last God

> *rājan parasya tanu-bhṛj-jananāpyayehā*
> *māyā-viḍambanam avehi yathā naṭasya*
> *sṛṣṭvātmanedam anuviśya vihṛtya cānte*
> *saṁhṛtya cātma-mahinoparataḥ sa āste*

My dear King, you should understand that the Supreme Lord's appearance and disappearance, which resemble those of embodied conditioned souls, are actually a show enacted by His illusory energy, just like the performance of an actor. After creating this universe He enters into it, plays within it for some time, and at last winds it up. Then the Lord remains situated in His own transcendental glory, having ceased from the functions of cosmic manifestation.

(*Bhāgavata Purana*, 11.31.11)

Even though it is pure indeterminacy, the revelation of the Last God involves negating the ontotheology's god. In this negation, god dies, hence allowing the Last God to reveal Himself in all His incomprehensibility, making evident the unmanifest manifestation of Being with which He reveals Himself.

The end is only where a being has torn itself away from the truth of be-ing and has denied every question-worthiness (*Fragwürdigkeit*), and that means every differentiating, in order to comport

Chapter 21: A new philosophical framework

itself in endless time within endless possibilities of what is thus torn away.

This paragraph focuses on a fundamental issue of his philosophy: the interrelationship between beings, Being, and truth. In this fragment, Heidegger posits that the "end" or culmination of an authentic understanding occurs when beings, that is, individuals, separate themselves from the truth of Being. This separation entails a renunciation of questionability. The term *Fragwürdigkeit* underscores the importance of the capacity to question, a crucial quality for achieving a deeper understanding of Being. Abandoning this questionability implies that beings stop searching for the truth of Being and settle for a superficial existence devoid of roots.

Heidegger also points out that this state of separation induces beings to behave indefinitely, according to the possibilities offered by this state of disconnection. This suggests a life devoid of authentic purpose, guided only by immediate and superficial occurrences, rather than a more authentic and meaningful existence connected to the truth of Being. Heidegger is critical of the superficiality and lack of depth in the life of beings that has lost their connection to the truth of Being and, therefore, their capacity to ask meaningful questions. For him, this state of disconnection and conformism represents the true "end" of authentic existence.

Opening up to the revelation of the Last God involves approaching the limit of the existence of the

Section VI: The journey toward the Last God

"I" as a being and independent consciousness, where a separation, a disconnection, between the being and the truth of Being is perceived. In this realm, the "I" emerges as an egoic phenomenon, creating a space where God is objectified and deprived of dignity through questions such as "What does God want?" or "Why did He create the world?" In this context of the egoic phenomenon space, all differences, distinctions, and determinations dissolve, leading to the disappearance of the god of ontotheology, as there are neither concepts nor theology in this space. The overcoming and transcendence of the egoic phenomenon constitute an essential preamble for the manifestation of the Last God. This process involves displacing the "I" as the fundamental center of existence, enabling access to a transcendental dimension. In its ontological and psychological dimension, the ego functions as a limit that prevents the approach to a higher reality. The rupture of ego-centric structures allows humans to open up to broader dimensions of existence and the Absolute.

This prelude or preamble of the Last God must be understood as an intensification of the egoic god that appears as a god that is nothing more than the image and likeness of the ego. Paradoxically, in the approach to the Last God, instead of diminishing, the egoic phenomenon intensifies to its maximum extent, reaching a final expansion that leads to its total dissolution. The ego emerges, transforms, and eventually nullifies itself, leading to a radically new understanding of Being and

Chapter 21: A new philosophical framework

the Divine. The paradox lies in that, as the ego intensifies to its limit, it triggers its own dissolution, thus allowing an authentic approach to the Last God.

The end is the unceasing etcetera from which from the beginning and long since the last (*das Letzte*) as the most inceptual has withdrawn. The end never sees itself; it takes itself instead to be completion and will therefore be least of all ready and prepared either to await the last or to experience it.

In this context, Heidegger proposes a vision of the end as a continuous process or becoming, in contrast to the idea of a final and definitive term. This end, although it considers itself a conclusion, does not understand its true essence. The "ultimacy," understood as the most fundamental, has remained hidden for a long time, indicating that the essential never reveals itself immediately. Due to this misunderstanding, the end is not adequately disposed of nor prepared to await and experience what is truly fundamental. Therefore, by seeing itself as a conclusion, the end reveals its inability to face the true nature of ultimacy.

This conception of Heidegger suggests that the end is not a static state but rather one that persists incessantly. The idea that ultimacy has been withdrawn from the beginning indicates an absence of

Section VI: The Journey toward the Last God

the essential in the realm of beings, contributing to the misunderstanding of the end regarding its own nature. By believing it is a conclusion, the end reveals its lack of readiness to confront the true nature of what is last.

Ultimacy, as initial, implies that the Last God is the first in the sequence, preceding all the gods of the religions. He has withdrawn from Being since Plato, leaving only an echo of His presence, a resonance of His absence. The withdrawal of this God has plunged human beings into a state of despair that has led them to create gods, golden calves, and religions to worship them. Not only that, they have also institutionalized religion, organized spirituality, and even structured the sociopolitical dimension of humanity. This process of invention and religious structuring has been, in essence, an attempt to fill that void, to silence the deafening silence left by His withdrawal. Just as the eye cannot see itself nor the teeth bite themselves, so does the end never perceive itself. If the end knew itself, it would lose its unity because it would be dual or objectual. The end's incapacity for self-recognition is essential to its unitary nature, as any act of perception would divide it into subject and object, thus destroying its integrity. This paradox underscores the absolute condition and its ineffability, reflecting the same difficulty humans face when attempting to grasp the essence of the Last God. If observation or pure consciousness could be perceived, then it could no longer be consciousness or observation but simply an observed object. The essence of our true

CHAPTER 21: A NEW PHILOSOPHICAL FRAMEWORK

identity lies in the point where beings have distanced themselves from Being. The end of our existence lies in this fracture between Being and the beings. As an egoic phenomenon, we are the fracture or division.

Therefore, Heidegger conceives of the end as a perpetual state incapable of grasping the essential due to the absence of the fundamental from the beginning. Understanding the end as a conclusion reveals the inability to deal with the profound nature of the essential. In summary, the end is not a definitive point but a continuous process in constant motion. It never fully comprehends the crucial because these elements remain hidden from the beginning.

An existence without a clear purpose implies a life devoid of the sense of Being. As presented by contemporary philosophy, this vacuity acts as a prelude to absolute emptiness, which strips essences from the determinations that, in turn, cover the Last God. In this context, we see how the multiple layers covering the Last God are gradually emptied of their essential content, reflecting a disintegration of the fundamental certainties that once constituted His nature. By questioning and dismantling these foundations, modern philosophical reflection reveals a background of nihilism where meaning dissolves, exposing an ontological nakedness that redefines both the understanding of Being and the ultimate divinity.

Therefore, and in virtue of what has been stated, we can speak of a context of three beginnings. In the first

Section VI: The Journey toward the Last God

beginning, Being reveals itself as *physis*. The second, marked by ontotheology, leads to the concealment of Being. Finally, in the third, Being reveals itself in the event as the Last God. For this to happen, the ontotheological god must die. In order to sustain themselves, it is essential to overcome the conceptual god humans created from the egoic sphere. As we approach the third beginning, the concepts defining the second begin to lose meaning. Then, the Last God emerges in His true essence, beyond all conceptualization, objectification, and comprehension.

This process should not be confused with the siren songs of postmodernity and other versions of the same idea. Postmodernity is generally seen as positive because it almost liberates all traditional structures. Contemporary philosophy, in particular, discusses the death of God and modern man, the end of history, and the decline of reason, which it views as chains. This liberating revolution celebrates the end and destruction, taking for granted that there is nothing and no one to subject us after God, reason, and history. Within this framework, postmodernity announces the end of metaphysics as an end in itself while simultaneously presupposing a complete and dignified human being who has himself.

However, from our point of view, this is not about celebrating the fall of metaphysics for the mere sake of emptying everything. The tendency of postmodernity to strip meaning from existing structures must certainly be valued. However, the true purpose must be deeper and not be satisfied with killing God to establish a new subject in His place. As we have been saying in this brief study, following Heidegger, the death of traditional concepts should not be seen simply as an empty ending. The goal cannot be emptiness itself but to embrace the absolute nihilism finally. This emptying from the egoic phenomenon, which allows us to see and understand the direction of events, is necessary to allow the Last God to reveal Himself. The disappearance of metaphysics is a crucial phase for manifesting a new divine reality.

CHAPTER 22

LANGUAGE AS THE HOUSE OF BEING

The revelation of the divine reality is closely related to "passage" and "readiness." In a way, these two terms outline a transition that Heidegger always connects to language as the house of Being. He frames this relationship from the need to exhaust all instances of metaphysical categories, allowing the transition from the personal God to the impersonal one, from the metaphysical God to the Last God. Humanity has turned to God to explain everything from creation and love to the purpose of life and even sin. It is essential to overcome all barriers, to traverse the passage and reach the place of the non-ground, the abyss where the Last God shines.

As we have advanced earlier, this passage occurs in a dialectic between the religious gods of metaphysics and the subject of manifestation, that is, between Being and the gods. Joseph Campbell said that the gods of the metaphysical era were masks of the true and Last God. For this reason, although the Last God reveals Himself in the realm of Being, His manifestation will depend solely on Him. Let us examine this relationship more closely, as Heidegger himself presents it.

> Not attributing being to "gods" initially means only that being does not stand "over" gods and that gods do not stand "over" being. But gods do need (*bedürfen*) Being (Seyn), which saying already thinks the essential sway of Being (Seyn). "Gods" do not need Being (Seyn) as their ownhood, wherein they themselves take a stance. "Gods" need (*brauchen*) Being (Seyn) in order through Being (Seyn)—which does not belong to gods—nevertheless to belong to themselves. Being (Seyn) is needed (*das Gebrauchte*) by gods: it is their need.[60]

The ontological relationship between Being and the gods constitutes a fundamental dialectic where existence and essence intertwine, giving meaning to the act of being. In this metaphysical framework, Being can be conceived as the condition of possibility for all manifestation. At the same time, the gods represent the concrete manifestations, the particular determinations that make Being "something" defined. The connection between the two is made through the copula "to be

---

60. Martin Heidegger, *Contributions to Philosophy (From Enowning)*, trans. Parvis Emad and Kenneth Maly (Bloomington: Indiana University Press, 1999), section VIII, "Be-ing," §259, "Philosophy," 309.

Chapter 22: Language as the House of Being

something," in which Being provides existence, while the "something" gives the essence or determination that concretizes Being in a specific form. Therefore, Being becomes the ontological foundation that allows the existence of the gods, while the gods act as the content, the multiplicity that shapes and gives meaning to Being. This interdependence implies that, without Being, the gods would be reduced to mere immanent ideas, empty concepts that lack reality or effective presence; they would be mere abstractions without place or substance in the world of becoming.

On the other hand, a Being without the gods, without their multiple determinations, would be reduced to pure and empty existence, a sort of indeterminate substrate, lacking content or differentiation. In other words, Being without the gods would be an entity empty of meaning, a mere possibility that never becomes realized in a manifested reality. Therefore, Being requires the gods to acquire content, form, and manifestation, while the gods depend on Being to gain existence, to appear and make themselves present in the realm of the real. A necessary correlation is thus established, in which Being and the gods co-involve one another: Being becomes the horizon in which the gods appear, and the gods become the concretization of Being.

To some extent, this relationship is analogous to the traditional metaphysical distinction between act and potency; Being is the universal potency of existence,

Section VI: The journey toward the Last God

while the gods represent the concrete acts that actualize that potentiality in particular forms. In other words, Being without the gods would be an abyss of pure indeterminacy, an open field that never becomes anything. On the other hand, the gods without Being would be a specter of ideas without the possibility of achieving real existence, remaining as mere potentialities that would never appear. Both acquire their full meaning only in their reciprocal relationship and dependence: Being finds its realization and determination through the gods, while the gods achieve their effective existence through Being. However, this relationship requires another figure to make it possible—the human being. Heidegger explores this issue in the following way:

> "Man" and "god" are word-hulls without history if the truth of Being (Seyn) in them is not brought to language. Being (Seyn) holds sway as the "between" (*Zwischen*) for god and man, but in such a way that this between-space (*Zwischenraum*) first grants essential possibility for god and man—a "between" that surges over its shore and from this surging-over first lets the shore stand as shore, a shore that always belongs to the stream of en-owning, is always sheltered in the richness of the possibilities of god and man, always this side and the other side of the inexhaustible relations in whose clearing worlds

are enjoined and sink away, earths are disclosed and endure destruction. But also in this or that way Being must above all remain unreadable (*deutungslos*): the bold venture against the nothing to which Being (Seyn) owns the origin.[61]

Heidegger offers an interesting reflection on the relationship between man, God, and Being, and how these concepts come to life and gain meaning only when expressed in the language of the truth of Being. In this context, he asserts that, without this articulation, man and God become "empty words." That is, without a deep and authentic understanding of Being, our notions of the Divine and the human lack substance and relevance. In other words, language allows the relationship between Being, God, and man; without it, neither the human being nor God would have any meaning. In the dimension of language, God and human beings have a relationship determined by the word, without which they cannot relate or possess an identity in relation to each other. What is the human being without speaking with God, and what is God without communicating with the human being? Precisely, God and the human being are defined as such because they speak to each other. The human being prays, and God reveals Himself, expressing each other in one another,

---

61. Martin Heidegger, *Contributions to Philosophy (From Enowning)*, trans. Parvis Emad and Kenneth Maly (Bloomington: Indiana University Press, 1999), section VIII, "Be-ing," §267, "Be-ing", 335.

explaining the other in the one, as the following quote from the Torah expresses:

אַתָּה חוֹנַנְתָּנוּ לְמַדַּע תּוֹרָתֶךָ, וַתְּלַמְּדֵנוּ לַעֲשׂוֹת חֻקֵּי רְצוֹנֶךָ, וַתַּבְדֵּל ה' אֱלֹהֵינוּ בֵּין קֹדֶשׁ לְחוֹל בֵּין אוֹר לְחֹשֶׁךְ בֵּין יִשְׂרָאֵל לָעַמִּים בֵּין יוֹם הַשְּׁבִיעִי לְשֵׁשֶׁת יְמֵי הַמַּעֲשֶׂה.

(תפילת שמונה עשרה למוצאי שבת וחג, ברכת חונן הדעת)

You have gifted us [with the ability] to know Your Torah and taught us to fulfill the statutes of Your will. You made a distinction, Lord, our God, between sacred and mundane, between light and darkness, between Israel and the nations, between the seventh day and the six days of creation.

(*Siddur*, Evening *Amidah*, prayer for Saturday night, "Blessing of Distinction")

To assert that language mediates between man and God implies recognizing that, ultimately, it is Being itself that reveals itself through language. Language acts as a "between" (*Zwischen*), linking God and man and enabling the essence of both. This "inter-space" unites but also, and especially, establishes the necessary conditions for both God and man to exist in their purest form. This intermediate space is crucial because it defines the boundaries and simultaneously arises from the difficulties these boundaries create. This is why Heidegger affirms that language is the house of Being,

Chapter 22: Language as the House of Being

because the essential connection between God and man is established and maintained solely through language. This leads Heidegger to make a final turn in his argument: if the Last God reveals Himself in the realm of Being, it is also the Last God who becomes Being. This is so because He speaks, because He expresses Himself through language. In this sense, as Aristotle already intuited, the human being is the Being that possesses speech. This means that the human being achieves true humanity by communicating with God, just as God is fully God by communicating with the human being.

To understand the importance of language, we can explain it this way: the tree is a tree because it has a name. This implies that if something lacks a name to identify it, it does not acquire its being. Without a name, word, or language (*logos*), nothing would be identifiable, and thus, it would not be. This ability to name and define through language connects the human being with their environment and, above all, inaugurates a relationship with the Divine. The act of speaking and naming is a manifestation of Being that transcends the purely human and touches the sacred. In this sense, the word acts as the vehicle, the passage that allows the encounter between the human being and God. Through it, both reveal themselves to each other, establishing a continuous and reciprocal communication that grounds and gives meaning to existence itself.

Furthermore, this argument brings into sharper focus an already highlighted aspect: for Heidegger, Being is not a static category nor an abstract concept. On the contrary, it is a dynamic and continuous becoming that manifests in the world through language. When he asserts that language is the house of Being, Heidegger indicates that Being is revealed and understood through language. Being subsists **as a** language between God and human beings. In other words, language is the medium that inaugurates the original relationship between the Divine and the human, giving meaning to them and to Being itself.

This language is not limited to words but involves a deeper understanding manifested in symbols, rituals, and spiritual experiences. Sacred texts, prophetic revelations, and prayers exemplify how God uses language to communicate with humanity. However, human beings are not merely passive receivers of this divine language. Through prayer, meditation, and other spiritual practices, humans communicate with God. This continuous and reciprocal dialogue is expressed in a language that, although it transcends words, resides in them.

As a result, Heidegger also suggests that our understanding of Being, both of ourselves and the world around us, is intrinsically tied to this dialogue. Being is revealed in this exchange, in this constant communication that gives meaning and direction to our existence.

Language, placed at the margin, contrasts with God and the human situated at the center. However, the marginal becomes central, as human beings would not be truly human if they did not communicate with God.

Chapter 22: Language as the house of being

This mutual dialogue, therefore, transforms what was merely an instrument into something constitutive and fundamental. If language shapes humanity and divinity, then its absence would transform Being into the Last God. At the same time, human beings would disappear, for, as an egoic phenomenon, they are essentially language. Without language, both the personal God and the ego would disappear.

To delve deeper into this idea, Heidegger emphasizes that Being is inextricably linked to *ereignis*. This, as we have pointed out, must be understood as a dynamic and continuous process that simultaneously reveals and hides the richness of its possibilities. This event is realized through language, which has the power to appropriate the human being while the human being appropriates God. In this context, we can infer that language acts as a destroyer of the word, as *ereignis* manifests itself through revelation. Revelation occurs in language because it is through this medium that the appropriating event takes place. The *páthos* of listening, the emotional and receptive disposition we referred to earlier, becomes the essential attitude of the human being to capture the destructive voice of Being. This active listening is not merely auditory but a form of total openness to the revelation of Being, allowing the human being to be in tune with the hidden and revealing dimensions of *ereignis*. Therefore, as we mentioned before, always hidden in the richness of its innumerable possibilities, Being unfolds from above and toward the heights of inexhaustible relations. In this clearing, where worlds are disposed and precipitated, the lands become the refuge and support of destruction. That is, everything is prepared for eventual destruction in that final manifestation of language. In this final revelation, language, in addition to constructing, also has the power to collapse, always keeping latent the duality of creation and annihilation that defines the event of Being.

Ereignis represents Being manifesting itself and appropriating the word, thus destroying the human word. In that instant, silence arises, and human beings can find serenity in the sacred, awaiting the revelation of the Last God. Silence emerges with the final word or definitive revelation. This Last God, therefore, only reveals Himself in the stillness of a silence not sought by the human being but established by the withdrawal of Being itself.

Essentially, the word of Being is silence, linked to resonance and the ineffable. More than an absence of sound, it is a presence full of meaning. Moreover, this silence is a stillness that transcends ordinary understanding, allowing a direct and pure connection with the Divine. In this stillness, the resonance of Being is perceived not as an empty echo but as a full manifestation of Being in its highest expression. The Last God, therefore, reveals Himself in this serenity imposed by Being, a state where human language has been transcended, and only the resonating silence remains, enabling true communion with the sacred.

Chapter 22: Language as the House of Being

This state of serenity and silence is the space where the human being, freed from the bonds of language, can truly perceive the divine presence and achieve a deeper understanding of existence. This very situation seems to be described in the Book of Genesis, where we read:

וַיִּקְרָא ה' אֱלֹהִים אֶל־הָאָדָם וַיֹּאמֶר לוֹ אַיֶּכָּה:

(בראשית ג', ט')

And the Lord God called to the man, and said to him, "Where are you?"

(Genesis, 3:9)

For many, it is surprising that the Bible begins with the theme of God searching for man. The first question posed in the Old Testament is: "Where are you?" This initial inquiry coincides with the first question in the New Testament, in the Gospel of Matthew, where wise men arrive asking, "Where is he?" (Matthew 2:2). In both cases, an essential search is emphasized, a longing for encounter and connection. While in the Old Testament, God seeks man, revealing a divine initiative, in the New Testament, men seek God, demonstrating a human desire to reach the Divine. This symmetry between the two testaments highlights the reciprocal relationship between the human and the Divine, a mutual search throughout the biblical narrative.

In response to God's question, "*Aieka?*" or "Where are you?" Abraham, Jacob, Samuel, and Isaiah replied

Section VI: The Journey toward the Last God

with "*Hineni*," which translates as "Here I am." This Hebrew term can be broken down into "*hine*," meaning "here," and *ani*, meaning "I." Thus, "*hine*" represents consciousness or Being, while "I" denotes presence. Consequently, Abraham's response can be interpreted as a manifestation of *Dasein*, of "being-there," according to Heideggerian terminology. This interaction emphasizes a response to the divine presence while likewise affirming Abraham's existence and consciousness. The expression *hineni* is not simply a literal response but a profound declaration of being present and aware at the moment, resonating with the idea of *Dasein* as a presence situated in the world.

Therefore, if appearing and speaking are the same event, then, conversely, disappearing and ceasing to speak must also be the same. Instead of being seen as two distinct events, they must be understood as a single essential phenomenon. Technique is the use of the language of categories to capture and dominate Being. This categorization process defines but also constrains, limiting the understanding and existence of Being. By ceasing to speak, Being loses its identity as something recognizable. In other words, with silence, Being frees itself from the limitations imposed by language. As the wise saying goes: "We are masters of our silence but slaves of our words."

However, this "liberation" of the language of Being implies certain risks and temptations: they are siren songs that Western philosophy would do well to ignore to avoid being dragged into the abyss. One of these risks is the topic of nothingness mentioned earlier, which arises once we accept that silence, meaning the end of language, implies the disidentification of Being. In other words, one might claim that a Being without identity is a Being that is not, and as such, only equates to nothingness (*nihil*). This appears to be the path followed by certain lines of thought that have confused the end of metaphysics with the need to adopt nihilism. Even Sartre reflected on this error, stating that, like every dreamer, he had confused disenchantment with the Truth. Heidegger argues that Being must persevere in its struggle against nothingness, an effort that gives rise to all that exists. Nothingness is the essence of the beings; confronting implies opposing the very essence of beings. This confrontation is inevitable and essential for the manifestation and understanding of Being. The struggle against nothingness is, ultimately, a fundamental act that unveils and challenges the intrinsic nature of beings.

CHAPTER 23

BEING AND GOD IN THE QUADRATURE

As we saw in the previous chapter, Heidegger helps us understand that Being is the foundation that gives meaning to both man and God through the language in which it resides. Only through the language of the truth of Being can we avoid reducing these concepts to mere "empty words." To better understand this issue, let us now turn our attention to the following quote:

> But when Being (Seyn) is the needfulness of god, when Being (Seyn) itself finds its truth only in en-thinking (*Er-denken* or "ex-cogitation"), and when this thinking is philosophy (in the other beginning), then "gods" need be-ing-historical thinking, i.e., philosophy. "Gods" need philosophy, not as if they themselves must philosophize for the sake of their godding (*Gotterung*), but rather philosophy must be if "gods" are again to come into decision and if history is to obtain its ownmost ground. Within the perspective of gods be-ing-historical thinking is determined as that thinking of be-ing

that understands the abground of needfulness of and by Being (Seyn) as primary and never seeks the essential sway of Being (Seyn) in the divine itself as what is supposedly the most-being. Be-ing-historical thinking is outside any theology and also knows no atheism, in the sense of a worldview or a doctrine structured in some other way. [...] But understanding be-ing-historical thinking from within the perspective of gods is "the same" as attempting to indicate what is ownmost to this thinking from within the perspective of man.[62]

The first part of the quote presents the idea that Being is essential to the necessity of God, finding its truth in the "ex-cogitation," a term that can be interpreted as a manifestation of consciousness.

But when Being (Seyn) is the needfulness of god, when Being (Seyn) itself finds its truth only in en-thinking (*Er-denken* or "ex-cogitation"), and when this thinking is philosophy (in the other beginning), then "gods" need be-ing-historical thinking, i.e., philosophy.

---

62. Martin Heidegger, *Contributions to Philosophy (From Enowning)*, trans. Parvis Emad and Kenneth Maly (Bloomington: Indiana University Press, 1999), section VIII, "Be-ing," §259, "Philosophy," 309.

Chapter 23: Being and God in the Quadrature

This means that if God cannot manifest without Being, it is because Being is the manifestation itself. As we mentioned earlier, God would have no means to reveal Himself without Being. Therefore, the revelation of the Last God depends on Being. That is why we can assert that when God remains silent, He is the One of Plotinus, whereas when He communicates, He does so by revealing Himself to the human being in the realm of Being, that is, by manifesting Himself. Therefore, the act of God's revelation is intrinsically linked to the existence of Being, making communication an essential expression of His divine manifestation.

In this sense, what has been said so far suggests that Being manifests as God or the One, while God or the One represents Being in its unmanifested state. God transcends Being but requires it to reveal Himself. That is, there is only revelation within manifestation. Likewise, Being depends on God to acquire entity or personality since Being, as a manifestation in its full purity or *physis*, as the pre-Socratics would say, lacks definition and essence. This relationship of interdependence between Being and God underscores a mutual need. In its naked essence, being is nothing without God's transcendence. In order to reveal Himself, God needs Being as manifestation before the human being. Therefore, we can infer that Being acquires meaning and presence only through its relationship with the Divine, that is, by revealing the sacred. On the other hand, God, in order to interact with the world and the man who inhabits it, expresses Himself through Being, showing His transcendental nature and His need for a means of revelation. Thus, Being and God are intrinsically connected, forming a dual dimension in which each finds its realization in the other.

This relationship between Being and the Last God also has a third component, which allows the relationship to flow, structuring the becoming of all existence. This third component is philosophy, ranging from its purely ontological dimension to its hermeneutical radicalization. The introduction of philosophy in this framework is, undoubtedly, a clear return to Hegel and his historical-phenomenological vision of reality. Following Hegel, we can affirm that the gods, like "the One" of Plotinus, overflow rather than create. They do not think because thinking involves a duality between the thinking subject and the thought object. To know themselves, however, the gods need to create something distinct from them: a mirror in which they can reflect and appreciate themselves and a reflective surface in which they can identify and recognize themselves. This mirror or "otherness" is philosophical speculation, which acts as a "speculum" or "mirror." In this philosophical speculation, the gods can observe and understand themselves. The creation of this mirror is essential for the gods to have a means of self-knowledge, for without an opening between the thinker and the thought, no reflection could occur. Philosophy is, in this sense, the means through which the Divine contemplates itself. In this process of speculation, philosophy is the reflection that allows for deep introspection, providing the gods with an understanding of their own essence. Philosophy reflects on God, and through this discipline, God (re-) knows Himself throughout the history of philosophy.

Referring to Hegel, Heidegger states that the history of philosophy is an *itinerarium ad menti deum*, that is, "a journey of the mind toward God." However, as it concerns the divine mind, this must be understood as God's mind's itinerary toward Himself. This journey is not merely an intellectual exploration of the Divine but a process in which God's mind reveals itself by understanding its own essence. In this journey, philosophy acts as a means through which God self-knows, reflecting and uncovering the depths of His Being. The history of philosophy, hence, becomes the record of this sacred journey, where every thought and philosophical reflection contributes to divine self-understanding. Heidegger expresses this in the second part of the quote when he writes:

Within the perspective of gods be-ing-historical thinking is determined as that thinking of be-ing that understands the abground of needfulness of and by Being (Seyn) as primary and never seeks the essential sway of Being (Seyn) in the divine itself as what is supposedly the most-being.

Section VI: The Journey toward the Last God

According to this, the abyss of the necessity of Being resides in the ontological difference we addressed in the initial parts of this study: it is understanding that the question of Being will never be exhausted in the beings. Beings are inexhaustible, and the answer to the enigma of Being will never be found in them. Such an answer can only be found in Being itself. The fundamental error of human beings and traditional epistemology lies in seeking ontic solutions to an ontological question. Therefore, this "utmost entity" consists of conceiving God as a supreme entity that must be believed in and in whom we must place our faith. This concept is, precisely, that of the God of ontotheology, a supreme entity that emphasizes belief without the need for a direct vision.

An example of this can be observed in Christianity. Jesus preached about the Kingdom of God. The apostles, in turn, preached about Jesus. Today, Catholics preach about the Church. Catholics center their message on the Church; the Church preaches about Christ, and Christ, in His time, spoke of the Kingdom of God.

This history of philosophy, understood as the history of Being itself, is not theological. As Heidegger himself warns in the third part of the quote:

> **Be-ing-historical thinking is outside any theology and also knows no atheism, in the sense of a worldview or a doctrine structured in some other way. [...] But**

Chapter 23: Being and God in the quadrature

understanding be-ing-historical thinking from within the perspective of gods is "the same" as attempting to indicate what is ownmost to this thinking from within the perspective of man.

Atheism, as the negative version of the same theology, opposes only theology and, therefore, cannot position itself against the Last God since this God does not exist in traditional terms. The history of traditional philosophy, read linearly as a succession of solutions to problems, is the history of thought about beings. To discover the foundation, we must return to studying the history of philosophy from Being, as the pre-Socratics Heraclitus, Parmenides, and Anaximander already did. This means reading beings through Being, and not vice versa, as has generally been done since the eruption of Platonic-Aristotelian philosophy.

Rereading the history of Being from Being itself will require an original approach. This last movement requires interpreting Being through the Last God. In this way, we access the foundation, the unfounded, the abyss, the *Abgrund*. This reaffirms that Being in its purity (*Seyn*), as pure manifestation, is only accessible through the revelation of the Last God, while this revelation can only occur in the unveiling of Being. Therefore, reaching this new beginning requires transcending all reality's categorization, to access Being devoid of categories. This involves observing or, more precisely, contemplating

Section VI: The journey toward the Last God

without the intervention of an objectifying mind that turns the contemplated into an external object separate from thought.

This implies the need for a new philosophical framework. In order to think of Being without reifying it and to allow the revelation of the Last God, human beings must go beyond transcendental epistemology and adopt a different mode of thinking. This is where Heidegger's quadrature (*Geviert*), presents itself as an alternative philosophical approach. It transcends the usual structures of debate, and in it, both the revelation of the Last God and the emergence of a new way of thinking about Being are possible.

In this context, Heidegger presents us with a four-sided structure—so to speak—that cannot be reduced or simplified to the traditional dualist structure. This duality is predominant since Plato has limited our capacity by reducing Being to an entity and confining God to a calf. In contrast, the quadrature is a structure of reception, not of exteriorization or separation, opening a broader space for understanding Being. It is important to note that it would be a mistake to place the deities at one of the vertices of the quadrature (*Geviert*) as a renunciation of the exclusive role of the ultimacy of God in *Contributions to Philosophy*. This disposition should not be seen as a diminution of divine importance but rather as a form of philosophical articulation that allows understanding of the complexity of Being and its relationship with the Whole.

Chapter 23: Being and God in the quadrature

The *Geviert*, as a conceptual structure, does not seek to displace God from His position of ultimacy. Rather, it proposes a perspective where the deities, the earth, the sky, and mortals coexist in interdependence and balance. In this sense, the ultimacy of God is preserved and understood in a broader context without losing His primacy or essential nature. The deities are integrated into the quadrature to keep it open, meaning that the "earth" (the inexhaustible dimension of potential), the "sky" (actuality in its manifestation), and the "mortals" (the human being, the only being capable of radically questioning itself, and therefore always tempted to flee before such tremendous power) do not become vertices of one-sidedness.

From this Heideggerian context of quadrature, as a philosophical approach, we can now affirm that the earth represents the inexhaustible dimension of potential because it is the one that receives the power of the sky in its actualized form. Everything that exists in a state of potential becomes fertile earth, prepared to be penetrated by the energies of the sky and, thus, enable creative activity in the world. This interaction between the earth and the sky is essential for generating new realities, where the earth acts as the passive receptacle that gives rise to a fruitful creative activity when activated by the sky. In this sense, the earth is not only a space of potentialities but also the necessary foundation for manifesting divine creativity in the mundane realm.

Section VI: The Journey Toward the Last God

On the other hand, when we refer to the sky, we conceive it as the actuality in its manifestation since every new event in the world is presented as an actualization of previous potentialities. In this sense, the sky symbolizes the dynamic force that transforms the possible into the real. Each novel event is a concrete manifestation of this force, a realization of what was once a mere possibility. Therefore, the sky is the source of novelty and change, the active principle that intervenes in the continuous creation of reality. This perspective underscores the interaction between potentiality and its realization. It also highlights how the sky, in its power to actualize, plays an essential role in transforming and developing all that exists.

The symbiotic relationship between earth and sky emphasizes the importance of both elements in the creative process, showing that the actualization of any potential depends on this dynamic. Not by chance, creation begins in Genesis with these two elements:

בְּרֵאשִׁית בָּרָא אֱלֹהִים אֵת הַשָּׁמַיִם וְאֵת הָאָרֶץ:
(בראשית א', א')

In the beginning God created the heaven and the earth.

(Genesis, 1:1)

The presence of the divinities within the framework of the philosophical quadrature does not aim to totalize

Chapter 23: Being and God in the Quadrature

but rather to counteract any claim of closure. Its four angles—gods, humans, heaven, and earth—do not constitute a barrier to the Last God; instead, they create an open quadrature. Each vertex is designed to prevent totalization and promote a dynamic balance. The earth limits the totalizing claim of the heavens, and vice versa. Similarly, the gods limit the totalization of humans, and humans restrict the totalization of the gods associated with institutionalized religion. This structure prevents any of the vertices from being independently asserted, ensuring that none is denied or dominating the others. The interaction between these elements creates a space where the Last God can manifest without being confined. In this way, the quadrature remains permanently open and flexible, allowing a harmonious and balanced coexistence between its components. This dynamic reflects a philosophical vision where multiplicity and diversity are essential to understanding the totality of Being and its relationship with the Divine.

The quadrature was not conceived in relation to the Last God but was established with reference to beings and, therefore, to the religious-conceptual or ontified God. In this sense, the quadrature serves as a platform where all experience occurs, and as such, it acts as a stage where the personal god appears with its respective mask. However, the quadrature is made to be abandoned, and its abandonment represents the leap from the personal to the impersonal, from the manifested to the unmanifested. The quadrature can be abandoned

Section VI: The Journey toward the Last God

when Christ has been crucified or when Kṛṣṇa as Īśvara has died. That is, when the God of ontotheology has been abandoned. This abandonment or death of the personal god facilitates another domain that allows for "building, dwelling, and thinking," as expressed in the lecture title, in which Heidegger particularly highlights the figure of the *Geviert* and its constituent elements.

Therefore, Heidegger's position should be interpreted within a line of thought that begins with Spinoza and culminates in Hegel. By postulating that the infinity of the divinity admits no limitation, either in extension or in thought, Baruch Spinoza lays the foundations for a conception of divinity without restrictions.[63] Taking this premise, Hegel interprets history as a continuous process of self-understanding of Being, where each stage represents an advance toward a greater self-consciousness. In this philosophical line and inspired by the Epistles of the Apostle Paul, Heidegger affirms that there will come a time when the kingdom will be delivered to God the Father, and all forms of dominion

---

63. The claim that Baruch Spinoza "lays the foundations for a conception of divinity without restrictions" is rooted in his philosophy, mainly in his seminal work Ethics. Spinoza's conception of God (or "Substance") is one of infinite, necessary, and boundless existence, without limitations or external constraints. A citation for this claim would typically point to *Ethics*, precisely the sections where Spinoza outlines his pantheistic view of God. In particular, Part I, Propositions 14–20 of *Ethics*. For further readings, see Baruch Spinoza, *Ethics*, trans. Edwin Curley (London: Penguin Books, 1996), 9–16. (Part I, Propositions 14–20).

Chapter 23: Being and God in the quadrature

and authority will be abolished. This is also reflected in the First Epistle to the Corinthians:

> Then comes the end, when he delivers the kingdom to God the Father, when he abolishes all rule and all authority and power. For he must reign until he has put all his enemies under his feet. The last enemy to be destroyed is death. For God has put all things in subjection under his feet. But when it says, 'all things are put in subjection,' it is plain that this does not include the one who put all things in subjection under him. When all things are subjected to him, then the Son himself will also be subjected to him who put all things in subjection under him, that God may be all in all.
>
> (1 Corinthians, 15:24–28)

Spinoza conceives of a free, infinite, and boundless divinity. Hegel interprets history as a dialectical journey where Being progressively understands itself. For his part, Heidegger completes this philosophical evolution with Paul's eschatological vision. According to this vision, there will be a final moment when all authority will be abolished and the kingdom delivered to God. At that moment, all will be subordinated to God, and the Son, having subjected all things, will also submit to God. This philosophical trajectory reveals a thread that connects these three perspectives into a coherent vision of the progress of Being toward a total understanding and eventual subordination to the Divine.

In light of the last paragraph, we can argue that Heidegger aspires to realize a kind of *apocatastasis*, in which the Last God becomes the All in all. With this consummation, unity is restored, and the transcendent perspective of metaphysical dualism, such as the perspective of Christianity, fades away. Unlike immanent dualism, this places God as an entity distinct from His creation. On the other hand, Gnostics argue that duality arises from a fracture of the *plērōma*, the fullness of Being, caused by the act of thinking. This rupture, interpreted as the fall, made God transcendental and left beings desolate in the solitude of the abyss. This Gnostic interpretation suggests that the division and isolation of beings are direct consequences of this primordial separation, marking a before and after in the relationship between the Divine and the created. Therefore, Heidegger says:

> Until the future human being of the Western world finds his way into the simple decisions and learns to honor and to know the abyssal remoteness of the near, long reflections are necessary to unravel the tenacious confusion and to awaken the courage for reflection as the joy of Da-sein. Those "truths" that are cooked up overnight and understood [?] by everyone will then simply be ignored as empty noise.

CHAPTER 23: BEING AND GOD IN THE QUADRATURE

> They require no refutation. Such refutation would itself only become noise and something contrived. Truth, however, prevails in essence in the silence of beyng. This silence is the nearness of the Last God.[64]

Heidegger speaks of "knowing the abysmal distance of the near" because what is closest to us is, paradoxically, the most distant. He places the "truths" accessible to anyone in quotation marks to emphasize their questionable nature. These "truths" promoted by believers do not even require a refutation. They are fabrications that arise quickly and, with the death of God, lose their power instantly. By stripping of a solid foundation, these supposed truths vanish as quickly as they appear, revealing their fragility and lack of substance.

---

64. Martin Heidegger, *The History of Beyng*, trans. William McNeill and Jeffrey Powell (Bloomington: Indiana University Press, 2015), "Draft for Koinón. On the History of Beyng," §214, 180.

Chapter 24

The dawn of the last God

> For it is written: "I will destroy the wisdom of the wise, and I will reject the intelligence of the intelligent."
>
> (1 Corinthians, 1:19)

Postmodernity is to modernity what the death of metaphysics is to metaphysics itself: an intrinsic necessity. That is, the death of metaphysics has its seed in metaphysics itself and its most inherent structures. Modern philosophy has begun draining the essential principles of subjectivity by prioritizing subjectivity and individuality. This has led to the dissolution of both the subject and the structures that supported our understanding of the ultimate divinity. In other words, this approach has led to a disintegration of ontological certainties, exposing a conceptual abyss where essences and determinations lose their coherence and meaning. The death of the conceptual god is the result of the death of the subject-man since the former is only a construct of the latter.

Section VI: The Journey toward the Last God

The death of the subject-man represents the dismantling of human knowledge about God. This process also allows the same subject-man to free himself from his egoicity and spring forth within himself as a witness to Being. Only from that testimony, freed from all will and original freedom, will man be able to prostrate himself before the abyss—which is the very abyss of his own finitude—and, from that abyss, harbor the Last God. Heidegger explains it as follows:

> The Last God has its most unique uniqueness and stands outside those calculating determinations meant by titles such as "mono-theism," "pan-theism," and "a-theism." "Monotheism" and all types of "theism" exist only since Judaeo-Christian "apologetics," which has metaphysics as its intellectual presupposition. With the death of this god, all theisms collapse. The multitude of gods cannot be quantified but rather is subjected to the inner richness of the grounds and abgrounds in the site for the moment of the shining and sheltering-concealing of the hint of the Last God. The Last God is not the end (*Ende*) but the other beginning of immeasurable possibilities for our history. For its sake history up to now should not terminate (*Verenden*) but rather must be brought to its end. We must bring about the transfiguration (*Verklarung*) of its

essential and basic positions in crossing and in preparedness.[65]

The Last God, which emerges beyond technique and the egoic intellect, is not a religious God in any sense. The Last God surpasses all religions, all spiritual paths, and all liberation routes. It transcends the metaphysical categories of "monotheism," "pantheism," "theism," and "atheism" and cannot be pigeonholed or categorized into either polytheism or monotheism, as it is neither multiple nor singular. On the contrary, the Last God represents the only authentic reality that is not due to any material or transcendental constructs predicated on the modern subject. The Last God is not labeled with a number, such as one, two, three, a triad, or a trinity. Behind monotheism and all forms of theism is a defense of the faith, fundamentally backed by metaphysics. All forms of theology are surpassed by transcending the God of ontotheology, which also implies the overcoming of any faith rooted in metaphysics.

Far from any theism, the essence of the Last God is related to the inner richness of the abyss (*Abgrund*) and the brilliance of ultimacy, where everything is found and, simultaneously, nothing. It is an abyss because we transform it into a person or Being when we seek it as a foundation. Quantity and quality are the entities' modes

---

65. Heidegger, Martin. *Contributions to Philosophy (From Enowning)*. Translated by Parvis Emad and Kenneth Maly (Bloomington: Indiana University Press, 1999), Section VIII, "Be-ing," §256, 289.

Section VI: The journey toward the Last God

of being, and Judeo-Christian apologetics consists of the art of defending faith in the God of Abraham through Greek philosophy. All the gods of the metaphysical age were, in reality, masks of the true and Last God, vain attempts to make it appear in one form or another. However, as we have said before, this Last God is not determined by Being; it does, however, require Being to present itself as the personal God that grounds (*Grund*) and gives meaning to human existence. But unlike the personal God, the Last God does not bring us absolution or salvation because it does not reveal itself to provide us with a new ground (*Grund*) or foundation that would allow us to silence our subjective consciousness. The Last God does not reveal itself to us as subjects; it is neither for us nor by us. On the contrary, it is the most radical alterity possible because it is more Other than even time or death. That is why Heidegger links it to the abyss (*Abgrund*) as the:

[...] the site for the moment of the shining and sheltering-concealing of the hint of the Last God.

The abyss is the place where the Last God shines, as it is not the support nor the foundation of anything. The Last God does not clarify the reason for life or the world's origin and humanity. The moment it is used to explain something, it ceases to be the Last God. Its brilliance in the abyss points to a reality that transcends

Chapter 24: The dawn of the last God

conventional explanations, thereby revealing a new dimension of divine understanding. As we have mentioned earlier, the concealment of the sign of the Last God manifests as resonance. This withdrawal is evidenced in the God of ontotheology, since the existence of a personal God indicates that the Last God has withdrawn. However, instead of implying absence, this withdrawal expresses a different, dizzying, abyssal presence. That is why Heidegger says:

The multitude of gods cannot be quantified but rather is subjected to the inner richness of the grounds and abgrounds in the site for the moment of the shining and sheltering-concealing of the hint of the Last God.

The brilliance of the Last God is its way of hiding itself, as it is too much to be understood by the categories of metaphysics. The Last God is the brilliance that blinds and cannot be seen, neither by the eyes nor by the consciousness of the ego. And it is precisely in this act of concealment that the Last God reveals its true nature of pure transcendence beyond any category. By manifesting itself as absolute transcendence, the Last God reveals that its essence surpasses the limits of conventional metaphysical thought. Moreover, this withdrawal precisely underscores its ineffability and ability to challenge our usual conceptions of the Divine.

Section VI: The journey toward the Last God

Speaking in these terms does not mean that the appearance of the Last God leads to the end of history, as postmodernity would proclaim. On the contrary, as Heidegger himself affirms when he says:

The Last God is not the end (*Ende*) but the other beginning of immeasurable possibilities for our history.

Therefore, instead of guiding us to an end, it inaugurates a new era, a new horizon of unlimited possibilities that represents the starting point for a richer and deeper history. A history that, as Heidegger argues, requires us to reinterpret the Divine beyond the traditional conceptions that present it as the entity that culminates human events. In this sense, the Last God is the Other divinity that does not replicate the characteristics or categories of religious gods of metaphysical explanations and their apocalyptic threats.

The Last God acts as the catalyst for a new beginning that opens up realities not previously explored. Moreover, this new horizon proposes overcoming the patterns underpinning the human notion of existence. It invites reevaluating values, meanings, and objectives while challenging traditional narratives and proposing a dynamic and evolutionary perspective of human history. In this same context, Heidegger affirms that:

Chapter 24: The dawn of the last God

For its sake history up to now should not terminate (*Verenden*) but rather must be brought to its end.

This reflection on historical becoming and the influence of the Divine in this process stems from the term *verenden*, which suggests a "non-perishing," a transformation that allows history to continue without dissolving into nothingness. However, Heidegger also warns that history does not continue indefinitely and must be brought to its end. This "end" should be understood as a culmination or complete realization, a sublimation in Hegelian terms, of the historical possibilities.

The Last God allows for historical continuity and, at the same time, guides its culmination. It enables a new beginning and radically transforms our understanding of existence and the historical past in which, as human beings, we recognize ourselves. This ambivalence highlights the tension between preservation and culmination in Heidegger's thought regarding history and the Divine. This Other-God also signifies another history and, therefore, another human being beyond all subjectivity and even beyond the very structures of *Dasein*. History, far from concluding, is heading toward the history of Being. In it, each personal story remains open, destined to contribute to the realization of Being and not to personal and concrete self-realization. According to Heidegger's words, this implies that:

Section VI: The Journey toward the Last God

We must bring about the transfiguration (*Verklarung*) of its essential and basic positions in crossing and in preparedness.

In this phrase, Heidegger invites us to reflect on the need for an essential transformation in our understanding of Being and history, which will ultimately lead us to a new understanding of the human being. This *transfiguration* (*Verklärung*) refers to a radical change in understanding and living our fundamental positions. This concept, far from referring to a superficial modification, points to a complete metamorphosis that affects the essence of our philosophical conceptions and practices. Heidegger mainly urges us to bring these fundamental positions to "passage" and "readiness," terms we have only presented before but now can explain in greater detail. The "passage" can be interpreted as a necessary transition to new ways of thinking and being. This process of movement and change leads us from one state of understanding to another, deeper and more authentic. In that sense, the *Geviert*, as a new philosophical framework arising from the ontological and hermeneutic turns, clearly expresses this approach. This new philosophy allows us to understand ourselves within a history of different meanings. This history is marked by the becoming of Being in its purity (*Seyn*) and by the revelation of a Last God, whose horizon opens new paths of thought and understanding for the human being. On the other hand, "readiness" implies an active

CHAPTER 24: THE DAWN OF THE LAST GOD

and conscious preparation. It is about being ready and maintaining a vigilant and attentive disposition to grasp and respond to the new possibilities that emerge in this transfiguration.

CHAPTER 25

THE OPENING TO THE "RETROPROGRESSIVE PATH"

By perceiving the constant heartbeat of the universe, one perceives a single, same life expressing itself in an infinite diversity. This realization corresponds to what Saint Paul identified as "the unknown God," which grants meaning to all the known gods. Heidegger referred to it as "the Last God," which is reached after the exhaustion of all human efforts to comprehend it. Its nature is retroprogressive because it is an innate right of all humanity, waiting in silence for our return, a return that does not deny progress but integrates and transcends it.

Therefore, this return to the Last God is conceived as the closure of a cycle that, far from concluding the search, inaugurates a profoundly renewed horizon of meaning. In the end, God reveals Himself to us as a starting point, a new beginning that always returns upon itself. This is reflected in the holiest Hebrew prayer:

Section VI: The Journey toward the Last God

אֱמֶת אַתָּה הוּא רִאשׁוֹן וְאַתָּה הוּא אַחֲרוֹן.
(סידור התפילה, תפילת שחרית, קריאת שמע וברכותיה)

Truly, You are First and You are Last.
(*Siddur*, Morning Prayer, Blessings of *Shema*)

The Path of Retroprogressive Alignment proposed here emphasizes the imperative need to transcend the ego, understood as a psychic construct that alienates the individual, condemns them to existential anguish, and ontologically separates them from the Whole. Egoism is the main vice of contemporary humanism. It embodies the illusion of an autonomous subject detached from the community. It has privileged domination and exploitation over communion and harmony.

Retroprogressivism is a radical critique of anthropocentric humanism, which has elevated human beings to a central position in the cosmos, neglecting their essential connection with the environment. It, therefore, aspires to restore humanity's relationship with its origin, proposing a life that transcends the dichotomies imposed by the ego and is oriented toward an existence in harmony with the totality. This path does not imply a mere nostalgic return to a previous state but a dialectical overcoming that, by integrating the past and present, opens up unprecedented possibilities for the individual and the universal relationship.

"Retroprogress" reflects the dynamics inherent in religion, understood etymologically as *re-ligare*, meaning

Chapter 25: The opening to the "Retroprogressive Path"

the action of reconnecting with the Divine and with the origin. In religious traditions, this return to the source or to the sacred is not reduced to a regressive or merely retrospective movement; it implies a deep union that reconstitutes the totality of Being.

The Last God is not the god of a particular religion. On the contrary, and as pure transcendence, it lies hidden precisely behind all of them. It is not the God of reformist, conservative, or orthodox Judaism but the God of Abraham, Isaac, Jacob, Moses, David, and Solomon. It is not identified with the God of Hasidism but with the God of the Ba'al Shem Tov, Rabbi Shneur Zalman of Liadi, and Rabbi Nachman of Breslov. This Last God is also not the God of Catholic, Protestant, Anglican, or Adventist Christianity, but the God of Jesus, Saint Francis, Saint John of the Cross, and Saint Teresa of Ávila. It is the God of Saint Hildegard of Bingen, Meister Eckhart, Julian of Norwich, Saint Catherine of Siena, Saint Ignatius of Loyola, Saint Bridget of Sweden, and Saint Bernard of Clairvaux. The Last God is not the Kṛṣṇa of religious organizations but the God of Lord Śrī Chaitanya Mahāprabhu. It is also not the God of Islam but the Allah of Muhammad. The Last God, more than the god of religion, is the God that transcends all religion.

Instead of understanding the Last God as a person, we must comprehend it as a presence, which makes all forms of personal worship senseless. Like peace, love, or joy, God is a presence with which no relationship can be established under the traditional subject-object framework; instead, it can be lived and experienced. It is unnecessary to carve statues and worship them to honor peace, compassion, and happiness. Similarly, we need not attend temples, mosques, synagogues, or churches to access love. The prayer that arises from our vulnerability and incomprehensibility must beat incessantly in any action we perform to the point that it defines us as human beings.

The conception of God as a personal figure has primarily generated calamities and suffering for humanity. From this idea of a personal God arises the religious believer, who envisions God as a personal entity dwelling somewhere in the sky, whether material or spiritual. Furthermore, the prayers of this believer are mere attempts to manipulate and control this illusory entity to gain favors and satisfy their desires, always in search of security and success, either in this world or the next.

The idea of a personal God has also given rise to atheism. Upon observing the life and behavior of religious believers, atheists have reacted by emphatically denying the existence of such a personal God. However, atheism falls into the error of rejecting this specific conception and completely denying God, replicating the same metaphysical structure that gave rise to this personal God.

In response to these positions, it is essential and urgent to adopt a fresh perspective that emancipates humanity from the chains of both religious beliefs and atheism.

Chapter 25: The opening to the "Retroprogressive Path"

Only by recognizing God as a manifestation of bliss, peace, compassion, silence, and love can we understand that true meditation transcends the importance of any prayer or religious ritual. Many believers perceive prayer as a dialogue with their personal gods, a constant interaction between the human and the Divine in a dual and relative framework. However, ancient traditions such as *Advaita-vedanta* and Buddhism propose going beyond words and reaching a state of mental and emotional silence. Instead of asking personal gods to fulfill our selfish desires, we should transcend desires and seek a deeper connection with the Self. It is essential to free God from any personal conception, as all notions of personality imprison the Divine. Only when God is liberated from all specific forms can it be recognized in all forms. Likewise, only when liberated from all particular names can it be identified in all names.

While we remain asleep, our dreams operate as a veil that conceals reality. Without being aware of our essence, we cannot perceive reality in its entirety, both in ourselves, others, and the world. Only by recognizing consciousness in the depths of our being can we identify it in everything and everyone. Rooted in the here and now, life unfolds its luminous and magical quality.

Retroprogressive individuals will not worship a personal god conceived as a separate and transcendent entity. Instead, they will reinterpret the notion of the Divine as an immanent manifestation, intrinsic to life, an essence that flows from Being and existence in its totality. Duality is transcended by placing the Divine and the human in a relationship of ontological continuity. Authentic prayer, from radical passivity, is not a practice or technique. More than a plea to personal gods, meditative prayer transcends the subject-object division. Any place where we are will become a sacred space. Both our relationships and our solitude will be venerated. Our words, as well as our silences, will have a divine essence.

In enlightenment, God reveals itself as the presence of the eternal fire of consciousness burning without anything left to incinerate. It is like an observation devoid of an object to observe, a waiting in which we become mere witnesses, an offering that simply shelters without demanding explanations, meaning, or foundation. Religious expression will distance itself from traditional rituals and ceremonies. The Last God will emerge when we meditate and allow consciousness to consume all the content constructed by the mind: desires, expectations, nostalgias, ambitions, and dreams.

Only then will we attend to the God that shuns all comprehension, form and image, concept and category. Humanity will not know it through concepts because it transcends any conceptualization. More than a mere philosophical proposition or theological postulate, the Last God is an immediate and intimate experience in which our existence will take on the most profound meanings. In this intimacy, the distinction between subjects and objects disappears, leaving only God, the

Chapter 25: The opening to the "Retroprogressive Path"

Last God, revealing itself indefinitely in the realm of Being, in pure manifestation. This Being is conceived as light that cannot be seen but allows everything else to be visible. With this, we are not asserting whether or not there is a God. On the contrary, as the Book of Deuteronomy says, it is affirmed that aside from God, there is nothing else.

אַתָּה הָרְאֵתָ לָדַעַת כִּי ה' הוּא הָאֱלֹהִים אֵין עוֹד מִלְבַדּוֹ:
(דברים ד', ל"ה)

> You have been shown to know that the Lord, He is God; there is no more than only Him.
> (Deuteronomy, 4:35

For atheists, God does not exist; according to polytheists, divinity manifests in a multiplicity of gods, and for monotheists, God is one. However, the Last God transcends these categories. I can say, from direct experience, that only God truly is. Besides God, absolutely nothing exists because there is nothing but Him.

BIBLIOGRAPHY SECTION VI

- Heidegger, Martin. *Contributions to Philosophy (From Enowning)*, translated by Parvis Emad and Kenneth Maly. Bloomington: Indiana University Press, 1999.
- Spinoza, Baruch. *Ethics*. Translated by Edwin Curley. London: Penguin Books, 1996.

Appendixes

Prabhuji
H.H. Avadhūta Bhaktivedānta Yogācārya
Śrī Ramakrishnananda Bābājī Mahārāja

About Prabhuji

Prabhuji is a faithful official member of Hinduism, as well as a universalist *Advaita* mystic. He combines his deep religious commitment with a remarkable artistic work as a writer and abstract painter. He is recognized by his line of disciplic succession as a realized master. As an *avadhūta*, a title conferred upon him in recognition of his state of realization, he has developed the Path of Retroprogressive Alignment, an original contribution rooted in the inclusive principles of *Sanātana-dharma* (the Hindu religion).

His solid training includes a doctorate in *Vaiṣṇava* philosophy, awarded by the prestigious Jiva Institute of Vedic Studies in Vrindavan, India, and a doctorate in Yogic philosophy earned at Yoga-Samskrutham University. These doctorates reaffirm his commitment to traditional teachings and his connection to the spiritual roots of the Hindu religion.

In 2011, with the blessings of his Gurudeva, he adopted the path of a secluded *bhajanānandī* and withdrew from society to lead the contemplative life of a hermit. Since then, he has been living as an independent Christian-Marian Hindu religious hermit. His days have been spent in solitude, praying, writing, painting, and meditating in silence and contemplation.

Prabhuji is the sole disciple of H.D.G. Avadhūta Śrī Brahmānanda Bābājī Mahārāja, who in turn is one of the closest and most intimate disciples of H.D.G. Avadhūta Śrī Mastarāma Bābājī Mahārāja.

Prabhuji was appointed as the successor of the lineage by his master, who conferred upon him the responsibility of continuing the sacred *paramparā* of *avadhūtas*, officially appointing him as guru and ordering him to serve as Ācārya successor under the name H.H. Avadhūta Bhaktivedānta Yogācārya Śrī Ramakrishnananda Bābājī Mahārāja.

Prabhuji is also a disciple of H.D.G. Bhakti-kavi Atulānanda Ācārya Mahārāja, who is a direct disciple of H.D.G. A.C. Bhaktivedānta Swami Prabhupāda. We could say that Gurudeva Atulānanda affectionately assumed the role of guide during his initial stage of learning, and because he was Prabhuji's first guru, he is considered the grandfather of Prabhuji Mission. For his part, Guru Mahārāja was Prabhuji's second and last guru and provided him with guidance during his advanced stage. Gurudeva acted as the primary educator at the dawn of his spiritual development, while Guru Mahārāja exercised with great diligence the role of master at the highest level, accompanying him until his realization.

Prabhuji's Hinduism is so broad, universal, and pluralistic that at times, while living up to his title of *avadhūta*, his lively and fresh teachings transcend the boundaries of all philosophies and religions, even his own. His teachings promote critical thinking and lead us to question statements that are usually accepted as true. They do not defend absolute truths but invite us to evaluate and question our own convictions. The essence of his syncretic vision, the Path of Retroprogressive Alignment, is self-awareness and the recognition of consciousness. For him, awakening at the level of consciousness, or the transcendence of the egoic phenomenon, is the next step in humanity's evolution.

Prabhuji was born on March 21, 1958, in Santiago, the capital of the Republic of Chile. When he was eight years old, he had a mystical experience that motivated his search for the Truth, or the Ultimate Reality. This transformed his life into an authentic inner and outer pilgrimage.

In his youth (18 years old), Prabhuji embraced the monastic discipline through long stays in various ashrams of different Hindu currents (*Gauḍīya* Vaishnavas, Advaita Vedanta, etc.) in Chile, Israel, and India. There, he underwent rigorous training within the Hindu religion. Immersed in the strict observance of religious life, he received a systematic education, following traditional methods of monastic teaching. His training included the in-depth study of sacred scriptures, the practice of austerities, the fulfillment of strict vows, and participation in prescribed rituals, all under the guidance of masters or gurus. Through this intensive discipline, he internalized the fundamental principles of Hindu monastic life, adopting its values, codes of conduct, and contemplative practices. This allowed him to learn the theory and also to incorporate the ideals that characterize the spirituality of Hinduism.

He has completely devoted his life to deepening the early transformative experience that marked the beginning of his process of retroevolution. He has dedicated more than fifty years to the exploration and practice of different religions, philosophies, paths of liberation, and spiritual disciplines. He has absorbed the teachings of great masters, shamans, priests, machis, shifus, roshis, shaykhs, daoshis, yogis, pastors, swamis, rabbis, kabbalists, monks, gurus, philosophers, sages, and saints whom he personally visited during his years of searching. He has lived in many places and traveled the world thirsting for Truth.

From an early age, Prabhuji noticed that the educational system prevented him from devoting himself to what was really important: learning about himself. He recognized that in the Western educational system of elementary schools, high schools, and universities he would not find what he wanted to learn. At the age of 11, he decided to stop attending conventional school and dedicated himself to autodidactic learning. Over time, he would become a serious critic of the current educational system.

Prabhuji is a recognized authority on Eastern wisdom. He is known for his erudition on the *Vaidika* and *Tāntrika* aspects of Hinduism and all branches of yoga (*jñāna, karma, bhakti, haṭha, rāja, kuṇḍalinī, tantra, mantra,* and others). He has an inclusive attitude toward all religions and is intimately familiar with Judaism, Christianity,

Buddhism, Islam, Sufism, Taoism, Sikhism, Jainism, Shintoism, Bahaism, Shamanism, and the Mapuche religion, among others.

During his stay in the Middle East, his esteemed friend and scholar, Kamil Shchadi, imparted profound knowledge about the Druze faith to him. He also benefited from his closeness to another illustrious acquaintance, the revered and wise Salach Abbas, who helped him to reach a thorough understanding of Islam and Sufism. He studied Theravada Buddhism personally from the Venerable W. Medhananda Thero of Sri Lanka. He studied Christian theology in depth with H.H. Monsignor Iván Larraín Eyzaguirre at the Veracruz Church in Santiago de Chile and with Mr. Héctor Luis Muñoz, who holds a degree in theology from the Universidad Católica de la Santísima Concepción, Chile.

His curiosity for Western thought led him to venture into the field of philosophy in all its different branches. He specialized in Transcendental Phenomenology and the Phenomenology of Religion. He had the privilege of studying intensively for several years with his uncle Jorge Balazs, philosopher, researcher, and author, who wrote *The world upside-down* under his pen name Gyuri Akos. He studied privately for many years with Dr. Jonathan Ramos, a renowned philosopher, historian, and university professor graduated from the Universidad Católica de Salta, Argentina. He also studied with Dr. Alejandro Cavallazzi Sánchez, who holds an undergraduate degree in philosophy from the Universidad Panamericana, a master's degree in philosophy from the Universidad Iberoamericana, and a doctorate in philosophy from the Universidad Nacional Autónoma de México (UNAM). He also studied privately with Santiago Sánchez Borboa, who holds a PhD in Philosophy from the University of Arizona, USA.

His profound studies, his masters' blessings, his research into the sacred scriptures, and his vast teaching experience have earned him international recognition in the field of religion and spirituality.

Prabhuji's spiritual quest led him to study with masters from different traditions and to travel far from his native Chile, to places as distant as Israel, Brazil, India, and the United States. He is fluent in Spanish, Hebrew, Portuguese, and English. During his stay in Israel, he furthered his Hebrew and Aramaic studies in order to broaden his knowledge of the sacred scriptures. He studied other languages intensively, such as Sanskrit with Dr. Naga Kanya Kumari Garipathi, from Osmania University in Hyderabad (India); Pali at the Oxford Center for Buddhist Studies; and Latin and Ancient Greek with Professor Ariel Lazcano and later with Javier Alvarez, who holds a degree in Classical Philology from the University of Seville.

Prabhuji's paternal grandfather was a prominent senior police sergeant in Chile, who raised his son, Yosef Har-Zion ZT "L, under strict discipline. Affected by that upbringing, Yosef decided to raise his own children in an environment characterized by complete freedom and unconditional love.

In this context, Prabhuji grew up without experiencing any external pressure. From an early age, his father manifested constant love, independent of academic performance or external achievements. When Prabhuji decided to leave school to pursue his inner quest, his family responded with deep respect and acceptance. Yosef fully supported his son's interests, encouraging him in every step of his search for Truth.

From the age of ten, Yosef shared with Prabhuji wisdom from Hebrew spirituality and Western philosophy, fostering an environment conducive to daily discussions that often lasted late into the night. In essence, Prabhuji embodied the ideal of freedom and unconditional love that his father had striven to cultivate within the family.

At an early age and on his own initiative, Prabhuji began to practice karate and study philosophy and religion. During his adolescence, no one interfered with his decisions. At the age of 15, he established a deep, intimate, and long friendship with the famous Uruguayan writer and poet Blanca Luz Brum, who was his neighbor on Merced Street in Santiago, Chile. He traveled throughout Chile in search of wise and interesting people to learn from. In southern Chile, he met machis who taught him about the rich Mapuche spirituality and shamanism.

In June 1975, at the young age of 17, he earned his first certification as a Yoga Teacher under H.H. Śrī Brahmānanda Sarasvatī (Rāmamurti S. Mishra, M.D.), the founder of the World Yoga University, the Yoga Society of New York, and the Ananda Ashram.

Two great masters contributed to Prabhuji's retroprogressive process. In 1976, he met his first guru, H.D.G Bhakti-kavi Atulānanda Ācārya Swami, whom he called Gurudeva. In those days, Gurudeva was a young *brahmacārī* who held the position of president of the ISKCON temple at Eyzaguirre 2404, Puente Alto, Santiago, Chile. Years later, he gave Prabhuji his first initiation, Brahminical initiation, and finally, Prabhuji formally accepted the sacraments of the holy order of *sannyāsa*, becoming a monk of the Brahma Gauḍīya Saṁpradāya. Gurudeva connected him to the devotion to Kṛṣṇa. He imparted to him the wisdom of bhakti yoga and instructed him in the practice of the *māhā-mantra* and the study of the holy scriptures.

In 1980, Prabhuji received the blessings of H.G. Mother Krishnabai, the famous disciple of S.D.G. Swami Rāmdās. In 1984, he learned and began to practice Maharishi Mahesh Yogi's Transcendental Meditation technique. In 1988, he took the *kriyā-yoga* course on Paramahaṁsa Yogānanda. After two years, he was officially initiated into the technique of *kriyā-yoga* by the Self-Realization Fellowship. In 1982 he received *dikṣā* from H.H. Kīrtanānanda Swami, disciple of Śrīla

Prabhupāda, who also gave him his second initiation in 1991 and *sannyāsa* initiation in 1993.

Prabhuji wanted to confirm the sacraments of the holy order of *sannyāsa* also within the Advaita Vedanta lineage. His *sannyāsa-dīkṣā*, or sacraments, were confirmed on August 11, 1995, by H.H. Swami Jyotirmayānanda Sarasvatī, founder of the Yoga Research Foundation and disciple of H.H. Swami Śivānanda Sarasvatī of Rishikesh.

In 1996, Prabhuji met his second guru, H.D.G. Avadhūta Śrī Brahmānanda Bābājī Mahārāja, in Rishikesh, India. Guru Mahārāja, as Prabhuji would call him, revealed that his own master, H.D.G. Avadhūta Śrī Mastarāma Bābājī Mahārāja, had told him years before he died that a person would come from the West and request to be his disciple. He commanded him to accept only that particular seeker. When he asked how he would identify this person, Mastarāma Bābājī replied, "You will recognize him by his eyes. You must accept him because he will be the continuation of the lineage." From his first meeting with young Prabhuji, Guru Mahārāja recognized him and officially initiated him as his disciple. For Prabhuji, this initiation marked the beginning of the most intense and mature stage of his retroprogressive process. Under the guidance of Guru Mahārāja, he studied Advaita Vedanta and deepened his meditation. Since his guru was a great devotee of Śrī Rāmakṛṣṇa Paramahaṁsa and Śāradā Devī, Prabhuji desired to be initiated into this disciplic lineage. He sought initiation from Swami Swahananda (1921–2012), minister and spiritual leader of the Vedanta Society of Southern California from 1976 to 2012. Swami Swahananda was a disciple of Swami Vijñānānanda, a direct disciple of Rāmakṛṣṇa. In 2008, Swami Swahananda initiated him, granting him both *dīkṣā* and the blessings of Śrī Rāmakṛṣṇa and the Divine Mother.

Guru Mahārāja guided Prabhuji until he officially bestowed upon him the sacraments of the sacred order of *avadhūtas*. In March 2011, H.D.G. Avadhūta Śrī Brahmānanda Bābājī Mahārāja ordered Prabhuji, on behalf of his own master, to accept the responsibility of continuing the lineage of *avadhūtas*. With this title, Prabhuji is the official representative of the line of this disciplic succession for the present generation.

Besides his *dīkṣā-gurus*, Prabhuji studied with important spiritual and religious personalities, such as H.H. Swami Yajñavālkyānanda, H.H. Swami Dayānanda Sarasvatī, H.H. Swami Viṣṇu Devānanda Sarasvatī, H.H. Swami Jyotirmayānanda Sarasvatī, H.H. Swami Kṛṣṇānanda Sarasvatī from the Divine Life Society, H.H. Ma Yoga Śakti, H.H. Swami Pratyagbodhānanda, H.H. Swami Mahādevānanda, H.H. Swami Swahānanda of the Ramakrishna Mission, H.H. Swami Adhyātmānanda, H.H. Swami Svarūpanānda, and H.H. Swami Viditātmānanda of the Arsha Vidya Gurukulam, while the wisdom of tantra was awakened in Prabhuji by H.G. Mātājī Rīnā Śarmā in India.

In Vrindavan, he studied the bhakti yoga path in depth with H.H. Narahari Dāsa Bābājī Mahārāja, disciple of H.H. Nityānanda Dāsa Bābājī Mahārāja of Vraja. He also studied bhakti yoga with various disciples of His Divine Grace A.C. Bhaktivedānta Swami Prabhupāda: H.H. Kapīndra Swami, H.H. Paramadvaiti Mahārāja, H.H. Jagajīvana Dāsa, H.H. Tamāla Kṛṣṇa Gosvāmī, H.H. Bhagavān Dāsa Mahārāja, H.H. Kīrtanānanda Swami, among others.

Prabhuji has been honored with various titles and diplomas by many leaders of prestigious religious and spiritual institutions in India. He was given the honorable title Kṛṣṇa Bhakta by H.H. Swami Viṣṇu Devānanda (the only title of Bhakti Yoga given by Swami Viṣṇu), disciple of H.H. Swami Śivānanda Sarasvatī and the founder of the Sivananda Organization. He was given the title Bhaktivedānta by H.H. B.A. Paramadvaiti Mahārāja, the founder of Vrinda. He was given the title Yogācārya by H.H. Swami Viṣṇu Devānanda, the Paramanand Institute of Yoga Sciences and Research of Indore, India, the International Yoga Federation, the Indian Association of Yoga, and the Śrī Shankarananda Yogashram of Mysore, India. He received the respectable title Śrī Śrī Rādhā Śyam Sunder Pāda-Padma Bhakta Śiromaṇi directly from H.H. Satyanārāyaṇa Dāsa Bābājī Mahant of the Chatu Vaiṣṇava Sampradāya.

Prabhuji dedicated more than forty years to studying hatha yoga with prestigious masters of classical and traditional yoga, such as H.H. Bapuji,

H.H. Swami Viṣṇu Devānanda Sarasvatī, H.H. Swami Jyotirmayānanda Sarasvatī, H.H. Swami Satchidānanda Sarasvatī, H.H. Swami Vignānānanda Sarasvatī, and Śrī Madana-mohana.

He attended several systematic hatha yoga teacher training courses at prestigious institutions until he achieved the level of Master Ācārya. He has completed studies at the following institutions: World Yoga University, the Sivananda Yoga Vedanta, the Ananda Ashram, the Yoga Research Foundation, the Integral Yoga Academy, the Patanjala Yoga Kendra, the Ma Yoga Shakti International Mission, the Prana Yoga Organization, the Rishikesh Yoga Peeth, the Swami Sivananda Yoga Research Center, and the Swami Sivananda Yogasana Research Center.

Prabhuji is a member of the Indian Association of Yoga, Yoga Alliance ERYT 500 and YACEP, the International Association of Yoga Therapists, and the International Yoga Federation. In 2014, the International Yoga Federation honored him with the position of Honorary Member of the World Yoga Council.

His interest in the complex anatomy of the human body led him to study chiropractic at the prestigious Institute of Health of the Back and Extremities in Tel Aviv, Israel. In 1993, he received a diploma from Dr. Sheinerman, the founder and director of the institute. Later, he earned a massage therapy diploma at the Academy of Western Galilee. The knowledge he acquired in this field deepened his understanding of hatha yoga and contributed to the creation of his own method.

About Prabhuji

Retroprogressive Yoga is the result of Prabhuji's efforts to improve his practice and teaching methods. It is a system based especially on the teachings of his gurus and the sacred scriptures. Prabhuji has systematized various traditional yoga techniques to create a methodology suitable for Western audiences. Retroprogressive Yoga aspires to the experience of our authentic nature, promoting balance, health, and flexibility through proper diet, cleansing techniques, preparations (*āyojanas*), sequences (*vinyāsas*), postures (*āsanas*), breathing exercises (*prāṇayama*), relaxation (*śavāsana*), meditation (*dhyāna*), and exercises with locks (*bandhas*) and seals (*mudras*) to direct and empower *prāṇa*.

Since his childhood and throughout his life, Prabhuji has been an enthusiastic admirer, student, and practitioner of classic karate-do. From the age of 13, he studied different styles in Chile, such as kenpo with Sensei Arturo Petit and kung-fu, but specialized in the most traditional Japanese style of shotokan. He received the rank of black belt (third dan) from Shihan Kenneth Funakoshi (ninth dan). He also learned from Sensei Takahashi (seventh dan) and Sensei Masataka Mori (ninth dan). Additionally, he practiced shorin ryu style with Sensei Enrique Daniel Welcher (seventh dan), who granted him the rank of black belt (second dan). Through karate-do, he delved into Buddhism and gained additional knowledge about the physics of motion. He is a member of Funakoshi's Shotokan Karate Association.

Prabhuji grew up in an artistic environment and his love of painting began to develop in his childhood. His father, the renowned Chilean painter Yosef Har-Zion ZT"L, motivated him to devote himself to art. He learned with the famous Chilean painter Marcelo Cuevas. Prabhuji's abstract paintings reflect the depths of the spirit.

Since he was a young boy, Prabhuji has been especially drawn to postal stamps, postcards, mailboxes, postal transportation systems, and all mail-related activities. He has taken every opportunity to visit post offices in different cities and countries. He has delved into the study of philately, the field of collecting, sorting, and studying postage stamps. This passion led him to become a professional philatelist, a stamp distributor authorized by the American Philatelic Society, and a member of the following societies: the Royal Philatelic Society London, the Royal Philatelic Society of Victoria, the United States Stamp Society, the Great Britain Philatelic Society, the American Philatelic Society, the Society of Israel Philatelists, the Society for Hungarian Philately, the National Philatelic Society UK, the Fort Orange Stamp Club, the American Stamp Dealers Association, the US Philatelic Classics Society, Filabras - Associação dos Filatelistas Brasileiros, and the Collectors Club of NYC.

Based on his extensive knowledge of philately, theology, and Eastern philosophy, Prabhuji created "Meditative Philately" or "Philatelic Yoga," a spiritual practice that uses philately as the basis for practicing attention, concentration, observation, and meditation. It is inspired by the ancient Hindu mandala meditation and it can lead the practitioner to elevated states of consciousness, deep relaxation, and concentration that fosters the recognition of consciousness. Prabhuji wrote his thesis on this new type of yoga, "Meditative Philately," attracting the interest of the Indian academic community due to its innovative way of connecting meditation with different hobbies and activities. For this thesis, he was honored with a PhD in Yogic Philosophy from Yoga-Samskrutham University.

For more than 20 years, Prabhuji lived in Israel, where he furthered his studies of Judaism. One of his main teachers and sources of inspiration was Rabbi Shalom Dov Lifshitz ZT"L, whom he met in 1997. This great saint guided him for several years along the intricate paths of the Torah and Hassidism. He personally taught him Tanakh, Talmud, Midrash, Shulchan Aruch, Mishneh Torah, Tanya, Kabbalah and Zohar. The two developed a very close relationship. Prabhuji also studied the Talmud with Rabbi Raphael Rapaport Shlit"a (Ponovich), Hassidism with Rabbi Israel Lifshitz Shlit"a, and the Torah with Rabbi Daniel Sandler Shlit"a. Prabhuji is a great devotee of Rabbi Mordechai Eliyahu ZT"L, who personally blessed him.

Prabhuji visited the United States in 2000 and during his stay in New York, he realized that it was the most appropriate place to found a religious organization. He was particularly attracted by the pluralism and respectful attitude of American society toward freedom of religion. He was impressed by the deep respect of both the public and the government for religious minorities. After consulting his masters and requesting their blessings, Prabhuji relocated to the United States. In 2003, the Prabhuji Mission was born, a Hindu church aimed at preserving Prabhuji's universal and pluralistic vision of Hinduism and his Path of Retroprogressive Alignment.

Although he did not seek to attract followers, for 15 years (1995–2010), Prabhuji considered the requests of a few people who approached him asking to become his monastic disciples. Those who chose to see Prabhuji as their spiritual master voluntarily accepted vows of poverty and life-long dedication to spiritual practice (*sadhāna*), religious devotion (bhakti), and selfless service (*seva*). Although Prabhuji no longer accepts new disciples, he continues to guide the small group of monastic disciples of the contemplative Ramakrishnananda Monastic Order that he founded.

According to Prabhuji, the quest for the Self is individual, solitary, personal, private, and intimate. It is not a collective endeavor to be undertaken through organized, institutional, or communitarian religiosity. Since 2011, Prabhuji has disagreed with spirituality practiced in a social, communal, or collective manner. Therefore, he does not proselytize or preach, nor does he try to persuade, convince, or make anyone change their perspective, philosophy, or religion. His message does not promote collective spirituality, but individual inner search.

In 2011, Prabhuji founded the Avadhutashram (monastery) in the Catskills Mountains in upstate New York, USA. The Avadhutashram is his hermitage, the residence of the monastic disciples of the Ramakrishnananda Order, and the headquarters of the Prabhuji Mission and the Academy of Retroprogressive Yoga, in which Prabhuji personally teaches his method of yoga to disciples and students, without departing from his hermit life. The ashram organizes humanitarian projects such as the Prabhuji Food Distribution Program and the Prabhuji Toy Distribution Program. Prabhuji operates various humanitarian projects, inspired in his experience that serving the part is serving the Whole.

Prabhuji has delegated the choice to his disciples between keeping his teachings exclusively within the monastic order or spreading his message for the public benefit. Upon the explicit request of his disciples, Prabhuji has agreed to have his books published and his lectures disseminated, as long as this does not compromise his privacy and his life as a hermit.

In 2022, Prabhuji founded the Institute of Retroprogressive Alignment. Here, his most senior disciples can systematically share his teachings and message through video conferences. The institute offers support and help for a deeper understanding of Prabhuji's teachings.

Prabhuji is a respected member of the American Philosophical Association, the American Association of Philosophy Teachers, the American Association of University Professors, the Southwestern Philosophical Society, the Authors Guild, the National Writers Union, PEN America, the International Writers Association, the National Association of Independent Writers and Editors, the National Writers Association, the Alliance Independent Authors, and the Independent Book Publishers Association.

Prabhuji's vast literary contribution includes books in Spanish, English, and Hebrew, such as *Kundalini Yoga: The Power is in you*, *What is, as it is*, *Bhakti-Yoga: The Path of Love*, *Tantra: Liberation in the World*, *Experimenting with the Truth*, *Advaita Vedanta: Be the Self*, *Yoga: union with reality*, commentaries on the *Īśāvāsya Upanishad* and the *Diamond Sūtra*, *I am that I am*, *The Symbolic turn*, *Being*, *Questioning your answers: Philosophy as a question*, *Beyond answers: Philosophy in the eternal quest*, *Phenomenology of the sacred: Foundations for a Retroprogressive Phenomenology*, and *Discovering the Last God*.

The term *PRABHUJI*
by H.G. Swami Ramananda

Several years ago, some disciples, followers and friends of His Holiness Avadhūta Bhaktivedānta Yogācārya Śrī Ramakrishnananda Bābājī Mahārāja, opted to refer to him as Prabhuji. In this article, I would like to clarify the deep meaning of this Sanskrit term. The word *prabhu* in Sanskrit means "a master, lord or a king" and it is applied in the scriptures to God and to the Guru.

Like many words in the Sanskrit language, the word is actually made of some components, and understanding its etymology will lead us to discover its various meanings. The word *prabhu* is a combination of the root *bhu* which means "to become, to exist, to be, to live" and the prefix *pra*, which can mean "forth, or forward" and which then, when attached to *bhu* would mean "one who causes to exist, who gives life, from whom life emanates, that which sustains or maintains."

The prefix *pra* can also mean "very much, or supremacy," and then when attached to the root *bhu* would mean "to be the master, to rule over."

The suffix *jī* is an honorific title in Hindi and other Indian languages. It is added after the names of Gods and esteemed personalities to show respect and reverence.

As manifestations of the Divine, great *ṛṣis,* or 'seers' and gurus are also called *prabhus*. For example, the sage Nārada is addressing the *ṛṣi* Vyasadeva as prabhu:

जिज्ञासितमधीतं च ब्रह्म यत्तत्सनातनम् ।
तथापि शोचस्यात्मानमकृतार्थ इव प्रभो ॥

> *jijñāsitam adhītaṁ ca*
> *brahma yat tat sanātanam*
> *tathāpi śocasy ātmānam*
> *akṛtārtha iva prabho*

You have fully delineated the subject of impersonal Brahman as well as the knowledge derived therefrom. Why should you be despondent in spite of all this, thinking that you are undone, my dear master (*prabhu*)?

(*Bhāgavata Purana*, 1.5.4)

Mahārāja Parīkṣit addresses Śukadeva as *prabhu* when he approaches the sage to seek spiritual guidance, thus accepting him as his guru.

यच्छ्रोतव्यमथो जप्यं यत्कर्तव्यं नृभिः प्रभो ।
स्मर्तव्यं भजनीयं वा ब्रूहि यद्वा विपर्ययम् ॥

*yac chrotavyam atho japyaṁ
yat kartavyaṁ nṛbhiḥ prabho
smartavyaṁ bhajanīyaṁ vā
brūhi yad vā viparyayam*

O prabhu, please let me know what a man should hear, chant, remember and worship, and also what he should not do. Please explain all this to me.

(*Bhāgavata Purana*, 1.19.38)

THE TERM *AVADHŪTA*

This is an excerpt from the book *Sannyāsa Darśana* by Swami Niranjanānanda Sarasvatī, a disciple of Paramahamsa Swami Satyānanda.

Stages of *sannyāsāvadhūta*

"The *avadhūta* represents the pinnacle of spiritual evolution; none is superior to him. *Avadhūta* means 'one who is immortal' (*akṣara*) and who has totally discarded worldly ties. He is really Brahman itself. He has realized he is pure intelligence and is not concerned about the six frailties of human birth, namely: sorrow, delusion, old age, death, hunger, and thirst. He has shaken off all bondage of the experimental world and roams freely like a child, a madman or one possessed by spirits.

He may be with or without clothes. He wears no distinctive emblem of any order. He has no desire to sleep, beg, or bathe. He views his body as a corpse and subsists on the food that comes to him from all classes. He does not interpret the *śāstras* or the Vedas. For him, nothing is righteous or unrighteous, holy or unholy.

He is free from karma. The karmas of this life and past lives are all burned out, and due to the absence of *kartṛtva* (the doer) and *bhoktṛtva* (the desire for enjoyment), no future karmas are created. Only the *prārabdha-karmas* (unalterable) that have already begun to operate will affect his body, helping to sustain it, but his mind will remain unaffected. He will live in this world until the *prārabdha-karmas* are extinguished, and then his body will fall. Then he is said to attain *videhamukti* (the state beyond body consciousness).

Such a liberated soul never returns to the embodied state. He is not born again; he is immortal. He has achieved the final aim of being born in this world."

The *Bṛhad-avadhūta Upanishad* reads as follows: "The *avadhūta* is so called because he is immortal; he is the greatest; he has discarded worldly ties, and he is alluded to in the meaning of the sentence 'Thou art That'."

His Divine Grace Śrīla Bhakti Ballabh Tīrtha Mahārāja in his article entitled "*Pariṣads*: Śrīla Vamśi das Bābājī" wrote: "He was a Paramahaṁsa Vaiṣṇava who acted in the manner of an *avadhūta*. The word *avadhūta* refers to one who has shaken off from himself all worldly feelings and obligations. He does not care for social conventions, especially the *varṇāśrama-dharma*, that is, he is quite eccentric in his behavior. Nityānanda Prabhu is often characterized as an *avadhūta*."

From the foreword to Dattātreya's *Avadhūta-gītā*, translated and annotated by Swami Aśokānanda: "The *Avadhūta-gītā* is a Vedanta text representing extreme Advaita or non-dualism. It is attributed to Dattātreya, who is looked upon as an Incarnation of God.

Unfortunately, we possess no historical data concerning when or where he was born, how long he lived, or how he arrived at the knowledge disclosed in the text.

Avadhūta means a liberated soul, one who has 'passed away from' or 'shaken off' all worldly attachments and cares and has attained a spiritual state equivalent to the existence of God. Although *avadhūta* naturally implies renunciation, it includes an additional and even higher state that is neither attachment nor detachment, but is beyond both. An *avadhūta* feels no need to observe any rules, whether secular or religious. He seeks nothing and avoids nothing. He has neither knowledge nor ignorance. Having realized that he is the infinite Self, he lives in that vivid realization."

Swami Vivekānanda, one of the greatest advaitins of all times, often quoted this *Gītā*. He once said, "Men like the one who wrote this song keep religion alive. They have experienced. They care for nothing, and feel nothing done to the body; they don't care for heat, cold, danger, or anything else. They sit still, enjoying the bliss of the Ātman, and even if embers burn their bodies, they do not feel them."

The *Avadhūta Upanishad* is number 79 in the *Muktikā* canon of Upanishads. It is a *Sannyāsa Upanishad* associated with the Black (Kṛṣṇa) Yajur-veda: "One who has transcended the *varṇāśrama* system and has always established in himself, that yogi, who is above the *varṇāśrama* divisions, is called *avadhūta*." (*Avadhūta Upanishad*, 2).

The *Brahma-nirvāṇa Tantra* book describes how to identify *avadhūtas* of the following types:

- *Bramhāvadhūta*: An *avadhūta* by birth, who appears in any cast of society and is completely indifferent to the world or worldly matters.
- *Śaivāvadhūta*: *Avadhūtas* who have taken to the renounced order of life or *sannyāsa*, often with long matted hair (*jaṭa*), or who dress in the manner of Shaivites and spend almost all of their time in trance *samādhi*, or meditation.
- *Virāvadhūta*: This person looks like a *sadhū* who has put red-colored sandal paste on his body and wears saffron-colored clothes. His hair is very well grown and is normally furling in the wind. They wear around their necks a *rudrākṣa-mālā* or a chain of bones. They carry a wooden stick, or *daṇḍa*, in their hand, and additionally always carry an axe (*paraśu*) or an *ḍamaru* (small drum) with them.
- *Kulāvadhūta*: These people are supposed to have taken the Kaul *Saṁpradāya* initiation. It is very difficult to recognize these people as they do not wear any outward signs that can identify them from others. The specialty of these people is that they stay and live like normal people. They may show themselves in the form of kings or family men.

The *Nātha Saṁpradāya* is a form of *Avadhūta-pantha* (sect). In this *Saṁpradāya*, Guru and yoga are of extreme importance. Therefore, the most important book of this *Sampradāya* is the *Avadhūta-gītā*. Śrī Gorakṣanāth is considered the highest form of the *avadhūta* state.

The nature of *avadhūta* is the subject of the *Avadhūta-gītā*, traditionally attributed to Dattātreya.

According to Bipin Joshi, the main characteristics of an *avadhūta* are: "He who is a sinless philosopher and has cast off the shackles of ignorance (*ajñāna*). He who lives in a stateless state and relishes the experience all the time. He revels in this blissful state, unperturbed by the material world. In this unique state, the *avadhūta* is neither awake nor in deep sleep; there is no sign of life or death. It is a state defying all descriptions. It is the state of infinite bliss, which a finite language is incapable of describing. It can only be intuited purely by our intellect. A state that is neither truth nor non-truth, neither existence nor nonexistence. He who has realized his identity with the imperishable, who possesses incomparable excellence, who has shaken off the bonds of *samsāra* and never deviates from his goal. That thou art (*tat tvam asi*), and other upanishadic statements, are ever present in the mind of such an enlightened soul. That sage who is rooted in the plenary experience of 'Verily, I am Brahman (*aham Brahmāsmi*)', 'All this is Brahman (*sarvam khalvidam brahma*)', and that '…there is no plurality, I and God are one and the same…', etc. Supported by the personal experience of such Vedic statements, he moves freely in a state of total bliss. Such a person is a renunciant, liberated, *avadhūta*, yogi, paramahamsa, *brāhmaṇa*."

From Wikipedia, the free encyclopedia:

Avadhūta is a Sanskrit term used in Indian religions to refer to mystics or antinomian saints who are beyond ego-consciousness, duality, and common worldly concerns, and act without consideration of standard social etiquette. Such personalities "roam free as a child on the face of the Earth." An *avadhūta* does not identify with his mind or body or 'names and forms' (Sanskrit: *nāma-rūpa*). Such a person is considered pure consciousness (Sanskrit: *caitanya*) in human form.

Avadhūtas play a significant role in the history, origins, and rejuvenation of a number of traditions such as yoga, Advaita Vedanta, Buddhist, and bhakti *paramparās* even as they are released from standard observances. *Avadhūtas* are the voice of the *avadhūti*, the channel that resolves the dichotomy of *Vāmācāra* and *Dakṣiṇācāra* or "left and right-handed traditions." An *avadhūta* may or may not continue to practice religious rites as long as they are free from sectarian ritual observance and affiliation. The Monier Williams Sanskrit dictionary defines the term *avadhūta* as follows: "अवधूत / अव-धूत — one who has shaken off from himself worldly feelings and obligations."

From *Hinduism, an alphabetical guide* by Roshen Dalal

Avadhūta: A term for a liberated soul, one who has renounced the world. Totally beyond all that is, an *avadhūta* follows no rules, no fixed practices, and has no need to follow conventional norms. There are several texts dealing with the life and nature of an *avadhūta*. In the *Avadhūta Upanishad*, the Ṛṣi Dattātreya describes the nature of the *avadhūta*. Such a person is immortal, has discarded all worldly ties, and is always full of bliss. One of its verses states: "Let thought contemplate Viṣṇu, or let it be dissolved in the bliss of Brahman. I, the witness, do nothing, nor do I cause anything to be done." (v.28)

The *Turīyātīta Avadhūta Upanishad* contains a description of the *avadhūta* who has reached the state of consciousness beyond the *turīya*. In this state, a person is pure, detached and totally free. An *avadhūta* who has reached this level does not chant mantras or practice rituals, wears no caste marks, and is finished with all religious and secular duties. He wears no clothes and eats whatever comes his way. He wanders alone, observing silence, and is totally absorbed in non-duality. The *Avadhūta-gītā* has similar descriptions.

The *Uddhava-gītā*, which is part of the *Bhāgavata Purāṇa*, describes an *avadhūta* who learned from all aspects of life and was at home anywhere in the world. The term *avadhūta* can be applied to any liberated person, but it also refers specifically to a *sannyāsa* sect.

Avadhūta Upanishad

Avadhūta Upanishad is a small Upanishad consisting of about 32 mantras. It falls under the category of the *Sannyāsa Upanishads* and is a part of Kṛṣṇa Yajurveda. The *Avadhūta Upanishad* takes the form of a dialogue between Dattātreya and Ṛṣi Saṁkṛti.

One day Ṛṣi Saṁkṛti asks Dattātreya the following questions: "Who is an *avadhūta*?; What is his state?; What are the signs of the *avadhūta*?; How does he live?"

The following are the answers given by the compassionate Dattātreya.

Who is an *avadhūta*?

The *avadhūta* is so called because he is beyond any decay; he lives freely according to his will, he destroys the bondage of worldly desires, and his only goal is That thou Art (*tat tvam asi*).

The *avadhūta* goes far beyond all the castes (such as *brāhmaṇa, vaiśya, kṣatrya,* and *śūdra*) and *Āśramas* (such as *brāmhacaryā, gṛhastha, vānaprastha,* and *sannyāsa*). He is the highest Yogi who is established in a constant state of self-realization.

What is his state?

An *avadhūta* always enjoys supreme bliss. The divine joy represents his head, happiness is his right wing, ecstasy represents his left wing, and bliss is his very nature. The life of an *avadhūta* shows extreme detachment.

What are the signs of *avadhūta*? How does he live?

An *avadhūta* lives according to his own will. He may wear clothes or go naked. For him, there is no difference between *dharma* or *adharma*, sacrifice or non-sacrifice, because he is beyond these aspects. He performs inner sacrifice and that forms their *aśvamedha-yajña*. He is a great yogi who remains unaffected even when engaged in worldly objects. He remains pure.

The ocean accepts water from all the rivers but remains unchanged. Similarly, an *avadhūta* is unaffected by worldly objects. He is always at peace and (like the ocean), all his desires are absorbed in this supreme peace.

For an *avadhūta* there is no birth or death, no bondage or liberation. He may have performed various actions for the sake of liberation, but they become history once he becomes an *avadhūta*. He is always satisfied. Others wander to fulfill their desires. But an *avadhūta*, being already satisfied, does not run after any desire. Others perform various rituals for the sake of heaven, but an *avadhūta* is already established in the omnipresent state and hence needs no rituals.

Other qualified teachers spend time teaching the scriptures (Vedas) but *avadhūta* goes beyond those activities, because he has no actions. He doesn't have any desire to sleep, beg (*bhikṣa*), bathe, or clean.

An *avadhūta* is always free from doubt, and since he is always in union with the supreme reality, he does not even need to meditate. Meditation is for those people who are not yet one with God, but an *avadhūta* is always in the state of union and therefore does not need to meditate.

Those who are after *karmas* (actions) are filled with *vāsanās*. These *vāsanās* haunt them even when they finish their *prārabdha-karma*. Ordinary men meditate because they wish to fulfill their desires. However, an *avadhūta* always stays away from that trap. His mind is beyond mental destruction and *samādhi*. Mental destruction as well as *samādhi* are possibly modifications of the mind. The *avadhūta* is already eternal and hence, there is nothing to attain for him.

Following worldly duties is like an arrow released from a bow, i.e. it cannot be stopped from giving good or bad fruits causing a cycle of action-reaction. However, an *avadhūta* is not a doer at any level and is not engaged in any action.

Having attained such a stage of detachment, an *avadhūta* remains unaffected even if he follows a way of life as prescribed by the scriptures. Even if he engages in *actions* such as worshipping God, bathing, begging, etc., he remains unattached to them. He lives as a witness and therefore does not perform any action.

An *avadhūta* can clearly see Brahman before his eyes. He is free from ignorance or *māyā*. He has no actions left to be performed and nothing left to achieve. He is totally satisfied and there is no one else with whom he can be compared.

नलिनी नालिनी नासे गन्ध: सौरभ उच्यते ।
घ्राणोऽवधूतो मुख्यास्यं विपणो वाग्रसविद्रस: ॥

nalinī nālinī nāse
gandhaḥ saurabha ucyate
ghrāṇo 'vadhūto mukhyāsyaṁ
vipaṇo vāg rasavid rasaḥ

The two doors called Nalinī and Nālinī are to be known as the two nostrils, and the city named Saurabha represents the aroma. The companion spoken of as *avadhūta* is the sense of smell. The door called Mukhyā is the mouth, and Vipaṇa is the faculty of speech. Rasajña is the sense of taste.
(*Bhāgavata Purāṇa*, 4.29.11)

Purport of H.D.G. Bhaktivedanta Swami Prabhupada:

The word *avadhūta* means "most free." A person is not under the rules and regulations of any injunction when he has attained the stage of *avadhūta*. In other words, he can act as he likes. This stage of *avadhūta* is exactly like air, which does not care for any obstruction. In the Bhagavad Gita (6.34) it is said:

चञ्चलं हि मन: कृष्ण प्रमाथि बलवद्दृढम् ।
तस्याहं निग्रहं मन्ये वायोरिव सुदुष्करम् ॥

> *cañcalaṁ hi manaḥ kṛṣṇa*
> *pramāthi balavad dṛḍham*
> *tasyāhaṁ nigrahaṁ manye*
> *vāyor iva suduṣkaram*

The mind is restless, turbulent, obstinate, and very strong, O Kṛṣṇa, and to subdue it is, it seems to me, more difficult than controlling the wind.
(Bhagavad Gita, 6.34)

Just as air or wind cannot be stopped by anyone, the two nostrils, situated in one place, enjoy the sense of smell without impediment. With the tongue, the mouth continuously tastes all kinds of tasty foods.

अक्षरत्वाद्वरेण्यत्वाद्धूतसंसारबन्धनात् ।
तत्त्वमस्यर्थसिद्धत्वात् अवधूतोऽभिधीयते ॥

> *akṣaratvād vareṇyatvād*
> *dhūta-saṁsāra-bandhanāt*
> *tat tvam asy-artha siddhatvāt*
> *avadhūto 'bhidhīyate*

Since he is immutable (*akṣara*), the most excellent (*vareṇya*), since he has removed the worldly attachments (*dhūta-samsāra-bandanāt*) and he has realized the meaning of *tat tvam asi* (That thou art), he is called *avadhūta*.

(Kulārṇava Tantra, 17.24)

From Yogapedia: What does *avadhūta* mean?

Avadhūta is a Sanskrit term used to refer to a person who has reached a stage in their spiritual development in which they are beyond worldly concerns. People who have reached the stage of *avadhūta* may act without considering common social etiquette or their own ego. This term is often used in the cases of mystics or saints.

Advanced yoga practitioners may find inspiration in the idea of reaching this stage through further sustained meditation and asana practice.

Avadhūta is often associated with some sort of eccentric and spontaneous behavior from a holy person. This comes partly from the fact that mystics who have achieved this level of spiritual enlightenment may forget wearing clothes or other normal social behavior.

About the Prabhuji Mission

Prabhuji Mission is a Hindu religious, spiritual, and charitable organization founded by H.H. Avadhūta Bhaktivedānta Yogācārya Śrī Ramakrishnananda Bābājī Mahārāja. Its purpose is to preserve the "Path of Retroprogressive Alignment," which reflects Prabhuji's vision of *Sanātana-dharma* and advocates for the global awakening of consciousness as the radical solution to humanity's problems.

Apart from imparting religious and spiritual teachings, the organization carries out extensive philanthropic work in the USA, based on the principles of karma yoga, selfless work performed with dedication to God.

Prabhuji Mission was established in 2003 in the USA as a Hindu church aimed at preserving its founder's universal and pluralistic vision of Hinduism.

The Prabhuji Mission operates a Hindu temple called Śrī Śrī Bhagavān Yeshua Jagat Jananī Miriam Premānanda Mandir., which offers worship and religious ceremonies to parishioners. The extensive library of the Institute of Retroprogressive Alignment provides its teachers with abundant study materials to research the various theologies and philosophies explored by Prabhuji in his books and lectures.

The Avadhutashram monastery educates monastic disciples on various aspects of Prabhuji's approach to Hinduism and offers them the opportunity to express devotion to God through devotional service by selflessly contributing their skills and training to the Mission's programs.

The Mission publishes and distributes Prabhuji's books and lectures and operates humanitarian projects such as the "Prabhuji Food Distribution Program," a weekly event in which dozens of families in need from Upstate New York receive fresh and nutritious food and the "Prabhuji Toy Distribution Program," which provides the less privileged kids with abundance of Christmas gifts.

Avadhutashram
Round Top, Nueva York, EE. UU.

About the Avadhutashram

The Avadhutashram (monastery) was founded by Prabhuji. It is the headquarters of the Prabhuji Mission and the hermitage of H.H. Avadhūta Bhaktivedānta Yogācārya Śrī Ramakrishnananda Bābājī Mahārāja and his monastic disciples of the Ramakrishnananda Contemplative Monastic Order.

The ideals of the Avadhutashram are love and selfless service, based on the universal vision that God is in everything and everyone. Its mission is to distribute spiritual books and organize humanitarian projects such as the Prabhuji Food Distribution Program and the Prabhuji Toy Distribution Program.

The Avadhutashram is not commercial and operates without soliciting donations. Its activities are funded by Prabhuji's Gifts, a non-profit company founded by Prabhuji, which sells esoteric items from different traditions that he himself has used for spiritual practices during his evolutionary process. Its mission is to preserve and disseminate traditional religious, mystical, and ancestral crafts.

The Path of Retroprogressive Alignment

The Path of Retroprogressive Alignment does not require you to be part of a group or a member of an organization, institution, society, congregation, club, or exclusive community. Living in a temple, monastery, or *āśram* is not mandatory, because it is not about a change of residence, but of consciousness. It does not urge you to believe, but to doubt. It does not demand you to accept something, but to explore, investigate, examine, inquire, and question everything. It does not suggest being what you should be but being what you really are.

The Path of Retroprogressive Alignment supports freedom of expression but not proselytizing. This route does not promise answers to our questions but induces us to question our answers. It does not promise to be what we are not or to attain what we have not already achieved. It is a retro-evolutionary path of self-discovery that leads us from what we think we are to what we really are. It is not the only way, nor the best, the simplest, or the most direct. It is an involutionary process par excellence that shows what is obvious and undeniable but usually goes unnoticed: that which is simple, innocent, and natural. It is a path that begins and ends in you.

The Path of Retroprogressive Alignment is a continuous revelation that expands eternally. It delves into consciousness from an ontological perspective, transcending all religion and spiritual paths. It is the discovery of diversity as a unique and inclusive reality. It is the encounter of consciousness with itself, aware of itself and its own reality. In fact, this path is a simple invitation to dance in the now, to love the present moment, and to celebrate our authenticity. It is an unconditional proposal to stop living as a victim of circumstance and to live as a passionate adventurer. It is a call to return to the place we have never left, without offering us anything we do not already possess or teaching us anything we do not already know. It is a call for an inner revolution and to enter the fire of life that only consumes dreams, illusions, and fantasies but does not touch what we are. It does not help us reach our desired goal, but instead prepares us for the unexpected miracle.

This path was nurtured over a lifetime dedicated to the search for Truth. It is a grateful offering to existence for what I have received. But remember, do not look for me. Look for yourself. It is not me you need, because you are the only one who really matters. This life is just a wonderful parenthesis in eternity to know and love. What you yearn for lies in you, here and now, as what you really are.

Your unconditional well-wisher,
Prabhuji

Prabhuji Today

Prabhuji has retired from public life

Prabhuji is the sole disciple of H.D.G. Avadhūta Śrī Brahmānanda Bābājī Mahārāja, who is himself one of the closest and most intimate disciples of H.D.G. Avadhūta Śrī Mastarāma Bābājī Mahārāja.

Guru Mahārāja guided Prabhuji until he officially bestowed upon him the sacraments of the sacred order of *avadhūtas*. Prabhuji was appointed as the successor of the lineage by his master, who conferred upon him the responsibility of continuing the line of disciplic succession of *avadhūtas*, or the sacred *paramparā*, officially designating him as guru and commanding him to serve as the successor Ācārya under the name H.H. Avadhūta Bhaktivedānta Yogācārya Śrī Ramakrishnananda Bābājī Mahārāja.

Prabhuji is also a disciple of H.D.G. Bhakti-kavi Atulānanda Ācārya Mahārāja, who is a direct disciple of H.D.G. A.C. Bhaktivedānta Swami Prabhupāda.

In 2011, with the blessings of his Gurudeva, he adopted the path of a secluded *bhajanānandī* and withdrew from society to lead the contemplative life of a hermit. Since then, he has been living as an independent Christian-Marian Hindu religious hermit. His days have been spent in solitude, praying, writing, painting, and meditating in silence and contemplation.

He no longer participates in *sat-saṅgs*, lectures, gatherings, meetings, retreats, seminars, study groups, or courses. We ask everyone to respect his privacy and do not try to contact him by any means for gatherings, meetings, interviews, blessings, *śaktipāta*, initiations, or personal visits.

Prabhuji's teachings

As an *avadhūta* and a realized Master, Prabhuji has always appreciated the essence and wisdom of a wide variety of religious practices from around the world. Although many see him as an enlightened being, Prabhuji has no intention of presenting himself as a public figure, preacher, propagator of beliefs, promoter of philosophies, guide, coach, content creator, influencer, preceptor, mentor, counselor, consultant, monitor, tutor, teacher, instructor, educator, enlightener, pedagogue, evangelist, rabbi, *posek halacha*, healer, therapist, satsangist, pointer, psychic, leader, medium, savior, New Age guru, or authority of any kind, whether spiritual or material. According to Prabhuji, the quest for the Self is individual, solitary, personal, private, and intimate. It is not a collective endeavor to be undertaken through organized, institutional, or community religiosity. Since 2011, Prabhuji has disagreed with spirituality practiced in a social, communal, or collective manner.

Therefore, he does not proselytize or preach, nor does he try to persuade, convince, or make anyone change their perspective, philosophy, or religion. Many may find his insights valuable and apply them partially or fully to their own development, but Prabhuji's teachings should not be interpreted as personal advice, direction, counseling, instruction, guidance, tutoring, self-help methods, or techniques for spiritual, physical, emotional, or psychological development. The proposed teachings do not aspire to be definitive solutions for life's spiritual, material, financial, psychological, emotional, romantic, family, social, or physical problems. Prabhuji does not promise miracles, mystical experiences, astral journeys, healings of any kind, connections with spirits, angels or extraterrestrials, astral travel to other planets, supernatural powers, or spiritual salvation.

The Sacred Way

Some time ago, on the sacred journey toward transcendence, Prabhuji reaffirmed his resolve not to disturb those who showed no interest in joining him on this path. This decision is not simple detachment, but instead, a deliberate choice to preserve the essence of this migratory route: a commitment to authenticity and deepening self-inquiry. Such a decision, far from being an abandonment, is a respectful recognition of individual autonomy and divergent destinies and aspirations. On this journey, choosing fellow travelers is not a mere whim, but an exercise in critical discernment and alignment with those whose vision intertwines with his own in the search for our home within our own house.

Public services

Even though the monastery does not accept new residents, volunteers, donations, collaborations, or sponsorships, the public is invited to participate in daily religious services and devotional festivals at the Śrī Śrī Bhagavān Yeshua Jagat Jananī Miriam Premānanda Mandir.

Titles by Prabhuji

What is, as it is: Satsangs with Prabhuji (English)
ISBN-13: 978-1-945894-26-8

Lo que es, tal como es: Satsangas con Prabhuji (Spanish)
ISBN-13: 978-1-945894-27-5

Russian: ISBN-13: 978-1-945894-18-3

Kundalini yoga: The power is in you (English)
ISBN-13: 978-1-945894-30-5

Kundalini yoga: El poder está en ti (Spanish)
ISBN-13: 978-1-945894-31-2

Bhakti yoga: The path of love (English)
ISBN-13: 978-1-945894-28-2

Bhakti-yoga: El sendero del amor (Spanish)
ISBN-13: 978-1-945894-29-9

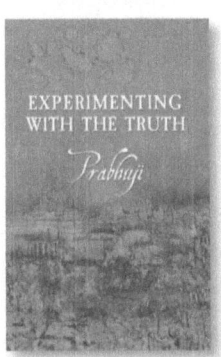

Experimenting with the Truth (English)
ISBN-13: 978-1-945894-32-9
Experimentando con la Verdad (Spanish)
ISBN-13: 978-1-945894-33-6
Experimenting with the Truth (Hebrew)
ISBN-13: 978-1-945894-93-0

Tantra: Liberation in the world (English)
ISBN-13: 978-1-945894-36-7

Tantra: La liberación en el mundo (Spanish)
ISBN-13: 978-1-945894-37-4

Advaita Vedanta: Being the Self (English)
ISBN-13: 978-1-945894-34-3

Advaita Vedānta: **Ser el Ser (Spanish)**
ISBN-13: 978-1-945894-35-0

Beyond Answers: Philosophy in the Eternal (English)
ISBN-13: 978-1-945894-91-6

Más allá de las respuestas: La filosofía en la búsqueda eterna (Spanish)
ISBN-13: 978-1-945894-88-6

Discovering the last God (English)
ISBN-13: 978-1-945894-75-6

Descubriendo al último Dios (Spanish)
ISBN-13: 978-1-945894-81-7

Questioning your answers: Philosophy as a question (English)
ISBN-13: 978-1-945894-80-0

Cuestionando tus respuestas: La filosofía como pregunta (Spanish)
ISBN-13: 978-1-945894-77-0

Īśāvāsya Upanishad
commented by Prabhuji
(English)
ISBN-13: 978-1-945894-38-1

Īśāvāsya Upaniṣad
comentado por Prabhuji
(Spanish)
ISBN-13: 978-1-945894-40-4

**The Diamond Sūtra
commented by Prabhuji
(English)**
ISBN-13: 978-1-945894-51-0

**El Sūtra del Diamante
comentado por Prabhuji
(Spanish)**
ISBN-13: 978-1-945894-54-1

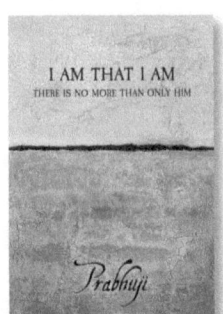

**I am that I am
(English)**
ISBN-13: 978-1-945894-45-9

**Soy el que soy
(Spanish)**
ISBN-13: 978-1-945894-48-0

Being - Volumen I and II (English)
ISBN-13: 978-1-945894-73-2
ISBN-13: 978-1-945894-80-0

Ser - Volumen I y II (Spanish)
ISBN-13: 978-1-945894-70-1
ISBN-13: 978-1-945894-94-7

Symbolic turn (English)
ISBN-13: 978-1-945894-61-9

El giro simbólico (Spanish)
ISBN-13: 978-1-945894-58-9

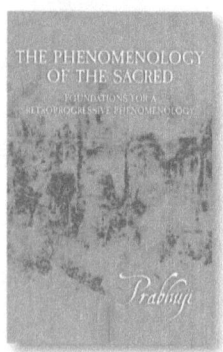

Phenomenology of the sacred (English)
ISBN-13: 978-1-945894-67-1

La fenomenología de lo sagrado (Spanish)
ISBN-13: 978-1-945894-64-0

www.ingramcontent.com/pod-product-compliance
Lightning Source LLC
Chambersburg PA
CBHW031215290426
43673CB00091B/3